Religion
Education
And
Life

Junior teacher's handbook

Sandra Palmer and Elizabeth Breuilly

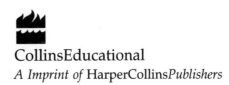

CollinsEducational
A Imprint *of* HarperCollins*Publishers*

ISBN 0 00312003–1
First published 1993 by Collins Educational,
London and Glasgow. A division of HarperCollins Publishers.

Reprinted 1994

Design by Derek Lee
Cover design by Leigh Hurlock
Cover artwork by Alice Bradbury
Series Editor Pat Green
Edited by Scarlett O'Hara
Production by Ken Ruskin

Typeset by Wyvern Typesetting Ltd, Bristol.
Printed and bound by Butler & Tanner Ltd, Frome, Somerset.

CONTENTS

ACKNOWLEDGEMENTS

Many people have contributed to this project over many years: so many that it is impossible to list them all. Faith communities have made us welcome in their homes and their places of worship, teachers have discussed ideas and tested material in their classrooms, individual members of faiths have read and commented on texts, although we should emphasise that any mistakes are our responsibility, not theirs.

The project began with a series of working parties, the members of which put in enormous amounts of work in writing, commenting, and contributing ideas. Working party members were (in alphabetical order) Vida Barnett, Sue Berry, Lucy Hall, Chris Halliday, Shelagh Hewitt, Jack Hogbin, Mary Ingram, Joanne O'Brien, Tony Philips, Ron Scrase, Angela Smith, Priscilla Trenchard, Peter Tucker, David Winston.

For faith advice and comments we especially thank Sister Ann Burgh, Douglas Charing, Ian Corbett, Mr Melvyn Flacks, Mrs P. Gill, Mr Habib ur Rahmam, Mr Halim, the Islamic Cultural Centre, Mrs Christine Malone, the Manchester Jewish Museum, Mr Werner Mayer, Mr and Mrs Panchmatia, Mrs Nila Pancholi, Stuart Polak, Ranchor Prime, Mr Abdus Salim, Daljit Singh and Raj Kaur, Mrs Charanjit Ajit Singh, Father Harry Stratton.

INTRODUCTION

REAL stands for Religion, Education and Life. It is a resource pack for religious education, a reservoir of suggestions for delivering religious education in the primary classroom via cross-curricular topics and resourced with stories and pictures. But this is not just a random collection of 'good ideas for RE': the suggestions are rooted in a consistent, coherent approach to the subject.

In the following discussion we have tried to anticipate some of the questions teachers might ask about this approach and about the REAL material.

What understanding of religious education is REAL based on?

We see R.E. as composed of two inter-related elements – the 'religious quest' and the study of religions.

The religious quest

'What is the meaning of life?'
'Is there a supreme being?'
'What's important in life?'
'What are my responsibilities to others?'

These and others are fundamental questions of meaning which we all explore consciously or subconsciously. The persistent 'Why?' of many young children is a way of seeking answers to such questions, as are activities such as choosing which football team to support and playing at being animals or playing at being grown up. We often live with 'answers' which are deeply ingrained in our culture and which we take for granted until experience, or contact with another view, calls them into question.

Religions have their own responses to these sorts of questions, answers which are expressed in their stories, rituals and doctrines. However, in a liberal, pluralist society with people belonging to many faiths and to none, there is no neat set of answers accepted by all, which can be passed on in a state school. Individuals need to acquire the skills and sensitivity to make up their own mind and develop their own thinking in the field of religion as in any other field of human enquiry.

One objective of RE is to help children develop those skills. For some children from homes with strong faith commitments this may entail reflecting on what that faith means to them and making it their own. For others the end result may be the emergence of a very individualistic faith, which may or may not include belief in the existence of God.

But we do not want this quest to be pursued in an entirely open-ended way. For example, we do not want the question, 'What are my responsibilities to others?' to produce the response 'None – I can treat them as I please'.

The basic values implicit in REAL are:

– the autonomy of the individual
– a positive approach to life and to change
– people are 'ends in themselves' not 'means to an end'
– the natural world should be treated with care and respect.

These values are implicit in the Agreed Syllabuses for religious education of most local education authorities.

The study of religions

People all over the world express their beliefs in their oral and written literature, their art, their rituals, their festivals and the choices they make in daily life. The second main element in religious education is learning about these particular expressions of faith. So, learning why Jews celebrate Passover, visiting the local church, or studying the Islamic ritual of wudu, are all part of learning about religion as a phenomenon as well as an influence in the lives of many people.

In hearing the stories of faiths and in learning about religious practices the children will gradually acquire a core of knowledge. By the end of the primary school we hope they will be able to group together the central religious details of each faith (e.g. the names of key figures, sacred writings, the place of worship, one main festival, and central stories).

However, more important than a body of

knowledge, the children should be building an understanding of faith as something which makes a difference to the lives of its followers. At the most superficial level, that will be in their celebrations. At a deeper level, it will affect the way faith communities respond to the questions of meaning posed at the beginning of this section. The children should also be gaining an awareness that religions make ethical demands on their followers.

In this study of religions, the children should also be gaining an insight into religious language and communication, seeing these as frequently metaphorical and symbolic. A child raised on a diet of myths and legends from different faiths, learns to recognise that the significance of the story lies in the ideas within it, rather than its literal, historical truth. Similarly, a sympathetic study of rituals can lead to an appreciation of their richness of meaning.

The quest for meaning and the study of religion

The quest for meaning and the study of religion are not two discrete components of RE but have a dialectical relationship. Children are led to their own exploration of meanings through studying other faiths. For example, in learning about Islamic views of humanity's relationship with the environment (chapter 1), the children have to think about their own relationship with the environment and their responsibility towards it. Conversely, reflecting on their own understanding and practice could give more insight into religious understanding. For example, becoming aware of the way meaning is conveyed through gesture could give a deeper understanding of gesture in explicitly religious contexts.

Skills in religious education

The skills which permeate this approach to RE are primarily those of discourse with yourself and with others. They are concerned with learning to think about questions of meaning and significance and to participate in discussions about them. This involves:

– being able to reflect on one's own experience,
– being able to articulate feelings and beliefs,
– being able to engage with the viewpoints of others,
– being able to enter imaginatively into stories,

whether myths and legends, or narrative accounts of religious practice,
– being prepared to ask questions and express doubts,
– being open to learning from others,
– being able to use metaphor and symbol.

All these skills are learnt not in isolation but by participating in the sort of religious conversation we hope this material will help to stimulate. There are ideas for starting points for discussions in each unit.

More than concepts and skills!

While religious education may involve gaining concepts and skills, we see it as more than that. Much of it is offering insights, ideas, images, and stories to the child. Some of these will be discarded immediately because they have no meaning for that particular child, some may have immediate effect, while some may lie dormant for years, gaining significance only later in life. This process is analogous to conversations we have. Some we forget almost immediately, however much we may have enjoyed them, and they have no effect on us; others we forget but in some way, however small, we have changed because of them; others linger in our memories to be recalled and given fresh meaning at a later date.

What religion is REAL based on?

Christianity permeates the project implicitly. The values in it are fundamentally Christian, although they are values shared by many who are not Christian. Both of the main authors are Christian. This means that Christian concerns have inevitably influenced the selection of materials, though we have attempted to listen to those of other faiths and the material has been checked by faith tutors.

However, the above understanding of RE entails a multi-faith approach, for an appreciation of the diversity of religion requires an encounter with more than one. We believe that children have much to gain in their spiritual development from the rich religious experience of humanity.

Most of the work is built on the five main faiths practised in Britain: Christianity, Hinduism, Islam, Judaism, and Sikhism. Buddhism is not included because it is not widely practised in Britain.

Christianity has the most substantial place in

this series. This breadth and weighting is in line with the 1988 Education Reform Act. Christianity has this place for two reasons. Firstly, because it is the faith which has most informed and shaped the ethos and culture of Great Britain. Much of Britain's art, architecture, literature and politics cannot be understood in any depth without a knowledge of Christian imagery and concepts. Second, it is the faith with which most children have had personal contact and which is part of all their environments. (We suggest that if the children at your school are mostly from another faith you build your initial work in RE on that faith, although sensitivity needs to be given to parents who may feel threatened when their children are in the minority.)

Is this multi-faith approach suitable for a school where only Christianity is represented?

Yes. Local Agreed Syllabuses may differ about the stage when it is appropriate to introduce a multi-faith content, as required by the Education Reform Act. We take the position that it is both possible and desirable to introduce the idea of different faiths early on. This can be done via examples which arise naturally in topic work and in stories from different faiths. Then children will grow up simply accepting the diversity of belief and practice, rather than it being introduced as something new and strange. Multi-faith teaching is all the more important where the children don't have any personal contact with people of other faiths, especially as the implications of living in a multi-faith society and world will have increasing significance as they grow older.

Why a cross-curricular approach?

Religion is a part of life, a dimension of it. Separating it out as a distinct programme of study, unrelated to any other areas of the curriculum, gives a distorted picture and can make it appear irrelevant to the children. Although the material could be used as an entity filling an RE period we hope that you will teach it in an integrated manner e.g. the topic 'Names' links with a general topic on myself. The topic 'Learning' links with a topic on 'Our School'. The chapter headings we have given lend themselves to integration with National Curriculum topics, especially in science and geography and local history work.

It is important when using this integrated topic approach that the activities should be developing the children's understanding of the subject of the topic, e.g. the RE work on homes increases the children's understanding of the home, as well as delivering RE.

It is a good idea to ensure that over the four years you teach about a major festival from each main faith at least once. In doing so you will be able to draw together aspects of the religion that you have mentioned before. As an introduction to each festival revise or introduce the main features of the faith (e.g. where do the people worship?). Tell other stories from the faith, especially about the key religious figures. These can be found in *A Tapestry of Tales*.

If possible, make sure that in each year RE is a substantial component of at least two cross-curricular topics, use some of the major topics outlined in this book.

What will I find in this project to help me deliver this RE?

REAL is fundamentally a resource and an approach to the teaching of religious education in the junior classroom. The fact that RE syllabuses are agreed at a local level makes it impossible to produce a definitive programme of study even if that were desirable. You will however find the following within the *REAL Junior Teacher's Handbook*.

Topics for RE in the classroom

These are based on the sort of topics which are popular in the primary school because they lend themselves to an integrated approach to the curriculum. They are not designed to be done in any specific order, but a faith which has not been mentioned before may need to be introduced before any further work on the topic can be undertaken.

Each topic is divided into units which focus on one aspect of the topic. Each unit contains two or more activities and frequently several points for discussion which explore or develop the concept.

☞ This symbol is used to identify a talking point or points which arise from the activities e.g. *Does an author always make up the story in a book or has she learnt the story from somewhere else?* Sometimes this symbol may denote an area for discussion or debate with the class.

All the material is designed to be used flexibly so that it can be adapted to the needs of children in a particular context. You may not think it appropriate to include all the units or activities outlined. You may wish to extend some of the ideas in other directions.

It is expected that these topics will be integrated with other areas of the curriculum, in the interdisciplinary approach that is common practice in primary schools. We have not made suggestions here for involvement of other curriculum areas except where they are directly beneficial for RE. The final section of each unit, called Cross-curricular Links, gives ideas for extending the activities into other curriculum subjects.

Because the material is open-ended it is quite possible for infant material to be adapted for junior classes, and vice-versa. (See the *REAL Infant Teacher's Handbook.*)

Information about religions

This is arranged in two ways. There are Faith Introductions to the five faiths and to Buddhism on pages 104–7. These are to fill you in on the general background to each faith so that you can put the other information we give you into context.

There are also Information Boxes throughout the topics, giving information which is specifically relevant to that topic. These are designed to make the information easy to use in preparation and teaching. The Information Boxes are a resource for you to adapt. Some of the material can be turned into simple narratives to introduce a ritual or a festival to the children. We have tried to anticipate questions children might ask and so have given you more detail than you would set out to use in a lesson. There are also recipes, prayers, etc. for you to use as you will.

Above all, the Information Boxes are there to help you become more familiar and feel more confident in teaching about faiths with which you may have had little contact. They are not there because all their contents should be taught to the children; it's up to you to decide.

A bibliography of children's books

All the books referred to in the topics are included in this bibliography but so are a few other books which we recommend because they explore basic concepts and issues in RE. These are books to be read over and over again throughout the year, and their value can lie as much at a subconscious level as in an explicit discussion of their content. They are stories which offer opportunities for conversation about questions of meaning and value (see also *A Tapestry of Tales*).

Other resources

A Tapestry of Tales: a separate anthology of traditional literature.

Many of the stories are a specific resource for the topics but there are some which are there for their intrinsic value to RE. They can be read repeatedly so that the children are familiar with them. In topic work where there is little or no RE you can use religious stories to raise questions of value and significance in the topic.

REAL Junior Assembly Book

This assembly book has classroom links as there are suggestions for classroom activities which can both contribute to the assemblies and follow on from them. There is direct reference to some of the topics. Much of the material in it could be adapted for classroom use.

A final word

REAL has been designed to help teachers with an important area of the curriculum and to smooth their path in teaching it. The material in the Teacher's Handbooks offers ways to approach RE through the context of different primary topics, but the material is there for you to use flexibly. We hope that it will be of assistance and will also increase your interest, enthusiasm and confidence in the subject.

FESTIVALS

Here is one element of religious life and education which every school in the country already tackles in some fashion or another. Even if your school has only looked at Christmas and Easter in the past, it is a foundation to build on. Of course, in many schools where a multi-cultural approach is already practised, it has been the festivals - Chinese New Year, Divali, Purim - which have proved to be the most popular and accessible way into other cultures and faiths.

This is because that is precisely what they are designed for. A festival is a way for a people, faith or culture to say, 'This is important to us. This is why it is important to us. Come and celebrate with us.' Festivals have arisen so that ordinary people, not scholars or priests, can rediscover, annually, certain fundamental truths which their faith holds to be vital. And the way these truths are put across is not through lengthy sermon but through song, dance, art and music as well as scripture reading. Festivals are designed to be a window into a faith as well as a means to make complex concepts easy to understand. Thus for teaching there can be no better way in than through festivals.

In this handbook, we give detailed ideas for a few festivals in the classroom, and the *REAL Junior Assembly Book* gives information about several festivals from different faiths which could be made the basis of classroom work where appropriate. The concept of festivals and celebration is an important one in RE, and many of the topics touch on this theme. However we would stress the following point: although a faith is saying in its festivals 'come and celebrate with us', we believe it is not possible to 'celebrate' a festival in the absence of at least a few people for whom it is real and part of their faith. It is still important to learn from the festival, and enjoy some of the stories, food and fun associated with it, but the experience will be different and should not be confused.

When you are considering using a festival for religious education, there are a number of basic points to bear in mind in order to get the best from the material, as well as treating the material with the respect it deserves.

What is the theme?
Is it the battle between good and evil as in Divali? Is it presenting a key belief in that faith such as the Divinity and humanity of Christ at Christmas? Is it recalling some major historical event such as Baisakhi in Sikhism? Look for the core idea which the festival enshrines and try to ensure that you do not lose sight of it by becoming too attracted to the forms by which it is expressed. Buddhists say that only a fool looks at the finger which points to the moon. It is so easy to reduce festivals to just food, festivities and fun.

Why this time of year?
Why does the festival fall at this particular time of year? In other words, what element in the natural rhythm of the year and of nature does the festival build on? This does not, of course, apply to Muslim festivals, because they follow a lunar year only. As the lunar year is 10-11 days shorter than the solar year, the Muslim calendar moves forward 10-11 days each year. Thus Ramadan which now falls in March/April, will in ten years' time be in December/January. However all other calendars of festivals do fall on the same dates or in the same seasons each year. Thus Easter being at the start of spring is in itself important because of the imagery which is used of new life. Likewise, Holi in Hinduism and Ching Ming in Chinese religion come at spring-time and the theme of new life is woven into their festivities. Turning to the autumn, Harvest Festival in Christianity and Succot in Judaism are times for recalling the bounty of God and of nature. Without the harvest time, these festivals would not exist. As so much symbolism and even colours are taken from the natural forces at work, at given seasons of the year, there is plenty of fruitful material here for the primary classroom.

Festive food

Third, there is the food - or at times the absence of it. In many festivals food plays a key symbolic or even representational role. For instance, chocolate Easter eggs for new life, or the rice dumplings of the Dragon Boat festival in Chinese religion, a symbol of the people's love for their honest official. Frequently these special foods are quite simple to make - such as the haman-tashen at the Jewish festival of Purim. These are simply pastry cases filled with poppy seeds and made to look like the three cornered hat of wicked Haman. Others are vehicles for the story which the festival tells, such as the different foods on the seder plate at Passover, or the roast lamb at Eid ul-Adha recalling the sacrifice of Abraham and Ishma'ail. At other times, the absence of food is important. In Buddhism, Christianity, and Islam there are set periods of fasting or abstinence which carry very important messages for a culture as materially dominated as our own. Children are notorious for their faddish attitude to food - especially unfamiliar food. Yet it is remarkable how a special food seems to be a bit more interesting and can begin to break down the barriers which different diets, smells and styles of cooking create for the average child.

A fund of stories

What story or stories are used to communicate the main point of the festival? Storytelling is a good way both to capture a child's attention and communicate complex ideas in an easily accessible manner. The power of storytelling and the matrix, which a diverse background of legends provide for a child, are beginning to be recognised in education. The great teaching systems of the world - the religions - never doubted their power, and thus all festivals have associated with them a rich fund of stories. Many of these stories appear in the book *A Tapestry of Tales*. With storytelling goes the possibility for art and for writing sessions. The creation of new stories around old ones is an essential feature of all living cultures, so encourage the children to make up their own legends based upon the themes of the festivals. Art is also much in evidence at festivals, be it the great temple paintings of the Chinese Buddhists and Taoists at festivals like the Hungry Ghost Festival, or the Eid ul-Fitr cards of Islam, there are plenty of opportunities for classroom work here.

A time for games

Maybe squirting coloured water, as happens at Holi, is not your idea of fun (though it probably is the children's!), but the dreidle from the Jewish festival of Hannukah or the 'hunt the egg' games from Orthodox Easter are perhaps a little safer.

Treasures of faith

The festival is a time when in two different ways the faith displays its treasures. In the first sense, the treasures are its teachings. For example, the belief in the power of the Holy Spirit at Whitsun for Christians is shown in the readings from the New Testament and the great Whitsun hymns such as 'Come down O Love Divine.' In Sikhism, the reading of the whole of the Holy Book, the Guru Granth Sahib is another testimony, this time to the belief that here one can hear the voice of God. In many of the Hindu festivals, the playing out of the great epics such as the Ramayana or the Mahabharata enables the audiences to be spoken to directly by the gods and by some of the most beautiful literature in the world.

The second treasure which is displayed alongside these scriptural treasures, are the actual treasures: the special communion cups and plates which are brought out for Christmas and Easter; the enormous Buddhist scroll paintings which cover temple walls during festivals such as Wesak; the most ornate Torahs which appear at festival times, as well as the magnificent scrolls of Esther for Purim; the seder plates at Passover; the lion dance costumes for Chinese New Year or Dragon Boat day; the church banners and priestly copes for Whitsun walks or Trinity Sunday processions. These are special treasures which we can all enjoy.

Enjoy yourselves!

Finally, there is the fun. Festivals are usually fun, although some are times of sadness, repentance or quiet, such as Good Friday, Yom Kippur or Lailat ul-Qadr, and others combine sadness or quiet with celebration such as the Martyrdom of Guru Arjan Dev in Sikhism. They naturally appeal to children and often the faiths have directed them primarily at children precisely because of the points we have made above about the ease with which festivals can communicate to children. Nor is it fun only for the children. For teachers too, using a festival as a focus for so many curriculum activities and life skills can be enormously rewarding, particularly if you are able yourself to join in with other people on these occasions.

Festivals in the classroom

In order to help you tackle festivals, we have put in some topics illustrating not just how these particular festivals can be used, but more importantly, how festivals in general can be used, practically. Below we also provide a list of major festivals, with a summary of the theme of the festival to give you a starting point.

Approximate dates are given, but these do vary as different faiths use different calendars. Muslim dates, as mentioned above, do not correspond to the solar year at all, but move forward each year. Approximate dates are given for 1993 - these will be about 10 days earlier each subsequent year.

Epiphany - January

This celebrates the visit of the 'wise men from the east' to the infant Jesus. It affords an opportunity to pick up after Christmas the themes of gift-giving and special journeys. (Eastern churches also celebrate Jesus' baptism at Epiphany, which falls on Jan. 12th in the Eastern calendar.)

Chinese New Year - January and February (*See topic in the REAL Infant Handbook*)

A great festival for schools because it is so visual - lion dances, dragon dances, drums, firecrackers, good luck money and signs, door gods, etc. Its meaning is the banishment and sorting out of the past year and the attempt to ensure that the New Year starts with as much good luck as possible. There are many stories about the twelve animal signs as well as numerous special foods.

Purim - February/March

This celebrates the story of the Jewish queen Esther, who saved her people from persecution at the hands of the wicked Haman. The story is read in the synagogue, while the children and adults, often clad in masks and silly costumes, make as much noise as possible every time the name of Haman is mentioned in the story.

Lent and Easter - February to April (*See topics in the REAL Infant and Junior Handbooks*)

The start of Lent is Ash Wednesday preceeded by Shrove Tuesday (Pancake Day). Lent is the Christian time of fasting or of giving up some pleasurable food or drink. The reason for this is to prepare physically and spiritually for Easter. It lasts 40 days (not counting Sundays) until Easter, thereby recalling Jesus' 40 days in the wilderness. Easter is the festival of the betrayal, death and resurrection from the dead of Jesus Christ. A time for celebrating new life and the victory of love over evil.

Hola Mohalla - February/March

Sikhs celebrate with sporting and martial competitions as well as games and music - a reminder that they must be ready always to defend the weak and uphold their faith.

Passover - March and April (*See topic in the REAL Junior Handbook*)

This is the Jewish celebration of God's freeing the Israelites from slavery in Egypt. Its main significance is that God shows his love for his chosen people but this carries with it responsibilities (as set out in the Ten Commandments). The Seder meal takes place during Passover.

Holi - March and April

Holi is the festival of love and of the harvest. It is a light hearted festival, chiefly renowned for the tricks played, such as squirting coloured water. The key figure is Krishna as the Divine Lover and Trickster.

Rama Naumi (Rama's birthday) - March/April

This Hindu festival celebrates the birth of Rama, the god Vishnu in human form, and the hero of the Hindu epic, the Ramayana. Beforehand the whole Ramayana is recited in the temple and there are periods of fasting.

Baisakhi - April 13th (*occasionally the 14th*)

The Sikh festival which celebrates the founding of the Khalsa is called Baisakhi. The heart of the festival is the love of God for all people regardless of caste, creed or colour, and the need to defend the helpless when they are in danger.

Ramadan and Eid ul-Fitr - March and April (*See topics in the REAL Infant and Junior Handbooks*)

This is the Muslim period of fasting and then celebration of being a Muslim and living in 'Islam' that is submission to Allah. The heart of this time is undergoing the deprivations of fasting in order to discipline both the mind and the body, and then the celebration of Eid which rejoices at the glory and blessings of Allah on those who worship him.

Whitsun - May/June

At this time Christians celebrate the coming of the Holy Spirit, when Jesus' disciples were filled with new enthusiasm and courage from God.

Dragon Boat Festival - June

This is the increasingly popular Chinese summer and water festival. At its heart is a story of honesty and virtue in the tale of Ch'u Yuen (see *A Tapestry of Tales*). The drama of the dragon boat races with their colour and vibrance adds to this.

Eid ul-Adha - June *(See topic on 'Journeys' in the REAL Junior Handbook)*

This Muslim festival recalls the obedience of Abraham and his son Ishma'ail to the Will of God. Its core is the idea of submission to God. Its joyfulness comes from God's mercy and providence (as shown in the gift of the ram).

Raksha Bandhan - August

Hindus exchange bracelets as a sign of friendship and protection. In some parts of India the day is celebrated as a festival for brothers and sisters.

Krishna's Birthday (Janmashtami) - August/September *(See also 'Birthdays' in the REAL Infant Handbook)*

Hindus gather at midnight to remember the birth of one of the most beloved Hindu gods, and his rescue from his uncle who wanted to kill him. At midnight everyone takes turns to push a decorated swing or cradle with a picture of the child Krishna.

Rosh Hashanah and Yom Kippur - September and October *(See topic on 'Time' in the REAL Junior Handbook, and the 'New School Year' assembly)*

This is the Jewish period of repentance and reflection. Its central purpose is to start the New Year (Rosh Hashanah) with due repentance and contrition for the failures and faults of the previous year. It is a time for new starts and better intentions. It is also traditionally the World's Birthday - a time to recall its beauty and bounty which we have so often despoiled, another reason for repentance!

Harvest Festival

A Christian celebration giving thanks for the harvest.

Succot - September/October

The Jews commemorate their journey from Egypt to the promised land, recalling the time when they lived in tents or temporary shelters. In Jewish homes and synagogues, temporary shelters are built of branches, and Jews use the shelter for as much of daily life as possible, eating and if possible sleeping in it. It is also a time to give thanks for God's provision of different species of plants.

Dusshera/Navaratri - October

The Hindu festival lasting nine nights, which celebrates different aspects of the goddess Devi. At its core is the diversity of that which speaks powerfully to individuals about the nature of the Divine - awesome; loving; warlike; compassionate; bringer of death and bestower of life.

Divali - October and November *(See topic on 'Light' in REAL Junior Handbook)*

Probably the most popular Hindu festival. At its centre is the celebration of the New Year and the clearing of old accounts, both financial and emotional, so that the New Year can start well.

Guru Nanak's Birthday - November *(See also topic on 'Birthdays' in REAL Infant Handbook)*

The birth of the founder of Sikhism is celebrated by reading through the entire scripture, the Guru Granth Sahib, by singing the hymns he wrote, and telling stories of him.

Hannukah - December *(See topic on 'Light' in REAL Junior Handbook)*

The Jewish festival of survival and of the enduring presence of God. Candles play a central role and the key story is about God's miraculous provision of oil to light the Temple light. Excellent for both a good story and good work on symbols and lights.

Advent and Christmas - December *(See topics in REAL Infant and Junior Handbooks, and topic on 'Light' in Junior Handbook)*

The Christian festival of Christmas needs to be placed in its context by looking at Advent as well. The central message is that through Jesus Christ God has reconciled the world to himself and has identified himself with our lives.

The above are some of the major festivals. There are of course many, many others. Your own class might bring up ones which have significance for a particular child. We hope that they will act as a spur to your own creative thinking in this most accessible and enjoyable area of multi-faith education.

THE LIVING WORLD

An approach to science which encourages children to take delight in the natural world and to treat it with respect implicitly conveys the belief that the world is of worth. Nevertheless an explicitly religious perspective on the topic can encourage children to think about what their relationship is to the natural world.

The topic could be used to focus on just one aspect of the living world, e.g. land or trees or animals.

Look, too, at the two 'Natural World' assemblies in the *REAL Junior Assembly Book*.

Unit 1
Living in harmony with the land

This unit takes different examples of the way different peoples all over the earth have lived in harmony with nature, rather than struggled against it.

Purpose
● to think about the land and the children's relationship with it

Ideas
★ Use the story of Edmund Hilary and Sherpa Tensing (see Information Box) to raise the question of whether the land is living.
★ Tell children about the notion of sacred land in the beliefs of Australian Aboriginals (see Information Box). Let them paint and draw land which is special to them – perhaps a local park, waste ground, some place in the garden.
★ Tell children about Chinese *Feng Shui* (see Information Box). If your school has a reasonably open aspect, or a view of the horizon, take them out into the playground to look at the surrounding area and identify dragons and tigers.
☛ *How much has local building been 'friendly' to the land? What are your ideas of friendly ways of building?*
★ Tell the Greek legend of 'Demeter and Persephone' (*A Tapestry of Tales*), with its theme of the land coming to life again in the spring.

Unit 2
Living in harmony with trees

Purpose
● to value trees
● to develop an idea of humanity being a part of nature rather than in conflict with it

Ideas
★ Tell the story of the Bishnoi of North India (see Information Box).
★ Ask the children to research the place of the tree in nature (not its direct use as a resource, e.g. as wood). For example, the trees' role in holding water in the soil, as a habitat for other species, etc.
★ Make a map of the local area, with children marking in the trees (or noticing the lack of them) on their way to school.
★ Have a fund-raising event to raise money to plant a tree in the school grounds for children to nurture. Let them research and vote on the most suitable tree.
★ Tell them about the Jewish saying of planting a tree for the future, and about Tu B'Shevat, the tree-planting festival (see Information Box). (See also the assembly 'Trees' in the *REAL Infant Assembly Book*.)

Edmund Hilary and Sherpa Tensing

The first two people to reach the top of Mount Everest were Edmund Hilary, a New Zealand scientist and explorer, and Sherpa Tensing, a Tibetan porter. Edmund Hilary proudly planted a flag, and rejoiced that he and his companion had 'conquered' the world's highest mountain. Tensing knelt down and prayed that the spirit of the mountain would forgive their disturbing this spot, which had been 'set apart' and unvisited.

Australian Aboriginals and the land

Australian Aboriginals see themselves as being an indivisible part of the land, which was sung into being by their Dreamtime ancestors at the beginning of time. The ancestors left their footprints and the marks of their journeys all over Australia, so that every rock, hillock or water-hole is part of the story, which is part of the life of the people. Thus every part of the land is sacred through its connection with the dreamtime ancestors. Some sites are particularly important because of their part in the story. Since Aboriginals see themselves as part of the land, they feel physical pain or illness when a site connected to their own particular ancestor is harmed.

One of the most famous sacred sites in Australia is the huge rock that rises a thousand feet above the desert floor, and changes colour during the day as the sun moves round it. It is known to white people as Ayers Rock, but to the Aboriginals as Uluru. Each boulder, waterhole, gully, plant and animal has a sacred meaning. For many years white people had control of the rock, and the Aboriginals were forced to move away; but recently, in response to great pressure from the Aboriginals, they have got back their sacred site. It is still a tourist attraction, but now care is taken that sacred sites are not trampled, destroyed, or covered with litter.

Feng Shui

The Chinese see the land as living, and having power over the lives of those living on it. They picture the land in terms of living creatures embodied in it: valleys are tigers, hills are dragons, rivers are snakes, and so on. It follows that it is very important to treat the land so as not to disturb or offend these powerful forces, but to work in harmony with them. So any building or cultivation must enhance, not destroy, the natural shape of the land. Dragons, in particular, need careful handling: you should not, obviously, build right in the dragon's eye, or tower over him.

The Bishnoi

The Bishnoi live in Rajasthan, in northern India. They are a Hindu sect which lays particular stress on not harming any living organism: they are vegetarian, they use only dead wood for firewood and inspect it carefully to make sure no insects are hiding in it. They protect all wildlife, and are prepared to die to protect their trees. In the last century, a local ruler wanted wood for fuel for his lime-kilns, so he sent his men to cut down trees in the Bishnoi lands. The Bishnoi ran to their trees and hugged them, making it impossible for the men to cut down the trees without hurting the people. The ruler sent in his soldiers who threatened the Bishnoi. Still they would not give up hugging their trees, and people were hacked to pieces before the ruler finally gave up in the face of this passive resistance. The Bishnoi lands are now green and fertile in an area of semi-desert, because they have taken such care of their trees.

Jewish belief about trees

The Jews tell a story of an old man who was hard at work planting a young fruit tree. A passer-by asked him, 'Why do you work so hard at this? It will be years before this tree bears fruit, and by that time you will almost certainly be dead.' The old man replied, 'When I came into this world, I found a fruitful world because my parents and their parents planted trees and tended them. So I am doing the same for my children and grandchildren.'

Jews also have a special festival for trees, Tu B'Shevat, the New Year for trees — it falls in January. On that day, Jews make a point of planting a tree, either where they live, or in the land of Israel, where many acres have been reforested and reclaimed from desert.

Unit 3
Living in harmony with animals

Purpose
● to explore our relationship with animals

Ideas
★ Tell the story of St. Francis of Assisi and his view of animals (see Information Box). Let them identify which animals they feel friendly towards and which ones they are fearful of.
★ Do a study on spiders, letting children who have negative feelings towards them express them but also exploring positive aspects. *Charlotte's Web* by E. B. White (Puffin) is a useful resource.

INFORMATION BOX

St. Francis of Assisi (see also *A Tapestry of Tales*) was brought up as a rich merchant's son in the twelfth century, but gave up all his riches and his settled home to serve God and the poor people. As well as preaching to everyone about the love of God, he was a great friend and respecter of animals, even the most humble, or those which seemed harmful. One story told of him is about how he once tamed a wolf that was terrorising a local village. When Francis spoke to the wolf as he would to a brother, it lay down before him. He spoke of all the living world as his brothers and sisters, and wrote 'The Canticle of the Creatures' in which he gives praise to God for his creation. (The hymn 'All creatures of our God and King' is based on this canticle.)

Unit 4
Having dominion over

Purpose
● to become aware of humanity's use of the natural world

Ideas
★ The starting point is Genesis, chapter 1: read from the Bible or tell it in your own words.

Note: Some Christians, Muslims and Jews, all of whom share this basic story, believe in its literal, historic truth. Many others see it as a myth embodying truth about the relationship between God, humanity and the rest of creation.
☛ *What does 'having dominion over' mean?*
★ Help children to find out what humanity has done to control the land, plants and animals (e.g. clearing, cultivating, fencing, zoning as wildlife areas, taming, training, caging, etc.).
★ Let the children find what use humanity has made of the land, plants and animals (e.g. building, cultivating, mining, for pleasure, food, medicine, paper, cloth, pets, clothing, working animals).
★ Children can then share the results of their research with the rest of the class.

Unit 5
Exploitation?

Purpose
● to introduce or develop the idea that dominion need not necessarily mean exploitation

Ideas
★ Use information in the boxes as an introduction. Discuss with the children what it is like to look after something precious for somebody else.
★ Read the story of 'The Student and the Ants' (*A Tapestry of Tales.*)

Unit 6
How can we care?

Purpose
● to appreciate that belief leads to action
● to learn how our efforts can help the environment

Ideas
★ Tell the children the story of 'Muhammad Washing by the River' (*A Tapestry of Tales*).
☛ *In what ways do we waste resources? What waste do we see in the world generally?*

Muslims, Christians and Jews all see humanity as being placed in some way 'over' the rest of creation, but having a responsibility for it. They express this in different ways.

Muslims describe humans as being the vice-regents of God on earth: they rule over the earth, but in God's name, and under his authority.

Christians use the image of a steward, who is in charge of his master's property. He is not expected to use it for his own ends, but to further the business of his master, and for the benefit of his master's dependants. This is the idea that God gives us good things, not as an outright gift, but rather He entrusts them to us.

To express the same idea, **Jews** tell this story: Adam, newly created, wandered through the garden where God had placed him, and saw the trees laden with delicious–looking fruit. He reached out a hand to pick some, but the branch withdrew out of his reach, the same happened with the next tree, and the next one. Puzzled and hungry, he wondered why the fruit was always out of reach. Then he heard a voice which said, 'Care for the garden and cultivate the trees, then you may eat.'

Muslim ways of caring

Islam has established principles for animal husbandry which embody the idea of humanity as God's Vice-regents on earth. For example, each animal killed for food is killed with the phrase 'Bismillah' – in the name of Allah. So it must not be killed wantonly or carelessly, but only for food. Once it has been killed, as much as possible of the animal should be used, and none wasted.

Many animals live in families as humans do. Any method of keeping them should not interfere with the natural family unit.

Aboriginal ways of caring

Australian Aboriginals try to keep the land and its animals and plants exactly as they were first created in the Dreamtime. Their songs are part of this, as each year they sing the story of the land to preserve its sacred life. But it also means taking as little as possible from any one place, whether food, plants or animals. Again, it is considered quite wrong to kill animals other than for food. No Aboriginal will kill the creature who is believed to be its ancestor, but even other creatures and plants are considered to be a gift from the ancestors, and are to be used carefully and with gratitude.

★ Ask children to research the consequences of wastage e.g. of paper, heat, lighting, water.

★ Start a recycling project.

★ Tell the children about Muslim and Aboriginal ways of caring for the living world.

➷ *In what ways could we take care of the land the school is on?*

In what other ways can we care for the earth?

★ Ask the children to research methods of animal husbandry used in Britain today, and to evaluate them in terms of the way the animals are cared for: e.g. egg production, milk production, beef production.

★ The children can make a class charter for care of the earth, based on their research.

CROSS-CURRICULAR LINKS

Science

Observe plants and trees in the school grounds.
Grow plants from seeds in the classroom.
Find out what plants need to live.

Make observations of pets. Find out what these animals need to live.

Make a book about how to look after your pet.

Find out what sorts of animals and plants live by the seashore, in the town, in the countryside. *Are they different?*

Make a visit to an environment different from your usual one. Compare it to your usual one. *Which do you prefer?*

History

Find out about the sorts of plants and animals people ate long ago.

Investigate plant and animal husbandry in the past.

How has the tree cover changed in the last 50 years? Find out from old photographs and maps from the library.

Investigate extinct animals and plants.

THE LOCAL AREA

Here we look at the local area in terms of its needs. There are plenty of opportunities for local surveys and geographical investigations in the community through this topic. It may also provide a means to establish links with the community perhaps through recycling campaigns.

Your local area is a rich resource for a number of topics – e.g. food, buildings, learning. It is also a valuable topic for RE in its own right, although much of the RE is implicit.

One way of drawing together all these themes would be for the class to prepare a guide book or series of booklets for newcomers to the district. This could be made available to new parents to the school, or presented for display and availability to the local library, or a place of worship. (Churches often have bookstalls.) Alternatively the class could mount a display in the classroom which was later transferred to a public place, covering the same sort of information. Although this would be a time-consuming task, it would obviously be an interdisciplinary study, and provide a lot of opportunity for developing research, language and display skills.

Also see 'A Guide' in the *REAL Junior Assembly Book*.

Unit 1
Where do you go?

The following areas might be covered although we suggest you try and elicit the list from the children rather than impose it on them. It is a long list so you may well wish to organise the children into groups or pairs researching one or two areas rather than the whole lot. Make use of the local library for reference material.

Purpose
• to develop an awareness of our interdependence ,
• to provide an opportunity to identify 'need'
• to look at the role of religion within the community

Ideas
★ Look at what basic needs are met locally and what has to be sought elsewhere. The children will need to identify what such needs are. For example ask the children to find out, perhaps from a survey, the following information.

�'ᴘ *Where do you go if you are ill? What are the names of local doctors, dentists, etc? Is there a local hospital?* (The problem of communities with poor access to hospitals could be raised.)

➲ *What transport facilities does the area offer?* (Thus linking the local area to the world beyond.)

➲ *What recreational facilities does the area offer?* These could be parks, pubs, cinemas, football clubs, museums, youth groups such as Brownies.

➲ *Where are there places to learn?* Find out about schools, ballet classes, Sunday schools, Adult Education Centres, etc.

➲ *Where do people meet to worship? What time are the services? What are the names of the leaders?* Find out about the other activities and services these places offer - (i.e. old people's clubs, mother's union, after school clubs, etc.). Remember, also, that people meet to worship in homes.

➲ *In what ways does the area provide for the disabled?*

➲ *Where can people go to find peace and quiet?* The local library, the local church if it is open, a corner of a park, etc.

➲ *Are there any dangerous places locally?* Think

about dangerous crossings, deep water, railway cuttings, etc.

➮ *Where can you find advice in the area?* For example, Citizen Advice Bureaux, the Library, Tourist Information Centres, etc.

★ Make a list of things which are special about the area. Find out if there are any local customs or folklore to discover about the vicinity.

➮ *Are there any local holidays?* (Wakes weeks for example.)

➮ *Is there a local festival? When is it held? What happened last year?*

➮ *What are the local buildings of interest?* This may well include purpose-built places of worship or local monuments and children could try and find out the story behind them.

★ Consider what the local area contributes to the wider community.

Look at produce, agricultural and industrial. Even the quietest suburban streets often have small pockets of light industry tucked away in them.

Look too, at services such as hospitals, schools, postal sorting offices, supermarkets, holiday homes, tourist attractions, an airport, etc.

Unit 2
An environmental campaign

This may well arise naturally out of studying the local area.

Taking up a local issue can give children the confidence that they can be authors of change, and responsible for the environment around them. It also demonstrates the relationships between the local area and government and political bodies. You may find that a local group such as the Community Association or a religious body, e.g. church or gurdwara, has already taken up the issue. You could join with them or enlist their assistance in your campaign.

Purpose
• to give a service to the local area

Ideas
★ Address a local issue such as: litter in a disused railway cutting; no place to play; timing of local

buses; lack of pedestrian lights at a busy crossing; lack of seating near shops for elderly or disabled people.

★ Try writing to a local newspaper explaining the problem.

★ Collect signatures for a petition among family and friends.

★ Make a display to show the merits of the case, and put it where it will receive a wide audience. This could initiate a discussion on where the most people would see it.

★ Invite a local councillor to the school to discuss the issue.

★ Discuss ways to raise funds where appropriate.

★ If the campaign is successful, stage a party to celebrate. However 'Rome wasn't built in a day', so children need to be aware that their contribution could be part of a long process.

CROSS-CURRICULAR LINKS
Geography
Write a plan of the local area. Decide what are the interesting things to see and incorporate these into the route. Use a map of the area to help with the planning. Try out one of the routes. Take a camera along and take photographs along the route, then put these in sequence. Make a display of the route and pictures.

Walk around the area speaking a commentary into a tape recorder. Play this to the class to see if everyone can guess the things being described.

Science
Go on a nature trail near your school. Find out about the plants and animals that live in your area.

Can you trace the route of various products to your local shops?

Try furniture, meat, tinned fruit and clothes, for example.

A PLACE OF WORSHIP

We take a church as our example for looking at a place of worship in the community. The same approach could be adapted to look at a mosque, temple, synagogue or gurdwara if you have one locally. (See Information Boxes, Faith Introductions, pp.104–33 and 'Visiting Places of Worship', p.134.) The Information Boxes give notes of some particular features to look out for in particular places of worship, but the best source of information is the community that uses the building. Get as much information as possible about the building before you visit, and talk with the person who is going to show you round beforehand.

When you arrange the visit ask if you can have copies of the church notices and if you can borrow a few hymn books and a copy of any Sunday School material.

'A celebration of a local religious building' in the *REAL Junior Assembly Book*, may be useful here.

Unit 1
The visit

When visiting any place of worship the children should be encouraged to behave respectfully – see Visiting Places of Worship, p.134.

Arm the children with sketch pads and note-books. This work could be undertaken by all children or divided among groups.

Purpose
● to give children first hand experience of a place of worship
● to gather information for use in the classroom

Ideas
★ Ask the children to draw: views from the outside; the doorway if it is an old church; as many objects/furniture in the church as possible; scenes from any stained glass windows; any memorial stones.
★ Ask them to map: the inside of the church and the layout of the building as a whole, finding out what other rooms there are.
★ Ask them to copy the information on the church notice board.
★ Back in school all this drawing and note-taking can be transformed into a display, the children

making paintings of the sketches. Alternatively some of the children could make a model of the inside and the outside of the church. Complement the display of the local church with post-cards, magazine pictures, etc. of a large variety of churches and their contents so that the children become aware of the similarities and differences.
★ The display could be the basis of a series of short lessons about the church, some of which might be run with the church.
★ In this process the centrality of the cross to Christians could be brought out. This might also be the time to look at some of the other features of Christian churches (see Information Box for some of them) to help children understand their significance. The children could, for instance, find out about the stories depicted in any stained glass windows.

Unit 2
The age of the Church

Purpose
● for children to be aware of the role the church has played historically in the community

Candles

Candles are often placed on the high table to symbolise God's presence. Roman Catholic, Orthodox and some Anglican churches have candles which individuals light. This may be done to honour a saint, and can also be a way of focusing prayer. The smoke is a visible symbol of prayer rising to God. (See also *REAL Junior Assembly Book*, p.12–13.)

Statues of Mary

Roman Catholic churches usually have statues of Mary. This is an opportunity to discuss how Mary is honoured and loved by many Christians because she is Jesus' mother. Each statue often has particular symbolism which the priest might explain.

Icons

See the topic on 'Messages Without Words', p.44, and the *REAL Junior Assembly Book*, p.49.

Other places of worship

In a mosque ask the children to look for and copy any Arabic calligraphy, and find out what it means.

A purpose-built mosque may have a minaret from which the call to prayer can be broadcast. This gives an opportunity to talk about Muslim prayer five times a day.

Mosques and gurdwaras, particularly, have places to wash before entering the main room. Make sure the children map these. There may be places to leave shoes before entering.

A gurdwara will always have somewhere to cook and serve food.

Outside a gurdwara note the Sikh flag – ask the children to draw the symbol on it.

In a synagogue, ask the children to draw the coverings on the Torah scrolls.

Ask the children to map the layout of the seating.

Ideas

★ Ask the children to make rough guesses about the age of the church (modern, medium old, very old) and to justify their idea with evidence from their observations. Look up dates in the church guide book if there is one.

★ Find out any stories about the building of the church from the guidebook, or by inviting in a local resident if it is a recent building.

★ Using old maps of the area compare the age of the building with other local buildings.

➥ *If the church is old, why do you think it has stood so long? Is it just because it is solidly built? If it is new, why would people want to build a church these days?*

★ Look at other places of worship and consider the building may well have had some other use before it became a mosque, gurdwara, etc. See if the children can find out or guess what the other use was. Trace the history which led to this change of use.

Unit 3
Who goes to church?

Purpose
• to think about why people go to church
• to see that people who go to church services have a broadly common faith

Ideas
★ Invite in a member of the congregation to talk to the children about why they go to church.
★ Invite in the vicar, priest or minister to talk about his or her role.
★ Ask the children to look at the information gathered from the church noticeboard and news bulletins to see if people go to the church for any reason other than the services; e.g. playgroups, Brownies, concerts, etc.

Unit 4
What goes on inside the church?

Purpose
• to develop understanding of Christian worship and see it as centering on God and Jesus

Ideas
★ Using the information from the noticeboard, ask them to decide when the church is most used.

Then tell them the story of the Last Supper and of Easter morning (*A Tapestry of Tales*), to explain why Christians worship on a Sunday, and why the service commemorating the Last Supper is often the most important one.

★ Ask children who have been to a Sunday church service to talk about their experience.

★ Did any of the children copy down the church hymn board? If so let the children look up the hymns to see if they know any of them. Read out the words of a hymn, and talk about them with the children. If you have a set of school hymn books, or enough copies of the church's for a group to use, ask the children to search through for their favourite hymns and make up their own notice boards.

★ If there were kneelers in the church ask the children what they are used for.

☛ *What sort of things do you think people pray for in church?*

★ You could also look at the Lord's Prayer. Although it is a difficult prayer to understand fully, many children will have heard of it and it is the central prayer of the Christian faith, taught by Jesus to his followers. The origin of the prayer is probably the easiest point to discuss with Junior children, but we have provided some commentary on the content for you to use if you wish (see Information Box).

★ The pulpit and the sermon: can the children guess for themselves why the pulpit is high up? A comparison may be made between a sermon and the headteacher's assembly talk.

★ Older children could be given a sermon topic to prepare and deliver to the class, e.g. 'Why should we be kind to others?', or 'What does the story of the Good Samaritan mean to you?'

★ The lectern and Bible: (see also topic on 'Writings', p.52).

☛ *Why is the Bible read in church?*

★ See if the children can identify stories they know from the Bible.

Notes on the Lord's Prayer
(For teachers to draw on as they wish.)

'Our Father who art in heaven,'
God is not an earthly father, but the words emphasise the intimate relationship between parent and children.

'Hallowed be thy name,'
Asking that God's name be honoured and thus treated with respect, as well as saying that God is holy.

'Thy kingdom come, thy will be done on earth as it is in heaven,'
Jesus taught that God's kingdom would come when people would obey God's laws. In Old Testament terms this meant peace, justice for the poor and widows, and compassion.

'Give us this day our daily bread,'
A prayer implying trust in God to provide; but also the word which is translated as 'daily', in Greek hints at the future kingdom of God when all will eat plentifully.

'Forgive us our trespasses,
As we forgive those who trespass against us'
The parable of the 'Unforgiving Servant' illustrates this (*A Tapestry of Tales*). In Christian thought acceptance and forgiveness of others is central.

'Lead us not into temptation,'
The translation 'Do not bring us to the time of trial' is probably a better one; it is asking God's protection from difficulties which may be too much to bear.

'Deliver us from evil,'
Again asking for God's strength to withstand the effects on us of things which are wrong.

Style and content of prayer differs between denominations although the Lord's prayer (see Information Box) is usually said. Prayers generally include praise of God, confession of sin, thanksgiving, and prayers for the church and the world, when the needs of the local community as well as the wider world community are put before God.

Other places of worship

As with the church, the furniture will give clues and starting points to discuss what goes on in the building. Note the niche which marks the qiblah wall in a mosque (the direction of Mecca). In general, look for a place where the scriptures are read; a place where a sermon is preached; indications of how people sit, stand or kneel to pray; a place for any musicians.

Unit 5
Sunday schools/children's church

Most churches have something for children which runs parallel to church services or takes place afterwards (see also the topic on 'Learning', p. 39). Sunday schools or children's churches vary enormously: some follow a commercially available programme, others are more individualistic. The best resource is the children's experience and yours if you have any.

Purpose
● to find out about Sunday schools and to look at their function

Ideas
★ If the local Sunday school does follow a programme look at one of the lessons with the children.

Unit 6
Weddings

(See Faith Introductions, pp.104–33 for information on weddings in other faiths.)
Remember some of your children may have unmarried parents.

Purpose
● to develop concepts of ceremony
● to begin to develop an understanding of Christian marriage

Ideas
★ Show children some wedding photos with a clear church background.
◓ *Do all weddings take place in church? Why do people want to get married in church?*
The answers will probably include that it is a nice looking place; but try and feed into the discussion the idea that many people want God to bless their marriage.
◓ *Why do they get dressed up in special clothes? Why do people get married? (An open question.)*

★ Encourage the children to talk about their experiences of attending a wedding, and their perceptions of what happened.
★ The subject matter lends itself to illustration.

Unit 7
Funerals

(See Faith Introductions, pp.104–33, for details about funerals in other faiths.)

Purpose
● to provide the opportunity to talk about death and bereavement
● to give a greater understanding of the role of the church

Ideas
★ Introduce the subject via any memorial stones or brasses seen in the church.
◓ *Why do people put up memorials to dead people?*
★ Lead on from this to how people feel when the person first dies, and how a funeral helps them to show their sorrow immediately, to remember what the person meant to them, and in a sense say goodbye.
★ Encourage children to talk about their own feelings when someone they knew died, and how other family members felt.
★ Play some sad music which might be played at a funeral; but also discuss with them how some people choose their favourite hymns to be sung at their funeral, if they know that they are dying.

> **Memorials**
>
> In a synagogue, look particularly for a memorial board for people who have died, with lights which are lit on the anniversary of the death.

Unit 8
Festivals in the Church

You will of course have seen the church at one particular point in time, during a particular Church season, so you will have to give the children other information about the church at other times of the year.

Purpose
- to develop an understanding of festival and ritual

Many Anglican and Roman Catholic churches use different coloured altar cloths, hangings and priests vestments for different seasons of the church's year. In the Anglican church, the general pattern is to use white for major festivals such as Christmas and Easter, red for preparatory periods such as Lent and Advent, purple for Good Friday and the rest of Holy Week, and green the rest of the time. Roman Catholic churches use a more complex system which may change according to the saint's day – red is used on the day of a martyr, for example.

Ideas
★ Start with asking the children about when they dress up, and when they dress up the house. Lead into 'dressing up' the church for festivals, and also 'dressing down' for Good Friday (see the topic on Easter, p.97).
★ 'Dress up' any model churches the class has made for the next festival.
★ Paint a picture of the inside of the church decorated for a wedding or festival.

CROSS-CURRICULAR LINKS

Geography
Consider the use of buildings, compare churches, hospitals, factories and schools. *What are the similarities and differences?*
List the facilities of the local area. *What does the area lack? How far away is the nearest hospital or college?*
Draw maps and plans of the local area.

Technology
Design furnishings, such as kneelers or hangings, which would be suitable for the building.

English
Interview some of the people who use or work in the building.

19

NAMES

The underlying themes of this section are: symbols, religious expression and diversity.

Whether we like our own name or not we have had it for longer than we have had any other sense of identity. Our name is the main way that people know us – even if they have never met us!

Even when there is no ritual, the choice of a name indicates the values and tastes of the parents or guardians. When a child is named within the rites and customs of a faith, the ceremony and the name together also give clues about traditions, customs and a way of life. The family name connects the child to a wider community as well as to the past.

A study of names can be an exciting activity for children. It is one way of exploring who we are – were we named after anyone? If so, who? Who was the first (or most famous) person to have our name? What does the name mean?

A study of names gives an opportunity to explore why names are given and some of the things they stand for. In this way we can start to consider how people try to understand and describe God or gods, e.g. the Lover, the Father, the Mother, the Just, etc. (See Information Box on p. 25.)

Here is an opportunity also to challenge the way in which children ridicule names (or other things) which are unfamiliar – one of the ways in which racism may be unwittingly transmitted.

It may be useful to get hold of a copy of the *Guinness Book of Names* and the *Oxford Dictionary of Christian Names* for help with this chapter.

The *REAL Infant Teacher's Handbook* looks at naming briefly in the topics on 'Babies' and 'Pets'.

This topic could be part of a general topic on **Myself**.

Unit 1

Me and my name

Purpose

• to involve all the children in the topic from the start

Ideas

★ Ask the children to write their name using decorated letters. (These could be used to make book covers or to caption a self portrait.)

★ See if they can draw a self-portrait using the letters of their name.

★ Make cut-outs of the letters of their name or initials, and rearrange them to form a pattern. Then see if others can decipher it.

★ Use children's names as rhythms for dance. Children can chant the name, and make a dance 'in celebration' of that person.

What do you know about your name? (e.g. famous people with the same name; original bearer of the name; geographical origin of the name; etc.)

What names would you call your children? Why?

If you weren't called by your name, what name would you choose?

★ Prepare for the next stages. Encourage the children to ask at home to find out how (and why) their names were chosen.

Unit 2
How was your name chosen?

The term 'Christian name' applies only to a name given at a christening, so it is best to talk of 'personal' or 'given' names.

Purpose
● to show some of the reasons behind the choosing of personal names
● to show that these may be from religious traditions

Ideas
★ Discuss with the children the difference between their personal names and those names determined by family, gender, etc. For examples the Sikh surname Singh (for boys) and Kaur (for girls).
★ Let the children discuss how the names were chosen and what other information the children found out at home.
➤ *Were you named after a relative or family friend ? If so whom?* (You may find that a lot of children have a 'middle' name, this is usually after someone else.) *Is that person alive or dead? Why were you named after that person? What do you know about the person?* If he or she is dead, the name lives on, discuss what might this mean. *Does the choice of names indicate anything about your parents' feelings?* Jewish parents often name children after a relative who has recently died. (This discussion may provide informal opportunities to discuss death or loss.)
➤ *Were you named after some other person admired by your parents?* Ask similar questions to those above.
★ Discuss naming in accordance with religious tradition, see particular notes on Sikh naming ceremonies ('Introduction to Sikhism', p.130). This would be the time to introduce the idea of naming ceremonies in a place of worship.
➤ *What other reasons for choosing a name can you think of?* e.g. after a place your parents are fond of? Because your parents liked the meaning of the name? Because your parents liked the sound of the name?
★ Conduct a survey of all the given names in the school, organised by age. These could be put into graph form to see whether trends and fashions become apparent. This may be more clearly seen if parents' and grandparents' names are also included.
★ Find out what people or events gave rise to these fashions, e.g. was there a popular film star at this time?
★ Use a globe or world map to locate the place of origin of some names.

Unit 3
The meaning of names

A book of names and their meanings would be useful here.

Purpose
● to show that many names were originally used to convey a specific meaning

Ideas
★ Drama can give an opportunity for children to take a new, meaningful name. If the drama involves setting up a new society, children can choose a name to express something about themselves; or in a drama about American Indians they can choose a meaningful name – Swiftfoot, Strongfighter, Wisethinker, etc., or a more allusive one – Running Water, Bright Sunrise.
➤ Talk about the most common sources of names. Possibilities include:
Religious tradition/scripture, e.g. Joshua, Jacob, Muhammad, Paul, Peter, Sarah, Elizabeth, Mary.
Folk heroes (recent or historical), e.g. Robin, Richard, Wendy, Florence.
Admirable qualities, e.g. Faith, Hope, Charity, Joy.
Flowers and jewels, e.g. Violet, Rose, Beryl.
Children's names may be grouped into the above or similar categories. Some names may crop up in many languages and cultures, for example, the name that in English is 'John'.

Unit 4
Family names or surnames

Purpose
• to reinforce ideas of names having meanings
• to think about where we may have come from (i.e. what our family might have been)

Ideas
★ Talk about the origin of family names: e.g.
Ancestry (-son, Mac-, O'-, Ben-, Ibn-, etc.)
Occupation (Thatcher, Cooper, etc.)
Place (Hawarth, Galway, de-, von-, etc.)
Also appearance, characteristics, class/caste, etc.
★ Take some names with fairly simple occupational meanings (e.g. Butcher, Cooper) and think how they might have 'advertised' themselves in the days when few people could read. Draw pictures to represent the different occupations.
★ Ask the children to make coats-of-arms with a pictorial representation of their names on them.
☛ *How is a surname passed on?*
★ Ask the children to find out what other families they are descended from (Mother's, mother's mother's, father's mother's and so on). This could be represented by a diagram (see page 23).
This is best avoided where some children do not know both their parents.
★ Discuss what else may be passed on in families. Family 'treasures' such as jewellery, orna-ments, furniture, pictures, for example. Also family mottoes and family stories, e.g. stories my mother learnt from her mother, or stories about great-grandparents or other ancestors.
★ Ask each child to make a 'family treasure chest' of what they would like to pass on to their children – 'family portraits' – (drawn or photographs) 'jewellery' made in various ways, a family motto. These might be things that they actually possess, or more likely things that they would like to have as family keepsakes.

Unit 5
Taking on a new name

People take on a new name for all sorts of secular reasons including simply not liking their own name. Chinese people often choose an English first name when they move to Britain. Other immigrants may adopt an English surname or anglicize their name to make it easier to pronounce, e.g. Fuchs to Fox. A similar adaptation to living in a new country comes with adding a family name as in the case of Pakistani Muslims or some Sikhs (see above under 'Family names').

Of course, the main reason people take on a new name in this country is that the majority of women take their husband's name at marriage.
Some children take their stepfather's name or receive the name of new parents at adoption. Obviously this is an area to be treated sensitively.

Family names

The practice of passing names on from father to children only developed gradually in Europe, and in many other parts of the world is not used at all. Members of the same family may not have any name in common. Pakistani Muslims, for example, do not usually use family names, but in Britain they often give children the same name as the father to conform with British practice. See the Faith Introduction on p.130 for the Sikh names Kaur and Singh. Some Sikhs add a family name to avoid confusion between families. Indian family names may derive from occupation, caste or sub-caste, geographical area, or from religious allegiance. As in Britain, names are now passed from father to children.

Nuns and monks usually take on a new name when they take their final vows. This is frequently after a saint.

Roman Catholic children are given an additional name at the time of confirmation.

Although the name given at Christian Baptism is usually a name already in use this may not necessarily be the case especially when the candidate is converting from another faith. In any case it is always a name associated with being a Christian.

Chinese children are given a new name when they start school. The Buddha is often asked to bless it. This will be their official name for the rest of their lives.

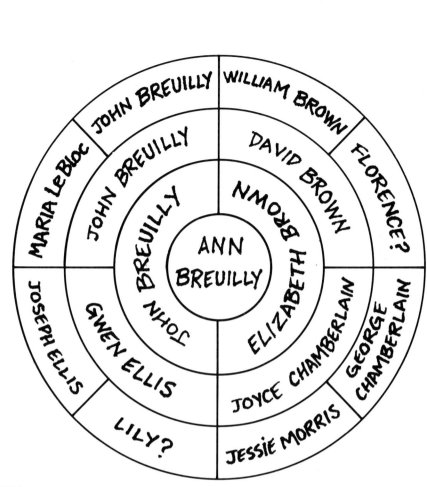

Ancestor diagram

Purpose

• to think about the new responsibilities that may be taken on at various stages in our lives
• to become aware that it is possible to start afresh or start an entirely new life

Ideas

👄 *Why do people take a new name?* (see notes and Information Box.)

★ Discuss sensitively if any of the children have ever taken a new name.

Unit 6
Titles and nicknames

Purpose

• to show that we are all given appellations other than our names and to explore what these mean in terms of our relationships with people and their perceptions of us

• to look at some of the titles given to some founders of faiths

Ideas

👄 *What do titles imply about our relationship with the title-holder?* (e.g. Mummy, Miss, Lord, Your Honour, etc.)

👄 *What do the titles suggest about the nature of the title-holders themselves?* (General, Reverend, Sergeant, etc.)

★ Names/titles of V.I.P.s, e.g. Her Majesty, His Holiness, Star of stage and screen, etc. Look at the Who?, What?, Why?, How?, etc. of these titles. *What is their significance?* (Some titles have lost much of their original meanings – for example: 'Rt. Honourable Friend' in Parliament.)

★ Discuss nicknames. *Why are they given?* These can sometimes be fun and friendly and affectionate especially in families but are also used to hurt, humiliate and isolate some children. The story of the Ugly Duckling is a good way to introduce a general discussion on the hurt such names can bring. Some children may well have nicknames within the family but may wish to keep these private. In Chinese tradition nicknames may have a special role (see Information Box).

★ Give some of the children or members of staff affectionate or praising titles in a light-hearted fashion e.g. James the Reader, Mary the Footballer, Mrs Smith the Wise One.

★ Self-chosen titles or nicknames. Look at some well-known stage-names for individuals or groups. *What are these people/groups trying to say about themselves (or their stage personae)?*

Chinese children are often given nicknames within the family. This may be for auspicious reasons e.g. a child is called 'little calf' expressing the hope that he will grow up to be strong like a bull, or a 'little pig' because pigs have large litters and his parents want more children. Some Chinese use the tradition of giving the baby an unflattering name, e.g. dogface, in order to trick the demons that might come and steal it away. This reflects the high rate of infant mortality in Chinese society until recent years.

Unit 7
Other kinds of names and titles

Purpose
• to look at the way some people are honoured by titles in religious tradition
• to note the respect given to some people's names

Ideas

★ Discuss with the children the use of the words Saint and Holy. Make a list with them of all the Saints they know of from reading, church names, etc. Your area may have its own local saints. If so you could try and find out their stories.

★ Read stories of people given special titles, e.g. 'Solomon the Wise', in *A Tapestry of Tales*.

★ Select some titles from the Information Box to talk about with the children. Your selection will depend on the past experience of the children.

Jesus is often called 'the Christ' meaning the anointed or chosen one of God. Jesus is also called 'the Son' because of the relationship Christians believe he has with God; also the Good Shepherd; the Lord and Saviour. Some Christians bow their heads at the mention of his name.

Mary is called 'Saint Mary', 'Our Lady', 'Mother of God', 'Blessed Virgin' (depending on the tradition of Christianity).

Moses is also called 'the Shepherd' but primarily 'Our teacher' as he gave Jews the Torah. Other Jewish leaders include Solomon the Wise, Elijah the Prophet.

Muhammad is called the 'Holy Prophet' and also the 'Messenger of God'. Muslims always say 'Peace Be Upon Him' when they say his name.

The founders of the Sikh faith are all called 'Guru' meaning teacher.

Siddartha Gautama is called 'the Buddha', meaning Enlightened or Awakened One.

Unit 8
Names and titles of God(s)

Purpose
• to look at some of the titles given to the deity worshipped
• to recognise that these are influenced both by language and by what people believe about God

Ideas

★ Tell the children about Muslim prayer beads and the 99 names of God. Use this to introduce some of the attributes given to God. You could also include here the fact that Muslims call God Allah for this is the Arabic word for God. Ask the children whether they know of any other titles given to God e.g. Father, Shepherd, Lord, King, Guru (Teacher) and what they think these might mean.

★ Unless you have Hindu children in your class, we suggest that you do not include the many names that Hindus use to personify God at this point. (See 'Introduction to Hinduism', p.113 for information on the Hindu concept of God.)

★ Ask the children to think of symbols associated

Names of God

In the Christian tradition, God has a variety of names – the Lord; Father; Creator; Lord of Hosts; etc. These often have historical connotations – Lord of Hosts arises from the battles of the Old Testament.

In the Sikh tradition God is chiefly called the True Guru and the Wonderful God.

In the Hebrew Bible there are many names for God but the most common is Yahveh. In later writings God is sometimes referred to as the 'Holy One' or 'Father in Heaven'.

Many Jews do not write the name of God, but put G-d instead.

Islam traditionally has 99 Most Excellent Names of God. In the Qur'an Muslims are advised to call upon these names (e.g. Surah 7.180):

'Allah has the Most Excellent Names. Call on Him by His names and keep away from those that pervert them.'

Amongst these are the Enduring; the Creator; the Recorder; the Guide. He is also known as the Destroyer; the Watcher; the Withholder; the Loving.

Muslim prayer beads

Muslims use prayer beads to help them concentrate when they praise God. They take each bead between their fingers and say a simple prayer. The prayers are: 'God is good. God is great. God is one.'

Muslims often carry the prayer beads in their pockets or hang them in the car. Then they can use them them when they have a quiet moment to spare.

with these titles e.g. a crook to symbolise a shepherd, or food to symbolize the provider. It is best to avoid drawing any human figure as this may cause offence.

★ Discuss with the children how God can be called a shepherd and a king at the same time. This can be an introduction to the concept of metaphor and figurative language, and the idea that God cannot be fully described in human language, so many names are used to express many different aspects of his nature.

CROSS-CURRICULAR LINKS

History

The children can explore their family trees. They will need to gather information from home and from older relatives. (Sensitivity may be required for children who may not be able to trace their family history.) Draw family trees.

Look at the origin of names. Children may be able to find out about the origin of their name from their parents or grandparents.

Geography

Find out about names which are connected with the locality. These may be names of shops, local businesses, street names, parks and libraries, etc.

WATER

This chapter looks at aspects of ritual and death, and at Islam.

Our sense of responsibility and how we relate to the physical world, of which water is an important part, is a fundamental religious question. Therefore much work on this topic under the heading of science, language, or drama, is implicitly RE when it allows children to explore this relationship. A more scientific study of water can also provide a background to understanding some of the symbolism of water in religion. This could be tackled at a later stage, using some of the suggestions below.

Look at the following aspects of water as essential to life. The Australian Aboriginal story 'Tiddalick' (*REAL Infant Assembly Book*) and the story of 'Muhammad Washing by the River' in *A Tapestry of Tales* further emphasise this. The symbolism of thirst used to express longing appears in Psalm 42, and in the encounter of Jesus with the woman at the well in John 4, but these ideas may be too difficult for many Junior children to grasp fully.

Talk, too, about how water is harvested and used and the effect that human action has on the water supply (e.g. destruction of the forest areas).

Discuss the children's own emotional reactions to storms, being at sea, etc. and follow on with the idea of water as potentially destructive in floods and storms.

Below we outline suggestions for the explicit RE in a topic on water. In this we concentrate on water's use in religion to suggest movement from one state to another – rites of passage in the widest sense. The use of water as an indication of this moving from one state to another is common in many faiths. We have used the Muslim wudu ceremony because it is the easiest for children to grasp.

Christian baptism is not covered, as the interplay of symbols is too difficult for children to grasp. For example, one symbol is of 'passing through water' from the kingdom of this world to the kingdom of God. Another is of 'rising from the waters of death' to 'new life in Christ'. There is also a concept of cleansing from original sin, but there is much disagreement over this, and to introduce it here could introduce undesirable ideas to the children. At this stage it is better to treat baptism as a naming and commitment ceremony. (See 'Babies' in the *REAL Infant Teacher's Handbook*.)

Unit 1
Wudu

This unit is to explain the notion of moving from one state of being to another. Washing in Islam is not a symbolic act, an 'outward sign' of an inward experience. Washing is part of the process which prepares the Muslim for prayer: body, mind and spirit are one, not viewed as separate entities.

Purpose
● to give children the opportunity to reflect on how their physical actions affect how they feel

• to develop an understanding of ritual linking the physical and the spiritual
• to increase understanding of Islam

Ideas

★ Ask the children to prepare short dramas or illustrate cartoon strips on the following sequences:
– Getting myself ready for supper after playing outside
– Getting up and ready for school
– Getting ready for bed
– Getting ready to go and visit Grandma
– Getting ready to go out to a party
Children will probably include washing in many if not all of the sequences.

Wudu – washing before Muslim prayers

If at all possible, Muslims always wash before prayer. Muslims emphasise physical cleanliness as well as the cleansing of the heart by this ceremony.
1) First the Muslim recites 'Bismillah rahmanir rahim' (In the name of Allah the most Merciful the most Kind) and then he washes both his hands up to the wrists three times making sure the water has reached up between the fingers.
2) Next a handful of water is put to the mouth and it is rinsed three times.
3) After this he sniffs water into his nostrils three times to clean them and then the tip of the nose is washed.
4) Then he washes his face three times from right ear to left ear and from forehead to throat.
5) First the right and then the left arm is washed thoroughly from wrist to elbow three times.
6) Next the Muslim moves his wet palms over his head from the top of his forehead to the back of his head.
7) The ears are cleansed next by passing the wet tips of the index fingers into the grooves and holes of both ears and passing the wet thumbs behind the ears.
8) He then passes the wet back of his hands over the nape of the neck.
9) Finally starting with the right foot he washes both feet to the ankle making sure the water has covered all the foot including between the toes.

★ Consider the practice of washing hands before handling sacred texts such as the Qur'an and before touching the images of the gods in Hinduism. The children may well be required or want to wash their hands before touching precious objects at home.
Then tell children about Muslims preparing themselves for prayer by washing (see Information Box). You could take the children through the wudu ceremony in mime. If you have a Muslim child in the class he may be able to demonstrate.
➥ *Why is washing so often a part of getting ready?*
Of course, cleansing is an important part of this, but try and encourage the children to go beyond this, perhaps by drawing on your own experience. *Does washing in the morning help you wake up? Does washing for dinner help you calm down after the excitement of games? Does a bath before bed help you relax?* Not all these things will ring true in every child's experience, but it will with some.
★ Brainstorm with the children lots of different things certain people might be thinking of before prayer time – e.g. a woman with a baby, a man in a shop, teenagers at school.
Then ask what would these people want to think about when they are praying?

Unit 2
Crossing the river Styx

In much of the ancient world, it was said that the soul had to cross the river dividing this world from the next. A coin was put into the dead person's mouth to pay the ferryman. This is another aspect of the association of water with change from one world (form of life) to another.

Purpose

• to explore further the use of water as part of a rite of passage
• to provide the opportunity to talk about death

Ideas

★ Ask the children to look at a map and to write down when a traveller would have to cross water on the following journeys:

Water

England – Belgium – Switzerland – Italy,
Egypt – Israel – Iran,
Istanbul – southern Greece – southern Italy.

➥ *Why are rivers and seas often boundaries?*

★ Tell them about the river Styx and Charon the ferryman. You could use the story of 'Orpheus and Eurydice' (*A Tapestry of Tales*) to illustrate this.

➥ *What might people have thought about on the journey across the River Styx?*

★ Ask them to draw pictures depicting the boat and the ferryman, and 'the soul' with a thought bubble giving the soul's thoughts as it travels to the next life.

CROSS-CURRICULAR LINKS

Science
Discuss the properties of water. Explore floating and sinking, boiling and freezing water and comparing different materials and the results of your experiments.

Make a list of who and what needs water and why.

History
Examine the history of water and sewage provision in Britain. Find out how people lived long ago. Ask older people what it was like for them. *How was the washing done? Do you think it was harder or easier to do the washing in your grandparents' time or great-grandparents' time?*

Geography
Look at a globe and find all the areas of water. *Is the world mostly land or water?*

Find out about the journey of water to your house. Write to the water authorities for more information.

Look at the importance of water transport in Britain.

28

FRIENDS

The themes of this chapter explore Christianity, relationships and feelings.

The making of friends marks the first move outwards from the family circle towards an awareness of a wider society. Our family is determined for us either by birth or adoption, but we choose our friends. At this age there is often a seemingly endless cycle of quarrelling and making up between friends. This also marks a stage where there may be the first real awareness of moral dilemma. Children may be torn between loyalty to friends, and the rules or norms of their family. Although the main focus of the topic is the relationship children have with others, it can be an opportunity to gain an insight into the character of the great religious leaders by reading some of the stories about them and looking at their relationships with others. Several of these can be found in *A Tapestry of Tales*.

Sensitivity needs to be shown to children who may feel they are without friends.

Many children's stories have an underlying theme of friendship, which you could pick up where relevant. Some examples where friendship features strongly are *The B.F.G.* by R. Dahl, *Woof* by A. Ahlberg, *The Sheep Pig* by D. King-Smith and *Charlotte's Web* by E. B. White. (See bibliography, p.137.) Also look at 'Friendship' in the *REAL Junior Assembly Book*.

Unit 1
Me and my friends

Purpose
- to reflect on the word friendship

Ideas
★ Working in pairs, the children could make 'Wanted' posters in which they identify the characteristics they think a friend should have.
★ Ask for contributions to a dictionary with definitions of friendship e.g. a friend is someone who plays with you.
★ Discuss the meaning of the proverb 'birds of a feather flock together'. *Do you think it's true? What other proverbs and expressions can you think of about friendship?* ('Fair-weather friend'; 'a friend in need is a friend indeed'; 'laugh and the world laughs with you, cry and you cry alone'; 'with friends like you, who needs enemies?') *What do they express about friendship?*
★ Some people think of God as their friend. Indeed some of the children in your class may have this sense of God themselves. This could be a time therefore to give the children the opportunity to talk about friendship with God. One idea of prayer is that it is like time spent with a friend, and that is how the friendship grows.

Unit 2
Friends outside school

Children have friends outside the home – children from the street, friends of the family, friends from a previous school, clubs, etc.

Purpose

• to further extend an understanding of friendship

• to show that places of worship are also places of friendship

Ideas

★ Invite the children to introduce a non-school friend to their classmates, not literally but by describing them either verbally or in writing. Encourage the children to think about what sort of person this friend is and why they like them, rather than describing them in purely physical terms. They could also be encouraged to think of friends across the age range, and to include people who might also be in their family.

★ From the previous activity or independently, compile a list with the children of places they might make friends.

★ Tell them about places where you have made new friends.

★ Ask the children to cut out pictures from old magazines, and find scenes in books and in the Pictorial Charts display pictures, of places where friends might meet – e.g. community centres, clubs, churches, mosques, etc. Look at how people meet and talk in their places of worship.

Unit 3
Quarrelling with friends

Purpose

• to give the children a chance to think about causes of quarrels and begin to learn how to avoid or handle them

Ideas

★ Make two puppets quarrel with one another. Ask the children to give reasons why the puppets are arguing, and suggestions as to how they could be reconciled.

(This activity is also suggested in the *REAL Infant Teacher's Handbook* topic on 'Family'. Even if it was used there, there would be no harm in repeating it for this important subject.)

★ Ask the children to work in pairs, or continue the above discussion to devise a puppet play in which the puppets argue and then make up. The puppets could be simple ones made by the children – e.g. out of paper bags or junk material.

★ If you have any drama work ongoing with the children introduce a quarrel into it, and let the children work out ways of resolving it. Quite what the quarrel is about will obviously depend on you, and the fictional situation you've created with them.

★ Suggest '**The Quarrel**' as a title for a story.

Unit 4
Loyalty to friends

Purpose

• to raise the question of loyalty to friends, and give children a chance to discuss problems which arise

Ideas

★ Loyalty is valued generally as a virtue. When you're out of luck you know who your true friends are. Discuss this idea together.

➥ *What if your friend is stealing or bullying a younger child, what do you do then?* This is a common dilemma for children.

★ Tell the story from the Ramayana of 'Rama and Lakshman' in *A Tapestry of Tales* which exemplifies loyalty between friends.

★ Tell the story of Peter's denial in the 'Easter Story' (*A Tapestry of Tales*), or the passage in C. S. Lewis's *Voyage of the Dawn Treader* p.120-121 (HarperCollins) where Lucy hears a friend make an unkind remark about her.

➥ *What makes people deny their friends?*

★ Pose some artificial 'what if' dilemmas for children – and ask them to work out a strategy. This could be done in a class discussion – or better still children working in pairs and then sharing their answers with the class. Stealing features high on the list, because it's a common problem with children of this age. You may find the most interesting results if you pair children of like temperament e.g. shy with shy. Some suggested dilemmas:

– *You see your friend take some sweets from the shop at the school disco. What do you do?*

– *Your friend boasts to a group of children that he has a computer (or whatever luxury item is popular at the moment) at home. You know he hasn't. What do you do?*

– Your friend has come to play. He wants to play with a computer game, you want to read a book. What do you do?

– You see your friend teasing another child. What do you do?

– A school rule says that no one is allowed out of the gate at lunch time, but your friend goes out. What do you do?

Unit 5
Unlikely friends

Telling a story set in another time and place can raise a sensitive issue without it being threatening to children in the class who might feel themselves to be outsiders.

Purpose
● to show children an example of someone befriending an outsider
● to extend an understanding of the character of Jesus

Ideas
★ Tell the story of 'Zacchaeus' in *A Tapestry of Tales*. Discuss the criticism Jesus received for being the friend of 'publicans and sinners' (see Information Box). Also look at the effect that Jesus's offer of friendship had on Zacchaeus. The children might like to draw before and after pictures of Zacchaeus.

> Zacchaeus in the story was an outsider in Jewish society because he was a tax-collector. He was therefore working for the Roman rulers, and because of the system under which such officials were employed, he made his own living out of the taxes he collected. The temptation to overcharge must therefore have been great.

Unit 6
A celebration of friendship

To conclude your topic on friendship, you could organise a class celebration. Discuss with the children the ways in which they would like to celebrate the existence of friendship, and their particular friends. Some suggestions are given below:

Purpose
● to celebrate friendship

Ideas
★ Make a large cake with some suitable decoration. If the class is small enough, or the cake is big enough, let each child light a candle in honour of his or her friends, or someone they would like to be friends with. The names can be spoken out loud, or kept private.
★ Make a friendship table or corner with pictures and writing about friends, or symbols which represent any particular friends. Perhaps you could light one candle in front of the table.
★ Learn poems and songs about friends and friendship, or write your own and present them as part of the celebration.
★ Drink a 'toast' in fruit juice to 'absent friends' – children could name them out loud or privately.

CROSS-CURRICULAR LINKS
Geography
Where do your friends live? Ask the children to describe the route from their house to their friend's house.

English
Write poems about friends. There are many books to read on the topic of friendship. The children can make a list of the qualities of a friend and using different colours and styles of writing, turn the words in a picture of their friend.

Art
The children can paint a picture of a friend, either from life, if the friend is at school, or from a photograph.

FOOD

Themes of celebration, ritual, diversity, sharing, and rules arise in this chapter. All the five major faiths Christianity, Hinduism, Sikhism, Islam and Judaism are linked with work on the topic of food.

A look at food provides opportunities for considering many aspects of religion: creation stories usually indicate how humanity should relate to the Earth and its bounty of food; scriptures or oral traditions may contain 'laws' concerning what may or may not be eaten; festivals and rites of passage are normally associated with special foods; food is eaten symbolically in some rituals and may be a symbol elsewhere; food is the subject of social and moral dimensions of religion – sharing and charity, greed and gluttony.

As it is so vast a topic 'Food' appears at both infant and junior levels. The following are covered at infant level – giving thanks for food, food as communication, food and community, food and celebration, and a special meal, the Sabbath, is covered in the topic on 'Family'. You may wish to include some of this material if your class has not done it earlier.

See also the assemblies on Food in the *REAL Junior Assembly Book*.

At this level two aspects of the topic are explored: religious rules governing permitted foods and preparation of food and the symbolic use of food.

Unit 1
Food and fads

The kind of food we eat depends to an extent on our circumstances, our culture and tastes. Sometimes these influences may be in conflict. An examination of these should lead to an understanding of the need for rules about food – rules which may be specific to one household or to an entire religious culture. Be careful that minorities in the class are neither offended by the discussion nor have their particular food customs presented as strange or distasteful.

Purpose
• to look more closely at the food we eat
• to think about rules concerning food

Ideas
★ Children can suggest 'ideal' breakfast menus and illustrate them, perhaps making up a 'still life' of the articles such as a corn flakes packet and a milk bottle to draw. From this data they can see that:

– A great deal of preparation, time and money would be involved to produce some of these menus. *Who would do the work – Mum/Dad, brothers, sisters, grannies, you?* Consider the problems of inconvenience, expense.

– Some children are going to hate food that others like. The same will apply in a family. Different ideal breakfasts will be needed in each home. This again is inconvenient and expensive.

– Some children may not be allowed to eat what others like most. These constraints may be applied for many reasons, e.g. health, religious belief, or expense. There may be general embargos or specifically breakfast ones, e.g. 'No you can't have chips and mushy peas at this time of the morning!'

★ You could raise the need for learning not to say 'Ugh' when people have something you don't like or haven't ever eaten!

☛ *Why can't we always have what we want? Why do we not all want the same things? What would happen* if we got what we wanted all the time? (This is a question about health as well as morality.)

➥ *Are there any items that no one in the class would eat?* Answers may include foods like spinach or similar items unpopular with children, but consider a consensus around 'what it's not right to eat', e.g. cats, the class gerbils, etc.

★ You could present the consensus reached above as a class rule. This rule can be challenged and explored further in drama. *In a situation of siege or scarcity what might people eat? Are the rules different if you are starving?*

★ Children can make books of **Things we can eat**, and **Things we can't eat**.

From this acceptance of rules of food it is possible to go on to look at the origin and reasons behind food-rules in different belief systems (see Information Box below).

Since the days of the Early Church, some **Christians** have avoided meat on Fridays as a means of aiding spiritual development by recalling Good Friday. The Lent fast has become the giving up of one or more foods or pleasures in order to feel closer to the suffering of Jesus in the last days of his life on Earth.

For **Jews**, food laws fall into two categories. The first category concerns animals which it is forbidden for Jews to eat. This includes all animals which either do not chew the cud or have not got cloven hooves; all fish or sea creatures which have not got both fins and scales and a wide range of birds. The second category covers the rules for the slaughter and preparation of food in the correct way to make it kosher or permitted. Adherence to these laws is a distinctive mark of Judaism and has helped to keep the Jewish identity and sense of a special relationship with God alive through years of persecution.

Muslims likewise have permitted foods called halal. Those which are forbidden come in four groups:
– that which has died by itself, been strangled, beaten to death, killed by a fall or gored
– all blood, as in black puddings
– pigs
– any food offered before images of the gods, or over which any name other than Allah's has been invoked.

These injunctions, laid down in the Qur'an, are a sign of belonging to God and of being in submission (Islam) to the will of God.

For many **Hindus**, the eating of any animal, bird or fish is seen to be wrong. Hindu belief teaches that within all sentient creatures there exists a spirit or form of soul, known as 'atman'. At death it is the atman which survives and is reborn. The atman, through countless rebirths, eventually escapes from the wheel of rebirth and is reunited with the Ultimate. However, the state of rebirth depends upon the actions of the person or creature during its previous lives. Hindu teaching stresses that to kill another creature for food is to commit a terrible crime against life. In any killing, the natural span of the atman is destroyed. Hence the prevalence of vegetarianism amongst Hindus.

A similar respect for living creatures is shared by **Buddhists**. For **Jains**, it goes even further, to the extent that Jain monks and nuns often sweep the ground in front of them to remove any ants or other insects, which might otherwise be trodden on.

Many people in the West are vegetarian and some are vegan (i.e. they do not eat any products of animals such as milk, cheese, eggs, or butter). They choose to do this not necessarily because they have religious principles, but because they object on moral or humanitarian grounds to the killing of animals, or to the conditions in which, say, battery hens are kept. Some people are vegetarian for health reasons.

Unit 2
Sharing food

Purpose
● to explore the notions and emotions involved in sharing
● to explore the symbolism of sharing food

Ideas
★ Tell the story of 'The Soupstone' (*A Tapestry of Tales*). Re-enact the story with children thinking of items to add to the soup.
★ Tell the story of 'Loaves and Fishes' (*A Tapestry of Tales*). Draw out the theme of the boy's willingness to share the little he had.
☞ Discuss, or role play, the situation where one child has a packet of crisps, sweets, etc., and her friend has not. *What will she do? Eat it all herself in front of her friend? Eat it later when her friend is not there? Or share it? What if other people join them? Why would you act in the ways suggested?*
★ Tell the story of 'Baucis and Philemon' (*A Tapestry of Tales*), drawing out that the old couple

were rewarded because of their willingness to share their food.
★ Tell the children about the Sikh Langar (see Information Box). See also the assembly 'Akbar' in the *REAL Infant Assembly Book*.
☞ *What would you bring to a communal meal?* Make sure that there is nothing which other people could not eat.
★ Look at other traditions where eating together is a sign of cementing friendship, e.g the Old English tradition that once you had eaten salt with someone, you could not turn against them. Since most food had salt in it, eating together at all was a pact between two people. You could compare this with the modern 'business lunch'.

Unit 3
Bread as a symbol

Bread is a staple food in Middle Eastern and Western diets. It is therefore often regarded as the most basic of all foods. In religious thought God provides the bread which sustains us. Bread represents the way in which God, or one's faith, feeds and sustains the spirit. Bread is also a food which can easily be eaten without utensils and so is easy to share with another. Sharing bread is a sign of friendship. Indeed the word 'companion' came from the French for 'with bread'.

Purpose
● to develop an understanding of the use of food in ritual, both symbolically and festively

Ideas
★ Ask the children to record what they eat in one day. Then you can compare these records with them to see how many children have eaten bread, potatoes, rice or pasta. The information could be presented in a graph and then used to discuss the idea of a staple food.
★ Make a collection of as many different sorts of bread as you can find. You may need to resort to pictures for some but obviously the more of the real thing the better as the children can then taste it. Your local bakers or delicatessen may be willing to give you some stale examples for display purposes.
★ Bake bread with the children and then eat the

The Langar

After every Sikh service or celebration in the gurdwara, a meal is served. All are welcome, Sikh or not, irrespective of whether they were at the service. The meal is prepared and served communally by the Sikh community. Some bring money to the service, others food, and some prepare and serve the food. (Incidentally, it is often the men who do the cooking and serving – Sikhism lays great stress on the equality of men and women.) The meal is always vegetarian to ensure that it is acceptable to all, no matter what their religious beliefs.

This practice originated with Guru Nanak, the founder of Sikhism, who lived in a society deeply divided between Hindu and Muslim, rich and poor, high status and low status. He insisted that anyone who came to see him should eat together first, and anyone who refused to do this could not visit the Guru. Thus all his visitors had to acknowledge their equality with others by sitting down to eat with them.

Holy Communion

The first Christians gathered together on the first day of each week, to share bread and wine in a simple meal. They met on the first day of the week, the day we call Sunday, because they believed that God raised Jesus from the dead on that day. At the last meal Jesus ate with his followers before his death, he asked them to remember him by sharing bread and wine.

Different traditions have different names for the Christian ritual in which bread is broken and then eaten: Communion, Eucharist, Mass, Lord's Supper. For all Christians the ritual remembers Jesus's command to his disciples 'Do this in remembrance of me' (Luke 22: 19-20) and his subsequent death by crucifixion. Beyond this, beliefs vary enormously and are often difficult for adults to understand, which is why we suggest that you stick to the one common tradition when discussing it with your class. In the major traditions the bread may only be consecrated by a priest.

The bread at Communion may be ordinary bread but is often a wafer, sometimes with a Christian symbol moulded into it. Your local vicar may be willing to give you an unconsecrated wafer to show your class or you can buy them from church suppliers (see Useful Addresses p.135). Although such a wafer would be unconsecrated it should still be treated carefully out of deference to the beliefs of some Christians.

Hallah

The hallah (plural hallot) is the traditional plaited bread used by Jews at the Sabbath meal and festivals other than Passover. It is a reminder of the grain that was once offered in the temple in Jerusalem. Since the destruction of the Temple in CE 70 the table in the home has become the altar at which the Jew offers his praise and service to God. Two hallot are laid on the Sabbath table because it is also a reminder to Jews of the story that God provided their ancestors with food (manna) in the desert – just enough for each day but on Friday there was a double portion so that they would not have to collect food on the Sabbath. The bread is blessed with the words: Blessed art thou, O Lord our God, King of the Universe, who brings forth bread from the earth.

This indicates the basic Jewish belief that God is the provider of all sustenance.

The bread itself is a rich mixture with milk and/or eggs. The following fairly simple version makes one good-sized loaf, sufficient for a class of thirty to have a piece each:
1 tablespoon vegetable oil
$\frac{1}{2}$ of 6 g sachet dry yeast (This recipe is based on the 'easy-blend' kind sold to be mixed dry into the flour. If using any other kind, adjust accordingly.)
1 teaspoon salt
150 ml warm water
2 teaspoons sugar
1 egg
500 g strong plain white flour
sesame or poppy seeds

1) Put the flour in a mixing bowl and stir in the dry yeast, sugar and salt.
2) Make a well in the middle and add the water, oil and the beaten egg, reserving a small amount of egg for brushing the surface later.
3) Mix well, adding more water or more flour if necessary to make a pliable dough.
4) Turn out onto a floured board and knead until pliable and not sticky. If poked with a finger the dough will spring back.
5) Return dough to the bowl and cover with a tea-towel. Put it in a warm place to rise for 1 hour. At the end of this time it should have doubled in size, and if poked with a finger, the hole will remain.
6) Turn dough onto a lightly floured board and knead for about 1 minute.
7) Cut into 3 equal pieces and knead each with a little flour until it is not sticky.
8) Oil a baking sheet.
9) Roll each piece into a sausage about 8 inches long.
10) Make a plait from the 3 pieces, sticking the ends firmly together and tucking them under.
11) Place on the baking sheet and let it rise for 45 minutes at room temperature.
12) Brush the top of the loaf with beaten egg and sprinkle with sesame or poppy seeds. Bake for 40 minutes at 190° Celsius, 375° Fahrenheit, Gas Mark 5.
13) Cool on a rack.

For information about matzah (unleavened bread) see the topic on Passover.

finished product together. Most general recipe books have a recipe for bread or you could try baking the traditional Jewish bread, hallah (see recipe in the Information Box).

★ Try to trace the process right to its very beginning on the farm. In a few places local farmers or mills will supply the grains of wheat and the whole class can participate by taking turns to grind it with a mortar and pestle. The end loaf will be very heavy and grainy but satisfying in more ways than one.

★ When you eat the bread together try doing so with some ceremony rather than by simply handing out the pieces. You could for instance sit the children in a circle, and then pass the bread from one child to the next, each one tearing off a piece to give to his neighbour. This would help give a small insight into the Christian Communion service (see Information Box).

★ Tell the story of the Last Supper in 'Holy Week, Easter and Whitsun' (*A Tapestry of Tales*) and tell the children how this became the origin of the Communion service (see Information Box). This could be used to initiate a discussion on the use of the bread in the service. We suggest you focus on the use of the bread as a way of remembering Jesus. The discussion could be led in the following directions:
– Why Christians want to remember Jesus
– Recollections of foods which remind the children of someone in particular or of a particular incident.

★ Some of the children in your class may have attended Communion services, which they may refer to by different names (see Information Box) and can contribute accounts of their experience and opinion of what is happening. (This may not always be the view the vicar would like them to have!)

★ If the children have made bread they will have had to use some yeast or other raising agent. Now introduce some unleavened bread, especially matzah, and take the opportunity to tell or recall the story of the Israelites' flight from Egypt and their celebration of it at Passover. The extent to which you do this will depend on whether they have already followed the topic on Passover. (See topic on 'Passover' p.89 for more details).

★ Show the children some hallah and describe its significance for Jews including the story of the provision of manna to the Israelites in the wilderness (see Information Box). Some supermarkets

and delicatessens do sell it or you could try making your own.

➥ Discuss with the children the derivation of the word 'companion' (see above) and what they think are the benefits of eating with a friend rather than alone.

Unit 4
Sweet food

Giving sweet food often is a way of wishing someone well, and sharing sweet food, such as cake, may be a way of sharing in the happiness of a person or couple.

Purpose
• to consider the symbolism of sweet food

Ideas
➥ Begin this section of the topic with a general discussion about sweets and sweet food. Your discussion could cover the following questions: *When do you eat sweets? Are you ever given sweets by adults? Why do some parents restrict the amount of sweets they give? If so, when and why?* (Grandparents may bring sweets as a treat to show love for a child but sweets can sometimes be given as a bribe to be good.) *On what occasions do your parents give or receive sweets? Why do you think that it's a general custom to give sweets (or fruit which is sweet) rather than savoury food like vegetables?* This might be the time to tell the children about the Hindu custom of always giving a baby something sweet as its first solid food as a way of expressing the hope that the baby will have a sweet life.

★ Show the children a map of the Middle East and tell them of the desert tribesmen who ride on camels and until recent years lived in huge tents (a few still do). Tell them of the tradition that all strangers were made welcome in the tents with a hearty meal. But first they drank bitter coffee followed by sweet tea. This symbolized that bitter times helped one appreciate the good times. The ritual invited the guest to remember happy times as well as wishing him or her a happy visit. Let the children taste bitter coffee followed by slightly honeyed tea.

★ The tale of this custom can be used to stimulate

the children to recall an occasion which was sweet to them – a time when they felt happy and the memory of it makes them feel happy. Some may even like to record these in their personal journals or in a class book.

★ Will someone in your class or a member of the school staff be having a birthday while you are in the middle of this topic? Perhaps it's time the class guinea pig had a birthday! If so bake a cake, preferably with the children, and share it. Then ask them why they think celebrations usually involve a cake and why it's nicer to have a big one that everyone shares rather than lots of little ones. Draw their attention to the ritual involved in the cutting of birthday cakes. (Lighting candles, singing 'Happy Birthday', trying to blow all the candles out at once, making a wish, sharing out the cake, and guests sometimes taking a piece of the cake home.)

★ Celebration cakes provide opportunities for further exploration of symbolism, beyond the fact that they are sweet. Birthday cakes have a candle to stand for each year of the life. Novelty cakes are often made to reflect the interests of the person whose birthday it is and festive cakes are generally bedecked with motifs of the occasion. The children could design a cake for someone they know. Collage would be an effective medium for the design as well as crayons and felt pens.

★ Ask the children to think of 'sweet' wishes to make for each other.

★ Children could design sweets, like the old 'Love Hearts', which had friendly messages on. Or cakes with 'sweet' wishes could be made. Iced hearts or smiling faces could decorate the cakes. Perhaps designs could be made on paper instead.

★ Make a sweet halva with the children, which will be similar to the Karah Parshad used in a Sikh service (see Information Box). Sikhs sometimes make this for parties, and may add raisins or nuts. It is important to emphasise that it is not Karah Parshad that you are making, since Karah Parshad can only be made by Sikhs, with special prayers, but the children will get an idea of what it is like to share this food.

Sweet food

When **Hindus** offer worship to the gods, they frequently offer sweet food such as fruit or honey to a statue of one of the gods – especially to Krishna, as stories are told about his liking for rich foods when he was a child. (See 'Krishna and the Butter' in *A Tapestry of Tales*).

It is common for children to be given sweets at a festival. At the **Jewish** festival of Simhat Torah the children walk round the synagogue, in procession, waving flags, and are given sweets. The **Muslim** festival of Eid ul-Fitr celebrates the end of the month of fasting, so sweets are especially welcome as a celebration.

It is common for **Sikhs** to give children sweets to celebrate any happy event. As part of any Sikh service, a special mixture of flour, semolina, sugar and butter is prepared, called Karah Parshad. This is prepared with special prayers, and mixed with a kirpan, the small sword or dagger that all Sikhs carry as one of the signs of their faith. At the end of the service, the Karah Parshad is shared out to all present. A small amount is put into everyone's hands, and children often follow, handing out napkins to wipe hands on.

The recipe below is for a sweet paste similar to **Karah Parshad**:

50 g flour
50 g semolina
100 g butter
100 g sugar
150 ml water

1) Melt the butter in a saucepan, and add the flour and semolina.
2) Stir for a few minutes over a medium heat.
3) Add the water, and stir well.
4) Add the sugar, and cook, stirring continuously, for about 15 minutes, or until it is a soft paste and the gritty, 'floury' taste has gone.

Unit 5
Ordinary food becomes special

Purpose
● to convey that the food itself may not be special but the special circumstances make it so

Ideas
★ Using the example of Karah Parshad (see Information Box above), you can explore with the children the idea that the same food can be quite ordinary, or have some special significance. When prepared normally, the butter and semolina mixture is a nice-tasting sweet. When prepared with special prayers, and stirred with a kirpan, it becomes Karah Parshad and is shared by all as part of the service.

★ Similarly, when Hindus prepare a meal, some of the food is offered to God at the home shrine. The offering makes the food blessed, and it is then taken and mixed with the rest of the food, so the blessing is distributed to all who share the food. By offering it to God it becomes special.

★ You could draw the parallel with the Christian Communion service pointing out that the bread, which may be ordinary bread from the bakers, becomes special because of the way it is blessed and used in the service.

★ Make an illustrated class book of symbolic foods and food for special occasions. This can be added to over a period of time as children track down the information from family, friends and other books. It could include recipes as well as explanations of the symbols or the stories associated with them (see Information Box).

★ Organise a class celebration – perhaps of a particular season, or the culmination of a large piece of work, or a school anniversary. Let each child make a collage on a paper plate of suitable food to bring to the party, and write about their reasons for choosing it – white or warming food for winter, a lattice tart to celebrate a weaving project, tree-shaped biscuits for Elm Road School, etc. Perhaps invite parents or other classes to come and share the celebration.

★ Learn some songs associated with food and special meals e.g. The Boar's Head Carol; Pace Egging Song; Sabbath songs; 'Mama will you buy me a . . . ?' in *Brown Bread and Butter*, ed. by A. McMorland (Ward Lock Educational) or 'The Street Market Song' in *Wake Up, Stir About* by B. Carson Turner (HarperCollins).

Symbolic food

★ Mince pies at Christmas were originally oval in shape, and represented the crib.

★ Hot cross buns are eaten at Easter, partly because they include many ingredients that have not been eaten during the Lent fast, and to represent the cross of crucifixion.

★ A lamb or a goat is eaten at Eid ul-Adha, as a reminder of the goat that was sacrificed in the place of Ishmael (see the 'Introduction to Islam' p.119).

★ Three-cornered pasties called Hammantaschen are eaten at Purim to represent Hamman, the villain of the story (see 'Introduction to Judaism' p.123).

★ See the unit on Passover for the symbolic food in the Passover meal.

INFORMATION BOX

CROSS-CURRICULAR LINKS

Science
Discover the effect of heat on various foods. Use different sources of heat, such as hot water, the oven, a toaster.

Talk about food hygiene. Write a food hygiene leaflet.

Investigate nutrition, sort pictures of food into categories e.g. bread/cakes, meat/fish, vegetables/fruit.

History
Look at changes in food consumption. Find out what parents or grandparents liked to eat and compare it with children's favourite foods today.

Geography
Find out where food comes from. *Where does the food come from before it gets to the shop?* Conduct a survey to find out where people buy their food. Investigate methods of transportation. *How is the food kept fresh?*

Technology
Make different shaped loaves. Use the recipes in this chapter. Try different materials to keep food hot or cold. *Which materials keep the food hot? Do the same materials keep the food cold too?*

LEARNING ABOUT LEARNING

This chapter deals with some of the great teachers of the five major faiths, it also looks at making priorities and seeks to develop some sense of an individual's own identity.

This topic ties in with the assemblies on 'The School Community' in the *REAL Junior Assembly Book*.

Learning plays an important part in the life of faith. Reflection, meditation and study, especially of sacred literature, are valued because they lead to a deeper understanding of the faith. Teachers are held in high esteem as those who can impart learning, and indeed the founders of faiths were primarily called teachers. However, this topic does more than observe one dimension of religious experience. It gives children the opportunity to develop a sense of themselves, asking them to reflect on themselves as learners. Also it asks them to think about an aspect of their relationships with other people.

The units in this topic are not dependent on each other, and it might be too much for children to work on all of them at one time. These are suggestions which can be incorporated into other studies, or used at odd times as the subject arises.

Unit 1
Learning in school

As school is the place most strongly associated with learning, we start the topic here.

Purpose
● to become aware of the range of learning which takes place within the school

Ideas
★ Be brave and ask the children what they think school is for. You may be surprised at the answers!

★ Ask the children to make a poster advertising all the things which can be learnt in your school. This could be done as a class activity or the children could work in small groups. You may need to have a brainstorming session first, to broaden their concept of what constitutes a learning activity.

Unit 2
Learning from each other

Purpose
● to realize that people can and do learn from people other than teachers
● to recognise that everyone has knowledge and skills they could share with others

➥ *What have you learnt from people other than teachers?* Perhaps a grandmother has taught them to knit, or a friend has taught them a playground song, or an older child showed them the route to the head's office when they first started in the school.

★ Read the stories *The Patchwork Quilt*, by Valerie Flournoy (Puffin), or *Badger's Parting Gifts* by Susan Varley (Picture Lions), which both deal with the value of learning something from another.

➥ *What have you taught someone else?* They may have helped a younger sibling to take her first steps, shown a friend how to kick a football, or taught a younger child to tell the time.

★ What have you as a teacher learnt from the children? Your class will probably be surprised to

learn that they have taught you something as well as vice-versa. One of your class may have taught you to count in their home language, or you may have learnt from a child's writing about a subject he is interested in. They may have shared a skill with you. This could be the time to publicly praise a child who lacks confidence for what that child has taught you.

★ Ask the children to think of something that they can teach you (e.g. the latest dance craze, a skipping game, etc.). They could work in groups to devise a 'lesson plan' which they then put into practice.

➲ *How do you learn from each other in the classroom? Do you help each other with spelling and writing, for example?* Maybe the children have worked together researching a topic and presenting material.

★ The story of 'Eli and Samuel' (*A Tapestry of Tales*) can be used to illustrate the idea of pupil and teacher learning from each other.

★ All the above items could be illustrated and given captions by the children to form part of a display on learning from each other. Reference could also be made to fictional people who have learnt from each other, if the class are familiar with the relevant books, e.g. Sophie and the giant learnt from each other in The *B.F.G.* by R. Dahl (Puffin), in *Heidi* by J. Spyri (HarperCollins) there is a mutual learning between three children, Barney and Stig exchange skills in *Stig of the Dump* by C. King (Penguin), and in the *Borrowers* books by M. Norton (Puffin), adults and children, big people and borrowers learn from each other.

★ Make a class **How to** book for which the children write contributions. Such contributions need not be made all at once, but pasted in long past the end of the time given to the topic. Similarly a class newspaper could have a **How to** page.

Unit 3
Places to learn

Purpose
● to share with each other skills acquired outside school
● to introduce children to the fact that religious

buildings are places of learning as well as worship, or to remind them of this

Ideas
★ On a map of the local area mark with flags places where children go for extra-curricular activities. Threads could lead to statements such as 'Jack learns the piano here', 'Alice is learning football here', 'Julie, Alan and Jane learn ballet here'. Of course some children will go out of the area for some activities, so you may only be able to indicate the direction in which they go. You could also note with the children that some lessons take place in homes, some in hired halls, fields, and some in purpose-built buildings.

★ Invite the children to prepare a short talk to give the class about their extra-curricular activities, they may well need your help to do this. Where more than one child attends the cubs, or swimming lessons etc., they could prepare a talk together. These talks could include showing pho-

---

Most places of worship have classes to help both adults and children to learn more about their faith.

Churches often run Sunday schools for children and/or classes at other times of the week. Adults learn from the sermon in a service, but may also attend classes or study groups during the week.

Sikh gurdwaras run classes for children to learn to read Gurmukhi, so they can read the Guru Granth Sahib. There are often also classes to learn the music, played on traditional instruments, which is an important part of a Sikh service.

Mosques run schools called madrassas, where children learn to pray and read the Qur'an in Arabic.

Jewish children often attend classes on Sundays where they learn Hebrew and study the Torah. Adults too attend study groups at the synagogue. One name for a synagogue is 'shul', which means 'school', and underlines the importance of the synagogue as a house of learning.

Hindu communities often run classes for children, either in someone's home or at the Hindu temple, where the children study the scriptures and learn songs. From time to time a scholar or holy man might visit the temple to give a lecture for the adults.

tos, cups won, or demonstrating a skill (e.g. showing how to place the hands in classical ballet, or playing a tune on an instrument). You will, of course, need to be sensitive to the possibility that not all children in the class may be engaged in such activities, but other children may have learnt skills at home, e.g. mending a puncture, making a cake.

★ Some of the children may attend Sunday school, or be learning Hebrew at the Synagogue. Supplement whatever they can tell you with information from the Information Box, and by looking at the Pictorial Charts display pictures.
➡ *Why do Muslim parents want their children to learn Arabic, or Jewish parents Hebrew?* (See the 'Introduction to Islam' p.119 and 'Introduction to Judaism' p.123).

Unit 4
Adults learning

Purpose
● to realize that learning is not simply a prerogative of the young. (This will have been partly demonstrated by you talking about what you have learnt from them.)

Ideas
★ Ask the children to ask their parents what they have learnt recently. Learning to drive is an obvious example of adult learning, but you could encourage them to include descriptions of smaller tasks, e.g. my Mum learnt how to put in a zip, my Dad learnt how to bake a sponge cake, or such things as programming the video, using a computer, etc.

★ Obtain some prospectuses from a local Further Education College. These could be used as a basis for discussion, but you could also make up some problems using the prospectus as a resource: e.g. *Mary wants to study French. She plays tennis on a Wednesday and babysits on a Friday, so when could she go to French lessons?*

★ The Information Box describes in brief some of the learning that takes place in services (sermons, scripture reading, discussion groups). The children could use this information as part of a general display or account of adults learning.

Unit 5
Learning from someone you have never met

Purpose
● to appreciate that you can learn from someone without them being physically present

Ideas
➡ Begin by asking, *How can you learn from someone you have never met?*
★ Think first about television. Ask the children what they have learnt from it. Ask if they learn only from quiz shows, nature and magazine programmes, or do they also learn from advertisements and cartoons. Discuss what attitudes they think they learn, as well as gathering information.
★ Identify with the children some books which they feel have taught them something. Where possible try and found out more about the author who has been an 'unknown' teacher. There may be more information on the dust jacket, or inside back page. The children could also write to an author, via the publishers, to make personal contact.
➡ *Does an author always make up the story that she writes in a book, or has she learnt it from someone else?* You will need to illustrate this idea using books in the class library – such as poetry anthologies, fairy stories, myths and legends. *Why do you think the author has bothered to record these stories?* Some of these were once passed on mainly by word of mouth. (This is useful background to a study of sacred literature which includes oral traditions which were recorded later.) See topic on 'Writing'.

Unit 6
Great teachers

Purpose
● to introduce or develop the idea that Jesus, Guru Nanak and Muhammad were teachers

Words learnt by heart

Islam

The Declaration of Faith:
There is no god but Allah and Muhammad is the messenger of Allah.
la ilaha illal lahu muhammadur rasulul lah

Sikhism

The Mool Mantra:
There is only one God, Truth is His name.
He is the creator, He is without fear, He is without hate.
He is timeless and without form.
He is beyond death, the enlightened one.
He can be known by the Guru's grace.

Judaism

The Shema:
Hear O Israel, the Lord our God is one God.
You shall love the Lord our God with all your heart, soul and strength.
(Deuteronomy 6:4-9)

Christianity

The Lord's Prayer:
Our Father, who art in heaven,
Hallowed be thy name.
Thy kingdom come, thy will be done, on earth as it is in heaven.
Give us this day our daily bread,
And forgive us our trespasses, as we forgive those that trespass against us.
And lead us not into temptation, but deliver us from evil,
For thine is the kingdom, the power and the glory,
For ever and ever,
Amen.
(This is the traditional version. More modern versions are easier to understand, but less well-known.)

Hinduism

A prayer from the Brihadaranyika Upanishad:
Lead me from the unreal to the real;
Lead me from darkness to light;
Lead me from death to immortality.

Ideas

☞ *What makes someone able to be a teacher? Do they need to have passed exams? Do they need a classroom and a blackboard? What makes some people better teachers than others?*

☞ Read the stories of Jesus, Guru Nanak and the Buddha from *A Tapestry of Tales*. Then pose the questions, *Why were Jesus, Nanak and the Buddha called teachers? Did they have certificates? Had they passed examinations? Why did people listen to them?*

★ Make a word list of the word teacher in many languages, and include 'rabbi' and 'guru'.

★ Tell one or more of the 'Parables of Jesus' (*A Tapestry of Tales*), pointing out how Jesus used stories when he was teaching.

Unit 7
How do we learn?

These ways of learning all have their place in religious traditions.

Purpose

● to help children identify some ways of learning

Ideas
Learning by example

☞ *What have you learnt by watching someone else?*

★ This idea could be developed in dance or mime. Children in groups could devise short dances with deliberate steps. Then each group could teach the others their own dance by example.

★ Tell the story of the woman leaving Mecca in *A Tapestry of Tales*.

★ Tell the story of Jesus washing his disciples' feet.

★ Tell the children about the hadith – the words and actions of Muhammad written down for Muslims to learn from (see 'Introduction to Islam' p.119). Muhammad was so obedient to God that his example can teach those who come after, even in seemingly small details of everyday life.

Using aids to memory

★ Ask if the children have any special ways of remembering e.g. tying knots in hankies, writing themselves a message. Perhaps this is rare at this age, but you could tell them of some. Religious examples are the tefillin and mezuzah (see Information Box in 'Rules and Justice' topic p.61). Prayer beads and rosaries also act as memory aids in reciting prayers.

Learning by rote

Religious stories and sayings were often handed down by word-of-mouth, and it is traditional in most faiths to learn passages of scripture by heart.

★ Ask the children whether they can remember any stories, poems, advertisements or songs by heart, and why they think this is so. It is usually because they have heard it so many times, and joined in so many times. This raises the point that a lot of learning is not achieved deliberately.

★ Use the Information Box on p.42 which contains items from faiths that are often learnt by heart (e.g. Lord's Prayer; Shema; Mool Mantra; beginning of Muslim prayer; Hindu prayer). The children could copy some of these out and decorate with borders, as examples of sayings learnt by heart.

★ Suggest that the children find something they want to learn by heart. This could be the years

their football team won the cup, a poem or song. Volunteers could then demonstrate newly learnt knowledge.

★ Have a concert of rhymes etc. that the children have learnt by heart.

CROSS-CURRICULAR LINKS

History

Look at pictures of school life in Victorian times. *What are the similarities and differences?* Have a Victorian schoolday.

Drama

Each child chooses a skill e.g. sewing on a button, making a cup of tea, mending a puncture, etc. Practise miming the skill and then perform the mime in front of the class. The class must guess the action.

Geography

Look at a map of the local area and find all the places where you can learn. Then investigate how you would get to the places. *What sort of transport would be best?*

MESSAGES WITHOUT WORDS

This chapter looks at worship and ritual; signs and symbols particularly in Christianity, Islam, Hinduism and Sikhism.

Although we often think of the spoken or written word as our main means of communication, much of what we 'say' is expressed without the use of words. Our beliefs and attitudes to life are often indicated by our clothing, our general appearance, gesture, facial expression and so forth. Gesture in particular can be formalized to convey very definite meanings, and in our religious life can express a great deal of our attitude to God and to fellow believers.

In this topic we are using the words 'sign' and 'symbol' in their loose, 'everyday' meanings. A detailed distinction is not necessary here. Also look at 'Plays Without Words' in the *REAL Junior Assembly Book*.

Units 2-4 look more specifically at the way art conveys 'messages without words'. The extent of the role of art in religion varies widely from faith to faith and, in the case of Christianity, for example, within one faith. Some faiths such as Hinduism and, to a large extent Christianity, make rich use of symbolism in their art. Islamic art tends to be simpler because of a prohibition on the use of images (see Introduction to Islam p.119). However there is a common idea that religious art is not purely decorative but is an offering to God. Conversely there is often a notion that God may be revealed or a blessing received through a painting or statue. This is particularly so of icons and Hindu statues of gods. Additionally, especially in pre-literate societies, paintings and statues were a means of teaching about the faith.

The idea of art as a gift is readily grasped by most children since they will have frequently presented their paintings as presents to parents and to each other. However they will probably need to be introduced to the role of symbolism, as their chief contact with adult art is likely to have been with representational or decorative art.

Unit 1
Signs around us

Purpose
● to enable children to recognise the way in which pictures and symbols in their everyday life act as 'pointers' to ideas

Ideas
★ Collect plenty of magazines and brochures and look at a large selection of commercial logos. Discuss why manufacturers have trade marks and why they chose their particular symbols. Find advertisements using symbols in old magazines and cut out the logos for a wall-chart quiz **Whose logo**?
★ Many publishers use animal symbols. Encourage the children to think of as many as possible for a **Book Symbol Zoo**. Look in the school library to make your list.
★ Make a mural of a shopping street where each shop displays a symbol to show what it sells.
★ If the school is in an urban area, ask the children to look out for symbols in shop-windows, on road signs, etc. on their way to school. Draw them, or make a list.

Design of religious buildings

Churches in Britain have traditionally been built in the shape of a cross, with the head of the cross pointing east – the direction of Israel, where Jesus lived. Many modern churches do not have this shape, and some older churches have additions which hide the plan. Most churches have a cross visible somewhere on the outside. Churches may also have a tower or spire, sometimes to house the bells so that they can be heard a long way off and draw people's attention, or to draw attention to the building, or as a symbol of aspiring to heaven.

There is no distinctive style of architecture for **synagogues**, but most will have a star of David or a *menorah* visible somewhere on the outside.

Hindu temple

Jewish menorah

Sikh symbol

Hindu temples in India are often built with stepped or curved towers, and are usually set near water, trees and gardens. In Britain there are very few purpose-built temples, and Hindu temples are set up in many different types of building.

A purpose-built **mosque** will usually have a dome or cupola and a minaret from which the call to prayer can be broadcast. There are separate entrances for men and women. Most mosques are decorated with intricate patterns or words from the Qur'an in decorative calligraphy.

The main sign of a **Sikh gurdwara** is the flag outside. It is always yellow, and shows the Sikh symbol. In the centre is the two-edged sword used in Sikh ceremonies. Surrounding this is a circle, reminding Sikhs that

God has no beginning and no end. On the outside are two swords or daggers, a reminder that Sikhs should be ready to defend their faith and fight for what is right. Every year at the festival of Baisakhi the flag is taken down, changed and washed.

Many religious buildings have been adapted for the purpose from some other building, for example a warehouse, a scout hut or a building of another faith. The clues to what goes on in the building can become very confused in this case, and can provide a challenging 'detective game'

★ Road signs carry very specific messages (see *The Highway Code*). Ordnance Survey maps also have their own symbols. You could join sheets of paper together and make a large floor map marking road signs at appropriate junctions, bridges, etc., and showing different features of the landscape with the Ordnance Survey symbols. Children can work in threes: one 'drives' a toy car along the road obeying the road signs; another is the passenger and has to comment on the passing scene – 'Now we're going through a wood'; the third child is the referee to see that signs are obeyed and features observed.

★ Architecture can incorporate signs of what the building is used for. Look at the local area, and at pictures of buildings, for signs in architecture. Find out if the children can recognise a building's function from the outside (e.g. multi-storey car park, theatre, supermarket, public toilet). Encourage them to isolate the clues which told them the answer. Using the Information Box, a visit to the local area, and pictures, look at some of the clues which religious buildings give to their purpose and to the beliefs of those who use them.

Unit 2
Symbolism in art

The use of symbol can be more fully understood by relating it to one's own experience. This section helps children to understand how a complex idea can be partially represented by a relatively simple symbol; it also encourages awareness of the limits of any particular symbol, and therefore indicates why several symbols may be used to represent one concept.

Purpose
● to begin an understanding of the use of symbols in religious art
● to affirm the children's own identities

Ideas
★ Ask the children to make portraits of themselves, their friends, or their family. Rather than concentrating on physical characteristics, see if they can include items which say something about the interests or personality of the subject

e.g. binoculars for a keen bird-watcher, football shirt for a footballer, etc. You could also venture into a use of colour and line e.g. red and jagged line for someone who is short tempered.

★ The children could design a shield based on something they think is important about themselves. Children may already have done this for their names (see page 22). If so, they could now do symbols for special skills and interests: cogs and wheels for someone interested in machines, a fish for a good swimmer; or an aspect of personality – a smiling sun could be someone known for a cheerful disposition, a streak of lightning someone who is over-hasty. The shields can be put together to form one huge class symbol – not forgetting a shield for the teacher! You could ask the class to suggest what this one should show.

Symbolism in religious art

Some of the richest and most easily accessible symbolic art is in the Christian and Hindu traditions. Almost any one of the 'old master' nativity scenes will furnish a variety of symbols. Look particularly at:

halos – a band of light around the head of particularly holy characters

colour – Mary the mother of Jesus is often dressed in blue to symbolise purity and virginity, or in rich robes to symbolise her position as 'Queen of Heaven'. Heavenly beings such as angels are often gold.

In Hindu art colour is also important – Krishna is usually shown with a blue skin to symbolise beauty. Shiva is often shown with several pairs of arms to symbolise the fact that he can do many different things at the same time. Gods and goddesses are shown carrying or wearing various objects which symbolise their functions and attributes.

Unit 3
A sense of the Divine

Purpose
● to look at the way art may communicate something about God, or awaken a sense of God in some people

Ideas

★ Over a period of time make a display with children of pictures that appeal to them and discuss why. Magazines and postcards are a good source for such pictures.

★ Look at reproductions of icons with the children. Tell them the story of 'The Robber and the Icon' (*REAL Junior Assembly Book*). *Are there any paintings or statues which make you think?*

Icons

Many Christians believe that an icon is like a misted-over mirror – through it you can see a faint reflection of heaven or a glimpse of God's holiness. And like a mirror you only see a part. The person praying can feel God's love and grace coming to them through it, almost as if he is talking to them. There are many miracle stories told about icons, in which God healed people or protected them from danger.

Most icons are of Mary with Jesus. But there are also many of Jesus on his throne in heaven, and of saints. An icon can only be painted by an icon painter who has the blessing of the church and when the painting is finished it is taken to the church to be blessed. The icon painter does not attempt to make the picture look real; on the contrary, the painting must be very flat with no shadows or depth to it. The eyes stare out at the viewer. The artist often uses gold paint in the icon. This is meant to be the golden light of heaven.

Some Christians have icons in their homes and some churches have a whole wall covered with icons. When the people come to pray they kneel before their favourite icon. Most churches in Russia, Rumania, Greece, and Ethiopia have icons, and a few do in Britain.

Unit 4
A gift of art

Purpose

● to explore the idea that religious art and architecture may be a means to praise God and to give God gifts

Ideas

◔ Discuss with the children why people give gifts, what they are 'saying'. The following are some of the points you could raise or draw out of them:

– giving gifts to show love and friendship

– giving gifts to say farewell e.g. to a departing teacher

– giving gifts to say thank you e.g. after a visit staying with friends

– giving gifts to say sorry

– giving gifts to show honour and respect e.g. to royalty

– giving gifts to bribe. (This is an important issue in its own right at this stage given the practice of some children to 'buy friendship'.)

★ This general discussion leads on to giving gifts to God. Talk with the children about gifts they have made themselves, whether it be a painting, or something three-dimensional, and discuss why people paint or commission paintings, statues, etc. for places of worship.

★ Make a gift or paint a picture to give to someone.

Unit 5
Clothes that talk

This unit builds on some of the ideas used in the *REAL Infant Teacher's Handbook* topic on 'Clothing', and reinforces the information conveyed in that topic.

Some of the items mentioned below are signs, which simply indicate something about the wearer (e.g., a Christian priest's 'dog-collar'). Others are symbols, which point to something beyond the item and the wearer (e.g., the cross, which symbolises the death and resurrection of Jesus.) The children do not need to have the difference articulated, but you should be aware of the slightly different functions of the different 'messages without words'.

Purpose

● to look at the distinctive qualities of religious dress

Ideas

★ Make a collection from magazines and books and from the Pictorial Charts display pictures, of

Fish symbol

Early Christians were persecuted for many years. The fish symbol arose as a secret means for Christians to identify themselves to each other. It is based on an acrostic on ICTHUS, the Greek word for 'fish':

Iesus
Christos
THeou
hUios
Soter

The words mean 'Jesus Christ, God's Son, Saviour'. The fish symbol also recalls Jesus' promise to his disciples that he would make them 'fishers of men'.

Clothing

See the 'Introduction to Sikhism', p.130, for the significance of turbans, and the 'five k's'. Young Sikh boys wear their hair in a topknot covered by a small cloth before they learn to tie a turban.

The clothing of Christian monks and nuns varies considerably between the different orders. The general principles are plainness, modesty, and a sign that the person is 'married to God'.

Buddhist monks traditionally wear robes of dark red or orange. This is a common Indian symbol for a holy man.

Most modern clerical dress as worn in Britain originates from eighteenth century gentleman's dress. The 'dog collar' is now a widely understood sign of a Christian priest.

Hairstyles and head coverings

There are a variety of ways of treating the hair or covering the head as part of religious expression. These are some examples:

1. Orthodox Jews, both men and women, normally keep their heads covered, particularly in the synagogue or when praying or reading the Torah. This is a sign of respect for God, whose presence is all around. Although any type of hat may be worn, men often wear the yarmulke (skull cap).
2. Hindu men who are devotees of Krishna may shave their head, as a sign of cleanness and austerity.
3. In the Rastafarian religion, which originated in Jamaica and which looks to an eventual return of black people to Africa, men wear their hair in 'dreadlocks', partly as a sign of religious allegiance and partly because they believe in living as close to nature as possible, and therefore do not cut or comb their hair, only washing it in pure water. They also refer to the passage in the Bible, Leviticus 21: 5, which forbids shaving hair and beard.
4. Anyone coming into the presence of the Sikh holy book, the Guru Granth Sahib, must cover his or her head as a sign of respect. Sikh males do not cut their hair or beard, as a sign of their allegiance to Sikhism, and the long hair is kept tidy with a comb, the kanga, and covered by a turban, or for young boys, a small piece of cloth.

– people in clothing which marks them out as belonging to a particular, non-religious, group, e.g. City businessmen and women, punks, building site workers, nurses, soldiers, children in school uniform, Brownies, Cubs, members of a sports team;
– people wearing distinctively religious clothing, e.g. a vicar in a dog-collar, a Sikh in a turban, a young Sikh with a topknot, nuns, Buddhist monks, Hassidic Jews.
☙ Compare the two groups of pictures, and the reasons for the clothing – including hairstyle (see Information Box). *Who are these people? How do we know? Why do they wear these clothes? What are their clothes saying about themselves? What can we tell about how they live their lives?*

☙ Talk about why people wear badges. Children could make a collection of badges, which you could supplement. *What does each badge say about the wearer?* (Membership of a group, admiration of someone or something, political beliefs). Look at specific religious examples, for example, the Christian cross or crucifix, fish symbol (see Information Box), Jewish star of David, Sikh kirpan worn as a badge.

Unit 6
Gesture

Purpose

● to develop an understanding of the use of gesture and stance in worship

Ideas

★ Paint faces showing different expressions.

★ Play a simple miming game with children in pairs. Each child has to guess the other's feeling from the expression on their faces.

★ Similarly, use hands to express emotions such as anger, fear, love.

➤ Discuss with the children how sometimes strong feelings are difficult to put into words. *How do you show it when you are feeling very angry? What are ways of showing love or friendship?*

Gestures of greeting

★ Try different ways of saying, 'hello' without using words. Suggest raising hats, nodding, shaking hands, saluting, hugging, etc.

★ Play a miming game in which children take a role which is expressed solely by greeting, e.g. a regal wave, a soldier saluting.

➤ Discuss with the children the way the relationship between the persons concerned may affect the method of greeting. Family members or friends may greet one another with a kiss, showing their affection for each other; soldiers salute superior officers and many people curtsey to the Queen both actions indicating respect.

★ Tell children the story of Jesus washing the disciples' feet in 'Holy week, Easter and Whitsun' (*A Tapestry of Tales*). The point of this story is that the gestures are the reverse of what one would expect in the relationship.

➤ Discuss the fact that greeting varies according to culture e.g. a common Hindu greeting is for each person to press his own hands together and make a small bow of the head; rubbing noses is a traditional greeting now being revived by the Maoris of New Zealand.

Gestures in places of worship

★ Talk about some of the ways people move in places of worship e.g. prostration before the Guru Granth Sahib, sharing the peace in a church, standing in line in the mosque (see Information Box). Of course you can also draw on children's own experiences. This may include genuflecting (bending the knee) in some churches.

➤ Discuss with the children the love and respect shown by these gestures.

Prayer positions

➤ Discuss with the children positions people adopt for prayer – including what they do in assembly. Can people pray to God without clasping hands, kneeling, etc.

★ Tell the children about the sequence of positions used by a Muslim (see Information Box).

Christians usually sit or kneel to pray and stand to sing while Jews sit to sing and stand to pray.

In the Communion service in many churches, the congregation exchange a handshake with those near them, as a sign of peace to each other.

When Sikhs enter the prayer room in the gurdwara, the first thing they do is kneel down before the Guru Granth Sahib, usually giving an offering at the same time. They are showing that they are in the presence of their Guru, whom they respect.

When Muslims meet to pray in the mosque they always stand and kneel side by side in rows, shoulder to shoulder. This underlines the brotherhood of all Muslims and their equality before God.

Unit 7
Messages in music

Purpose

● to provide a background to understanding music as a message to God

Ideas

★ Ask the children to send messages to each other with the use of simple percussion instruments e.g. about the weather – drumbeats echoing the rain or try to make warm sunny sounds or send a message which suggests how they are feeling.

Sequence of Muslim prayer

All prayers are said in Arabic. We give approximate English translations.

1. Stand upright and say, either out loud or in your mind, how many prayers you intend to say.
2. Raise the hands to the ears (women and girls to the shoulders) saying:
    'Allah is most great.'
3. Place the right hand on the chest saying:
    'Oh Allah, glory and praise are for You, and blessed is Your name, and exalted is Your majesty; there is no god but You.

    I seek shelter in Allah from the rejected satan. In the name of Allah, the most merciful, the most kind.'

Then recite the opening chapter of the Qur'an:

    'All praise is for Allah, the Lord of the Universe, the most merciful, the most kind; Master of the day of judgement. You alone we worship, from You alone we seek help. Guide us along the straight way – the way of those whom You have favoured, not of those who earn Your anger nor of those who go astray.'

Say any other passage from the Qur'an.

4. Bow from the hips, placing hands on knees, saying:
    'Allah is most great.'
5. Stand up from bowing, saying:
    'Allah hears those who praise Him. Our Lord, praise be to You.'
6. Kneeling bow (prostration) with forehead, nose, palms of both hands, and knees touching the floor, saying:
    'God is most great',
then, three times,
    'Glory to my Lord, the Highest.'
7. Kneel upright with hands on knees, saying:
    'Allah is most great.'
8. Repeat 6 again.
9. The whole sequence is repeated. Adopt a half-sitting, half-kneeling position with one foot under the body, saying:
    'All prayer is for Allah and worship and goodness,
    Peace be on you, O prophet, and the mercy of Allah and His blessings,
    Peace be on us and on the righteous servants of Allah,
    I bear witness that there is no god but Allah,
    And bear witness that Muhammad is His servant and messenger.'
Recite a blessing on Muhammad and his family, follow by a confession of sins and asking Allah's forgiveness, then say:
    'O Lord, make me and my children steadfast in prayer. Our Lord, accept the prayer. Our Lord, forgive me and my parents and the believers on the day of judgement.'
10. Look to the right and then to the left (whether praying alone or in a group) saying each time:
    'Peace and mercy of Allah be on you.'
Private prayers may be said after this.

★ Listen to short excerpts of music and discuss with the children what the music makes them think of. Your selection is best taken from the school record library. Classic examples are Beethoven's 6th Symphony 'The Pastoral' or Mendelssohn's 'Fingal's Cave' Overture.

You may have had a discussion earlier about how words are sometimes inadequate to show how someone is feeling. Music may be one way of expressing this, even if it is only the repetition of a simple phrase.

Unit 8
Music as gift

Purpose
● to introduce an idea that music can be a gift showing affection

Ideas
➤ *Do you have a song which is special to you because of the person who taught it to you?* Perhaps it was by a grandmother or a favourite aunt. *What songs would you give to a baby and why? What songs would you give to a friend?*

Messages in music

In **Christian and Jewish** liturgy music is both an offering to God of praise and thanksgiving and a means of conveying a mood in a service. Thus processional hymns are usually triumphant with a strong rhythm whereas music during the partaking of the bread and wine in a Communion service is more likely to be quiet and meditative.

In **Sikhism** music has been part of both teaching and worship from the beginning, when Guru Nanak composed hymns which he sang with his friend Mardana. A large part of the Sikh service consists of music which is designed to calm the spirit and centre the thoughts on God.

There is no music in **Muslim** worship.

In many faiths music or sound is a link with the spiritual world. Sound in itself is like a spirit because it is clearly present yet cannot be seen. Sound can fill a room while at the same time the room is filled with people. Sound is often thought of as belonging to another world which overlaps with this one. Sound can therefore be understood as a way of linking the physical world with the spiritual world. At the simplest level it takes messages to the gods as well as taking the worshipper out of himself into a spiritual realm. In the **Hindu** faith, for example, chanting the sacred sound 'om' unites the worshipper with the very essence of the universe. Chanting sounds, especially sacred ones, is seen as partaking in the creative power of Brahma (see 'Introduction to Hinduism', p.113).

It is likely that most children will discuss how particular pieces of music make them feel in their music lessons, as well as experiencing creating their own music. The focus in this topic is music as a message rather than a study of religious music extensively.

★ Make a class graph to show children's favourite hymns. Use the opportunity to discuss why we sing hymns.

★ Using percussion instruments, have the children make up their own simple song to give to someone, perhaps a new baby sister, a new teacher in the school, etc. Some of these could be sung. Such a song need only be one or two lines.

★ If there is someone new to the school whom you wish to welcome, or someone who is leaving, this would be the time to offer a gift of song in a school assembly.

CROSS-CURRICULAR LINKS

Science
Find out how animals communicate. *Do they use sounds only?*
Develop work on the senses. *Which sense do you think is the most important?*
Devise some experiments to prove your theory.
Discover all the ways there are to send messages, by radio, telex, phone or fax. *Can you find out how these machines work?*

English
Invent a symbol and advertising slogan for your school. Work in groups and produce a brochure to attract new pupils to your school.

Drama
Can you communicate with your friend without using words? Invent a new language of your own with a few friends. *Can the rest of the class understand what you are saying?*

WRITINGS

This topic considers the idea of sacred or holy which is important in Christianity, Islam, Judaism, Sikhism and Hinduism.

Scriptures are an important focus and resource for all world religions. This unit aims to introduce children to the scriptures of the major faiths covered in the REAL material, at the same time as putting them in the context of the way we use and value books of all sorts in our culture. The particular value given to scriptures by the faiths underlines both the beliefs and the everyday practices of their believers.

Because of the physical respect that is shown to the Qur'an and Guru Granth Sahib, even books of translations or excerpts should not be distributed to the children. We suggest the Bible for classroom activities because there are no such restrictions on its treatment (although deliberate disrespect should of course be avoided) and also because it will probably be the most familiar. A translation of the Bhagavad Gita, Hindu scriptures from The Mahabharata, would also be acceptable to hand round.

Unit 1

What are books for?

Purpose

• to appreciate the wide variety of books that exist, and their many different purposes

Ideas

Show a selection of books of different types, and discuss with the children what they are and what is in them (e.g. mathematics textbook, story book, children's picture book, poetry book, music book, telephone directory, cookery book, instruction book for a video recorder, guide book). Then ask the children to consider each one and answer the following questions (and any others they think relevant):

– What is in it? – How is it written? (In lists, numbered points, paragraphs, picture captions, lines of poetry, musical notation, etc.)

– What language is it written in? (Many instruction books contain more than one language.)

– Where is it kept? (Book case – in which room? telephone table, kitchen drawer?)

– What is it used for? – Who uses it?

Distribute a selection of books to the class, and ask them, individually or in groups, to explain why someone would read it – for pleasure (if so, what sort of pleasure?), for information, for guidance, etc. As part of this, present the Bible and explain to children why people read it (see Information Box). You could talk about other sacred books too (see Information Box).

★ Show pictures of one or more of the following: Bible or Torah study; Muslim prayer; Hindu prayer; Sikh naming ceremony. Pictures of these are in the Pictorial Charts display pictures resource pack. Explain some of the ways the scriptures are read: as prayer, for guidance, for meditation, for stories about a beloved person (see Information Box).

★ Play a game with the children entitled **What book**? Children (and teacher) take it in turns to ask *What book would help you if you were ...?* Adjust the rules to suit the class, but make a rule that the questioner should have a plausible answer in mind; or alternatively, questioners try to think of a situation in which there is no book which would help, and others try to show that there is. Some examples are:

What book would help you if you were bored? What book would help you if you were lost in a strange town? What book would help you if you felt sad? You could introduce one or more sacred books here.

See also the Introductions to Faiths, pp.104–33.

HOW THE SCRIPTURES ARE USED

People look to their scriptures for guidance, inspiration and encouragement. In particular:

The Bible

Many Christians make a point of reading a passage from the Bible every day, and it is also read in church services. In it they find:
– Stories of how God has acted in the past, both in bad times and in good;
– Stories of people who obeyed God;
– Songs and poems in praise of God, or asking for God's help;
– God's words spoken by prophets;
– Accounts of the life and sayings of Jesus;
– Accounts of the activities of the early Church;
– Advice and guidance given to the early Christians by their leaders.

The Torah

Many Jews read the Torah at home, either in Hebrew or in translation. In the synagogue there is a passage of the Torah set for each Sabbath of the year.

Jews lay particular stress on studying the Torah in order to learn more about God's laws. They meet to study and discuss the Torah on the Sabbath and mid-week. There is a long tradition of discussion and argument to draw out the exact meaning of any passage in the Torah, and its application to present-day circumstances.

The other books of the Hebrew Bible are also read as encouragement and guidance, and because they record and celebrate the special relationship that God has had with the Jews throughout their history.

The Guru Granth Sahib

Although very few Sikhs own a copy of the Guru Granth Sahib (see Information Box below), many have a book of some of the hymns from it, which they read every day.

They also know by heart many of the hymns in the holy book, and sing them in their daily prayer time. In the gurdwara, passages from the Guru Granth Sahib are read during every service, and at festivals it is read all the way through by a team of readers.

Sikhs turn to the Guru Granth Sahib for guidance with any problem. They sometimes open the book at random, and take whatever hymn is found as a word of guidance. When a Sikh child is named, the Guru Granth Sahib is opened at random, and a name chosen beginning with the first letter of the hymn on the right-hand page.

The Qur'an

Muslims believe that the Qur'an contains the very words of God, revealed to the prophet Muhammad, and that it contains everything that people need to know in order to live lives in submission (Islam) to Allah. All Muslim daily life, all Muslim laws, all Muslim commerce and business life, is based on the Qur'an. From quite a young age children learn passages from the Qur'an by heart, and many adults can recite much of it from memory. Passages from the Qur'an are used in prayer, are quoted in everyday life, and are written in beautiful calligraphy on the walls of mosques and houses.

The Hindu Scriptures

There are many different Hindu scriptures (see 'Introduction to Hinduism' p.113) and all may be used in different ways in Hindu life. The priests may use one holy book to know how ceremonies should be performed and what prayers to say. Others might turn to the Upanishads to help them ponder more deeply the meaning of life. Many read, recite and re-enact the great epics with their depiction of the battles between good and evil.

The sound of the scriptures in their original Sanskrit is particularly important, and chanting prayers from the scriptures is an important part of Hindu worship. Many people chant prayers which they do not understand word for word, but they know that their praying is producing the sacred sound of the scriptures.

Unit 2
Precious books

Purpose
• to understand some of the different ways a book can be important or precious
• to understand the value given to the scriptures of different faiths

Ideas
★ Ask the children to make a list of their favourite books, giving their reasons for liking them. Encourage them to include photo albums, mementos of visits, books about pop stars, etc.
★ Bring in yourself, or ask another adult to bring in, some book or collection which has special personal or family significance, e.g. an album of wedding photos, a 'baby book' recording a child's birth and development, the diary or letters of a relative, or a book given by someone special. Tell the children about it, and let them look at it, but with great care – perhaps two or three at a time, after washing their hands. This will emphasize to them its importance, as well as serving the practical purpose of avoiding damage. Discuss why it is important to you.
★ Encourage the children to find and copy out favourite passages from books, poems, sayings, songs, for their own **Commonplace book** (see Information Box). Each passage should be done in their best handwriting, and decorated or illustrated. You might during the course of the topic read out various passages as suggestions for the book. Make sure that there are poetry books available for browsing through. Read some of the stories from different scriptures in *A Tapestry of Tales*.
★ Using pictures, or where possible the actual books, introduce children to one or more of: the Bible, the Torah, the Guru Granth Sahib, the Qur'an. Explain their importance to the faith, and the way they are treated (see Information Box).
★ Visit a mosque, synagogue or gurdwara to see how the scriptures are treated and used (see Information Box below for what to look for).
★ Show children reproductions of illuminated pages of the Bible, and explain that the pages were decorated like this because the words of the book were so precious.

Unit 3
How and when was it written?

Purpose
• to appreciate the different ways in which books, including scriptures, are written or collected
• to learn of the antiquity of some scriptures

Ideas
★ Ask groups of children to find out about the author and when and where various books the class is familiar with, were written. Try to select books which give a variety of dates and countries of origin: for example, Heidi, Anansi stories, *Treasure Island*, the Narnia stories by C.S. Lewis, as well as more modern books. Also include some collections and anthologies. Children could start by looking at the date of publication inside the book, and any information about the author on the dust jacket. Public libraries and publishers would be able to furnish more information. If a book was not originally written in English, draw out this fact, and look at who translated it.
★ Tell the children one or more of the stories of how scriptures came to be written or collected. Use information from the Information Box on the origins of different scriptures.
★ Make a time chart of the books the children have investigated, showing when they were written. Use a long roll of kitchen paper (perhaps take it up the wall and along the ceiling) to mark in the dates of the different scriptures (see Information Box).
★ Tell the children about translations of the Bible (see Information Box) and compare the same passage in two different English translations. Contrast this with an explanation of how Muslim, Jewish and Sikh children go to special classes to learn the language of their scriptures so that they can read them in the original.

HOW THE SCRIPTURES ARE TREATED

The Bible

The most important thing about the Bible for most Christians is that it should be read or heard, and understood, by as many people as possible. This is why the Bible is translated into thousands of different languages, and great efforts are made to make copies available to all. Although no Christian would deliberately treat the book disrespectfully, it is regarded as being there to be used freely. However, in Orthodox churches, the gospels are in beautiful, richly decorated bindings, and are treated with great respect. The priest kisses the book before reading it, and takes it round the church, where the congregation bow to the gospels.

In Protestant and Roman Catholic churches, there is usually a lectern from where the Bible is read, and this will be in a prominent place where all will be able to hear clearly the passage being read. There may be a particularly large copy of the Bible on the lectern, which is sometimes old and precious. In many churches the congregation stand while the gospel is being read, in order to show respect for the words, as the Word of God.

The Qur'an

An Arabic copy of the Qur'an is always treated with great respect, because it contains the very words of God. It is kept on a shelf by itself, which must be higher than any other book in the room. When used, it is handled with great care, often using a bookrest in order to avoid any damage. Muslims always wash their hands before handling the book.

The Guru Granth Sahib

The Guru Granth Sahib is regarded as a living Guru, and is treated with the same respect as a highly honoured and loved teacher. It always has a room of its own in any place where it is kept. (This is why few Sikhs own a copy.) Whenever it is moved from one place to another, it must be accompanied by five members of the *Khalsa* (see 'Introduction to Sikhism', p.130). One of them carries the Guru Granth Sahib above his head.

In the gurdwara the Guru Granth Sahib rests on cushions and is covered by embroi-dered cloths. It is on a raised dais and under a canopy in the centre of the prayer hall. As each person comes in, he or she approaches the Guru Granth Sahib and bows low before it, giving a gift of food or money which is used for the upkeep of the gurdwara and for the communal meal after the service. During the service there is always one person who sits behind the Guru Granth Sahib and waves the *chauri* over it: this consists of long hairs embedded in a handle. In India this would be a very necessary service to a respected Guru, in keeping flies away.

The Torah

Every synagogue owns a set of Torah scrolls. These are written on long strips of parchment and rolled up. The task of writing out the Torah scrolls is a very skilled one, and can only be done by a Jew well-versed in the Law. A set of Torah scrolls is never thrown away when worn out, but buried in the cemetery. The scrolls are kept in a special cupboard, the ark, at the east end of the synagogue, closed by a decorated door or a richly embroidered curtain. Each scroll is kept in a velvet or silk cover, also richly embroidered, and is adorned with silver ornaments and bells. There is also for each scroll a special pointer to be used when reading it, to avoid touching the scroll with a finger.

When the Torah is read in the synagogue, it is often carried round the congregation, and is then lifted high so that all can see it, before being taken to the *bimah*, a lectern in the middle of the synagogue. It is an honour to be chosen to read out the passage for the day in a synagogue service.

The Hindu Scriptures

The books themselves are not treated in any particular way, apart from respect for what is in them.

Commonplace books

In the eighteenth and nineteenth centuries, a popular hobby amongst upper-class ladies was to collect and copy out passages of poetry and other writing into a book. The book was decorated or illustrated, and best handwriting was used. It became a collection of favourite passages.

History of the Scriptures

The Jewish Bible and Christian Old Testament is a collection of writings made by many different authors at different times. Much of the material is a recording of oral traditions which existed long before they were first written down. The events recounted about Abraham may have occurred around 2000 BCE (Before Common Era), and the freeing of the Israelites from Egypt around 1250 BCE. In 622 BCE the Jews found a 'Book of the Law' which had been lost, and several other books were revised. The books of the prophets were still being written up to about 160 BCE.

All the books were written in Hebrew, and are read in Hebrew by Jews today, although many use translations as well.

The Christian New Testament

The earliest Christian writings are almost certainly the letters which St. Paul wrote to the new Christians in different parts of the Mediterranean world, starting around 50 CE. Up to that time the accounts of the life of Jesus existed only in oral form. The story spread as people who had known Jesus told others about him. Some of these traditions may have been written down at about the same time. Around 70-80 CE the gospels that we know today were written in Greek.

It was only gradually that the church decided which writings were to form part of the Christian scriptures, together with the Jewish Bible.

From very early times there was a tradition of translating the Bible into languages that ordinary people could understand. The first translations were into Latin, and then later into the native languages of Europe. The 'Authorised Version', or 'King James Bible', so called because King James I authorised its use in churches, was published in 1611. There are now many modern translations of the Bible into English, and many scholars still working on translations into hundreds of languages of the world.

Hindu

Not much is known about the authorship and writing of the Hindu scriptures in Sanskrit, but they are known to be very ancient. The *Vedas* were probably written about 1200 BCE, the *Upanishads* about 800 BCE, and the Ramayana during the 9th century BCE. The *Mahabharata*, from which comes the *Bhagavad Gita*, the most loved of Hindu scriptures, was written in the 6th century BCE. Again, all these were almost certainly oral traditions before they were written down.

Muslim

The first revelations of the Qur'an were given to Muhammad in 611 CE. The whole book was compiled shortly after his death in 632 CE. The Qur'an is written in Arabic, and is not generally used in translation, although translations into English and other languages have been made, mainly for the benefit of non-Muslims or converts.

Sikh

The Guru Granth Sahib is a collection of the hymns and poems written by several of the Sikh Gurus, starting with Guru Nanak who first began to preach and sing in 1490 CE. It also includes poems and hymns by non-Sikh writers. It was compiled in 1603-4 by Guru Arjan. He had a quiet room built where he would not be disturbed, and sent messengers all over India asking people if they had any written records of the Gurus' hymns. When the collection was finished it was placed in the Golden Temple in Amritsar, with great rejoicing. Many years later Guru Gobind Singh added the hymns written by his father, Guru Tegh Bahadur. When Guru Gobind Singh died in 1708 he told the Sikhs that from that time on the Guru Granth Sahib was to be their Guru. The book is written in Panjabi, in a special script called Gurmukhi.

Compare these three different translations of the same passage: (Luke 2 : 4-7)

King James version:
And Joseph also went up from Galilee, out of the city of Nazareth, into Judaea, unto the city of David, which is called Bethlehem; (because he was of the house and lineage of David:) to be taxed with Mary his espoused wife, being great with child. And so it was, that, while they were there, the days were accomplished that she should be delivered. And she brought forth her first-born son, and wrapped him in swaddling clothes, and laid him in a manger; because there was no room for them in the inn.

Jerusalem Bible (a modern translation intended to keep as close as possible to the original Greek):
So Joseph set out from the town of Nazareth in Galilee and travelled up to Judaea, to the town of David called Bethlehem, since he was of David's House and line, in order to be registered with Mary, his betrothed, who was with child. While they were there the time came for her to have her child, and she gave birth to a son, her first-born. She wrapped him in swaddling clothes, and laid him in a manger because there was no room for them at the inn.

Good News Bible (a modern translation intended to be as easy as possible to understand):
Joseph went from the town of Nazareth in Galilee to the town of Bethlehem in Judaea, the birthplace of King David. Joseph went there because he was a descendant of David. He went to register with Mary, who was promised in marriage to him. She was pregnant, and while they were in Bethlehem, the time came for her to have her baby. She gave birth to her first son, wrapped him in strips of cloth and laid him in a manger – there was no room for them to stay in the inn.

Unit 4
Simhat Torah

The Jewish festival of Simhat Torah (see Information Box) is taken as an accessible example of a faith treasuring and celebrating its scriptures.

Purpose
● to appreciate that the scriptures are seen as a precious gift to be celebrated

Ideas
★ Tell children about the yearly cycle of reading the Torah, and the festival (see Information Box). Ask the children to choose one of the scriptures they have learnt about and make a flag celebrating it, with suitable patterns and symbols (not pictures). Make a display of the flags.

The Torah is read in synagogues every Sabbath, with a passage set for each Sabbath in the year. This means that the complete Torah is read through in a year. Simhat Torah is the Sabbath in October when the cycle is completed and starts again. The theme of the festival is giving thanks to God for the gift of the Torah, without which people would not know God's will. The Torah scrolls are carried in procession round the synagogue, with singing and dancing. The children follow on, waving flags. The emphasis is on great enjoyment.

CROSS-CURRICULAR LINKS

Technology
Find out how a book is made, follow the whole process from manuscript to bound copies.
Make books in the class.

Geography
Look on maps and globes and find the countries where religions originated. (Pictorial Charts have a wall chart showing the origins of world religions.)

RULES AND JUSTICE

There are many different sorts of rules, e.g. rules which apply to a particular game, rules which are part of the civil law, rules which form a code of morality, rules which apply only to a particular home or school. This topic looks at rules in different areas, in an attempt to explore some of the fundamental questions behind law-making such as:

Why do we have rules? Why should we keep them? What happens if we don't? Who makes the rules? What happens if you do not know the rules? Are rules always just?

This topic explores the subject by looking at how rules operate in different contexts. It is not expected that children of this age group would be able to draw out abstract principles.

Units 4–8 look explicitly at aspects of religious and moral rules. The debates about the origin of the moral law, and where religion ends and morality begins have occupied the minds of philosophers for many centuries. Here we look at some aspects of religion and morality without engaging the children directly in the debate, although some may start asking questions themselves. You will probably find the levels of reasoning about morality vary widely and include comments such as, 'I don't do that because I'll be punished if I do', or 'I don't want to do that because people won't like me'.

Drama is a good way of exploring the necessity for rules in a community. You could remind the children of a drama which you have already performed, or develop alongside this topic a drama about building a new community.

Also see the assemblies on 'Justice' and on 'Owning' in the *REAL Junior Assembly Book*.

Unit 1

Rules in games

Purpose
• to look at key questions such as why we have rules and who makes them

Ideas
★ Children can work in small groups or pairs and see if they can remember and record the rules of a game they enjoy. These can be put together to make a class book on games. There may not always be agreement, in which case the rules may have to be checked against a higher authority – the lid of the box, a book of the rules, etc. Possible games to choose are cricket, football, chess, Scrabble, draughts, Monopoly, hop-scotch.

★ With the children in groups, ask them to devise a new game which they can then teach to another group. This task will be easier if children are given an item or two around which to build their game, e.g. a ball, a hoop, some small models, a squared board.

★ If the above task proves successful you could then see if one group could learn another group's rules, not by explanation, but by watching the game being played.

☛ *Why do we have rules in games?*

What happens if you do not know the rules, or if someone keeps breaking them?

Do all games have rules? What about when you make up a game to play? Are there some rules even then?

Unit 2
Traffic rules

Purpose
• to focus on the need for safety
• to consider the function of government in rule-making

Ideas
★ Give the children the following outline and ask them to make up rules:

On the planet Anarchiston, there are problems on the roads. There are two types of vehicle: the Whizzers, which can go very fast, have very responsive steering and good brakes; and the Crawlers, which go rather slowly, have very difficult steering, and no brakes (the driver has to judge the distance within which they will gradually slow to a stop). Crawlers are necessary because Whizzers can only carry two people at the most. There are also pedestrians who have to cross the roads from time to time.

Ask the children to devise 'Rules of the Road', or a highway code, answering such questions as:

Should both types of vehicle use the same road?
Should there be a speed limit for whizzers?
Should traffic keep a specified distance apart?
If a Whizzer and a Crawler are both approaching a crossroads, which should give way?
How should pedestrians cross the road?
What qualifications should be required to drive each type of vehicle?
What penalties should there be for breaking the rules?

☛ *Why was there a need for rules? The children made up the rules for this planet, but who makes up the rules for ours?*
★ *What are the rules in this country?* Ask each child to ask his parents for the five most important traffic rules, and see to what extent the lists coincide.
☛ *What is the significance of everyone driving on the left (or the right)?*
Why is the speed limit lower in a town than on a motorway?
Why should people wear seat-belts?
What happens if you break the rules? (Encourage the

children to go beyond the legal penalties involved.)
★ Some traffic rules are not the law of the land (punishable by a fine or imprisonment) but should be obeyed for safety's sake. Discuss the existence of such rules with the children. Practise the Green Cross Code, either in the hall with children pretending to be cars, or in small supervised groups doing the real thing.

Unit 3
School rules

Purpose
• to explore aspects of rules in a context which is common to all the children

Ideas
★ Ask the children to write down the school rules they think the following people would make:
a dinner lady,
a school secretary,
a school child,
a parent of a child in the school,
a caretaker.
★ Ask the children to write down what school rules they think do, in fact, exist.
☛ *Why are rules against stealing and fighting in the playground enforced in most schools?*
What happens if you break school rules?
Why are there sometimes rules about uniform?
Who makes the school rules?
★ Discuss with the children the need to know the rules, to avoid getting into trouble unwittingly. Ask the children to write a story or make a play called 'But I didn't know it was wrong!' Should people be punished for breaking a rule they did not know about?

Unit 4
Where do rules come from?

Purpose
• to encourage children to articulate their own moral code, and their reasons behind it

• to introduce the Ten Commandments to the children, in context, as part of the Jewish faith
• to show that while there may be overlap between them, there exists a variety of religious rules
• to explore the role of authority in rule-making

Ideas

We suggest you follow this section in the order given.

★ Tell the children the story of Moses receiving the Ten Commandments, called 'Mount Sinai' in *A Tapestry of Tales*, without telling them what these commandments are.

★ Ask the children to write their own 'five commandments'. Compare these lists and discuss with the children the reasons behind their choices.

★ They could write out their commandments on slabs of clay.

★ Now show them the Ten Commandments (see Information Box). Some explanation may be needed for words like 'Sabbath', if you have not already studied it, and 'adultery'.

➡ *Where does this list overlap with yours? Are there different types of rules in this list?*

★ Remind the children of who keeps the Sabbath now. Spend a session with them looking more

closely at the way Jews obey the 4th commandment and keep the Sabbath. (See the topic on 'Food' and the topic on 'Family' in the *REAL Infant Teacher's Handbook* and look at the 'Introduction to Judaism').

★ Look at the summary of the law given by Jesus (Mark 12 : 28-31), or alternatively, ascribed to one of his questioners, a lawyer (Luke 10 : 25).

'You must love the Lord your God with all your heart, with all your soul, with all your strength, and with all your mind, and your neighbour as yourself.'

★ Tell the story of the Good Samaritan, from 'Some Parables of Jesus' (*A Tapestry of Tales*). (Note: it was the Samaritan, the traditional enemy of the Jews, who was the good neighbour). *What does 'neighbour' mean?*

★ Tell the story of Muhammad receiving the Qur'an, called 'Muhammad' (*A Tapestry of Tales*) to demonstrate that different faiths have different laws even though some may coincide. The food laws of Jews and Muslims (see topic on 'Food') can provide an illustration of this.

➡ *Where do Jews or Muslims believe these rules come from? Who makes them?*
Who makes the rules in our society? Ask the children about both personal and communal rules.

The Ten Commandments

These laws which were given to Moses on Mount Sinai summarize the most important points of the Jewish law. There are many more laws in the Bible which go into more detail. The ten are:
You shall have no other gods but me.
You shall not make a carved image or any likeness of any creature; you shall not bow down and worship them.
You shall not utter the name of the Lord your God to misuse it.
Observe the Sabbath day and keep it holy; you shall do no work that day.
Honour your father and your mother.
You shall not kill.
You shall not commit adultery.
You shall not steal.
You shall not bear false witness against your neighbour.
You shall not covet anything that is your neighbour's.

Unit 5
What motivates people to keep the law?

This aspect has been explored to some extent, by children thinking about the reason behind particular laws. This is the more positive side of keeping the law. Although in Christianity, Judaism and Islam there are elements of punishment, there is also a strong emphasis on being motivated by love of God and compassion for one's fellow-creatures.

Purpose
• to think about positive reasons for keeping laws
• to reflect on their own motivation

Ideas

★ Find the story of 'The Robber and the Icon' in the *REAL Junior Assembly Book*. Talk with the children about the robber's change of heart when he realized he was hurting people.

★ The story of 'Zacchaeus' (*A Tapestry of Tales*) is another example of a man who resolved to keep moral laws after he had encountered Jesus' teaching.

★ Tell the children about the Jewish Shema (see Information Box). Explain that for Jews love of God is the foundation for keeping the law.

★ Read some verses from Psalm 119. Talk about the idea of laws being something to give thanks for.

➲ *What do you do for people because of love, for example, for friends, parents, grandparents?*

Unit 6
Remembering to keep the law

Purpose

● to reflect on how the children can remember to be obedient

● to develop the idea that religious law may cover every aspect of life

Ideas

★ Use the Information Box to find out what laws the Jews must remember to keep. This does not just mean the Ten Commandments but also the dietary laws (see 'Food' topic) and civil laws. (See 'Introduction to Judaism' for more details of the Jewish Law.) These laws are outlined in the book of Deuteronomy.

Shavuot

The Jewish festival of Shavuot, or Pentecost, as well as having a harvest element, is a rejoicing and thanksgiving for the Torah, the law. The Jewish people celebrate their being chosen by God to receive the privilege of hearing and keeping his laws. They teach that it is the law that makes them a special people and enables them to be truly free.

★ Find out from the children if they have any methods to remind them about an instruction, e.g. tying a knot in a handkerchief, or repeating a rhyme over and over.

★ The children can write what they think is the most important rule of life on a small scroll. These can then be put in a small decorated box and hung around the doorway to the classroom.

The Shema

The first commandment for the Jews is also the most important:
'Hear O Israel, the Lord our God is one God. You shall love the Lord our God with all your heart, soul and strength.'
Jews call these words the Shema. The Torah tells Jews to write the words on their hearts and minds, to fasten them to their hands and to write them on their door-posts and gates.

The tefillin

A scribe writes the words of the Shema in Hebrew, sometimes with other words from the Torah, on tiny scrolls. These words are then placed in small boxes called tefillin, with straps or tapes attached. When it is time to pray on a weekday the Jewish man or boy straps the tefillin to his forehead and to his left arm. On his forehead the words of the Shema are close to his mind, and on his arm they are close to his heart and the straps fasten them to his hands. The tefillin remind him to obey God in everything he thinks, feels and makes. Look at the Pictorial Charts display picture which shows the tefillin being fastened to a boy's arm.

The mezuzah

Once Jews used to carve the words of the Shema, in Hebrew, onto their door-posts. Today, they put smalls scrolls written with the words of the shema into small boxes called mezuzah and nail the mezuzah to the door-post while they say a blessing. There is usually a mezuzah on every door-post in a Jewish home except outside the bathroom and lavatory. Every time a Jew looks at the door-posts he should remember to keep God's laws.

Unit 7
Submitting voluntarily to a law

The word 'Islam' means 'submission' and the Islamic faith centres around submission to the will of God. Undertaking voluntarily to keep certain rules is a feature of other religions, too. When Sikhs join the Khalsa (see 'Introduction to Sikhism') they are agreeing to live by certain rules of dress and behaviour. Many children will belong to clubs such as cubs, girls' brigade or a

INFORMATION BOX

Monks and nuns are people who give up ordinary life to dedicate themselves to a religious life. They do not marry, and are committed to the community in which they live, rather than to their own family. They do not own personal property. Hindu and Buddhist monks and nuns are dependent on alms for their support. Some Christian orders are also dependent solely on alms, although some monasteries own property which supports the community. (This in turn would originally have been a gift).

The basis of most Christian monastic life today is the Rule written by Saint Benedict in the 5th-6th century. He called it a 'little rule for beginners', and in it he laid down rules for every detail of the monks lives: how they should work, as well as how they should pray; how the abbot should be chosen, and what degree of authority he had. Since the time of Benedict many revisions of his rule have been written to suit changing times, but his guiding principles have remained the model – to allow everyone in the community to draw closer to God.

The reasons behind the monastic life vary. For some orders, particularly Christian, the freedom from normal family responsibilities is seen as enabling the monks and nuns to devote themselves more fully to helping others, with teaching, medical work, etc. Others see themselves as praying or performing religious ceremonies on behalf of the rest of the world. For others, particularly Hindus, the aim is to free oneself from the distractions of the world in order to concentrate on God or the gods.

rugby club, where becoming a member involves agreeing to obey certain rules.

Purpose
● to realize that many people will submit voluntarily to keep strict rules

Ideas
★ Find out which children belong to clubs, and ask a representative of each club to describe what sort of club it is, its rules, and any joining ceremony it has.
★ Using books from the library, ask the children to find out about the clothing rules which all Sikhs are encouraged to observe, particularly if they belong to the Khalsa. (See also the 'Introduction to Sikhism', p.00) Tell the children the story of 'The Khalsa' (*A Tapestry of Tales*).
➥ *Why do Sikhs join the Khalsa?* (They believe it to be the way to serve God best). Look, also, at the fact that belonging to the Khalsa involves abstinence from alcohol, tobacco and drugs.
★ Look at the example of monks and nuns in various traditions such as Christian, Hindu and Buddhist.
★ Look at the story of the life of 'Saint Francis' in *A Tapestry of Tales*.
What did Francis give up to serve God?
★ Talk about monks and nuns today, perhaps taking Mother Teresa of Calcutta as an example (see Information Box in the Money chapter). Talk about vocation – the sense of being called to serve God. *Who are they promising to obey?*

Unit 8
Breaking the law and forgiveness

Purpose
● to understand more about the ideas of forgiveness and to be able genuinely to say sorry

Ideas
★ Tell the story of The Prodigal Son or The Unforgiving Servant from the 'Parables of Jesus' (*A Tapestry of Tales*). In Christian thinking genuine repentance for breaking the law brings forgiveness. Older children may be able to discuss

whether and under what circumstances a judge could pardon a criminal.

★ Tell 'The story of Jonah' (*A Tapestry of Tales*). The story looks at the repentance of Nineveh, God's forgiveness, and Jonah's reaction to that forgiveness.

➥ *Why was the city of Nineveh not destroyed? Why was Jonah so angry about this? How would you feel in his situation?*

★ Ask the children to recall what happens if traffic rules, game rules, or school rules are broken. Ask them if these are 'crimes' against particular people.

★ Look at the Jewish Yom Kippur ('Introduction to Judaism' p.123) and talk about its theme of recollection and repentance. Another festival which emphasises reconciliation and forgiveness is the Muslim Night of Forgiveness (Lailat ul-Barah), two weeks before the fast of Ramadan, when Muslims seek forgiveness from anyone they have wronged.

★ Ask the children to devise plays or write poems on the theme of forgiveness. If you have a drama in progress, it might be possible to introduce someone (the teacher?) who has done harm and is repentant. *How should that person be treated?*

The Qur'an specifically states that if a Muslim is faced with the choice of starving or eating food which is normally forbidden, he should eat. The law is not given to harm anyone.

Jews, too, are instructed not to adhere to the law so closely so as to endanger their own life. The book of 1 Maccabees recounts how a party of Jews were attacked on the Sabbath and offered no resistance. They were massacred, and those who heard about it decided that in future they would defend themselves if they were attacked on the Sabbath.

The famous athlete Eric Liddel caused much comment by refusing to run an Olympic heat on a Sunday, because of his Christian beliefs. But much later in his life, when he was held prisoner by the Chinese along with a number of young men, he helped to organise football games on Sundays, as this was the only day that the men were allowed any exercise at all.

CROSS-CURRICULAR LINKS

English

Write out some questions to ask a policeman/woman who has come to visit the school.

In groups, discuss and write down five rules which you have all agreed are the most important rules for conduct in the classroom.

Geography

Find out about the traffic rules which apply in your town. Draw a diagram showing the flow of traffic through the area. *Can you improve on this system?*

Technology

Write out a list of rules for the kitchen to use when you are doing any cooking. *Can you make another list for the workbench, to keep everyone safe when you are using tools?*

Unit 9

Times to disobey

Purpose

● to open up the question of whether it is sometimes right to break rules

Ideas

★ Tell the story of Gandhi's civil disobedience, and how he cleaned latrines (*A Tapestry of Tales*).

➥ *When is it right to break rules?*

★ Look at other examples where 'the law' accommodates unusual circumstances (see Information Box).

MONEY

Themes of commitment and giving are considered here, particularly in relation to the Christian and Islamic faiths.

The attitude of religions to wealth varies, not only between but also within different religions: it can be seen as an obstacle to faith or a blessing from God, an attachment to the world or a privilege which brings responsibility.

Unit 1
What is money?

Coins are worth, as metal, a great deal less than their face value; notes are even more worthless. Their value lies in what they symbolise. This section also brings out why money is needed in a large community, to simplify the process of exchange of goods and services.

Purpose
● to look at money as an example of a symbol

Ideas
◉ Show children a collection of foreign coins and/or notes. *Would you accept these as pocket money? Could they be spent at your local shop? Why not?* Add some British coins. *Can you spend these? Why? What do the words on a British note mean?* Show the children, from a distance, a coin and a piece of ordinary writing paper with words on. *Which would you rather have? What if the coin is 2p and the piece of paper is an IOU for 20p? Which would you rather have now? What makes the difference?*

★ Examine the need for money through drama. This would be more interesting if it was part of a long-term drama project, rather than one created for the day.

In your drama, create a new community. This could be a group of people on an island after a shipwreck, or explorers on a space station, or a community in an imaginary country the children have devised themselves. Groups of children can be made responsible for producing one sort of food or commodity (e.g. fruit, meat, shoes, houses). The need to exchange and thus value

product against another should arise and with this the need for some kind of coinage. The next step would be to introduce services and ask the children to judge their relative value.

★ Research the history of coinage with the children.

Unit 2
Attitudes to money

In our society, wealth is often regarded either as something to be desired and respected, or as something to be despised. From a religious viewpoint it is the attitude to money which is most important. A frequent misquotation is 'Money is the root of all evil', but the correct quotation, 'The love of money is the root of all evil' shows that motive is the main consideration.

Purpose
● to look at the different ways wealth is regarded
◉ *Do you need to be rich to be happy? Does being rich make you happy?*
◉ Use the story of 'King Midas' (*A Tapestry of Tales*) to stimulate discussion. *How did Midas think he would feel if he had a great deal of gold? How did he feel when he got it?*
★ Make a class frieze or display of pictures showing a range of activities that can be enjoyed with little or no money e.g. singing, playing, reading, games, meeting your friends.

People who give up wealth
★ Tell the children one or more of the following: the story of Saint Francis; the story of 'Prince

Siddharta, the Buddha' (*A Tapestry of Tales*); Oscar Wilde's fairy story 'The Happy Prince' in *The Happy Prince and Other Stories*. (Puffin Classics).

★ Tell them about people today who give up the right to money – monks and nuns who take a vow of poverty – and perhaps focus on Mother Theresa of Calcutta (see Information Box). *Why do you think these people have done this?*

Mother Teresa

Mother Teresa of Calcutta was born in Yugoslavia but is Albanian. At the age of 18 she joined a missionary, teaching order of nuns. She became principal of a school in Calcutta teaching well-to-do Bengali girls, but in 1946 felt called to go and help 'the poorest of the poor' in Calcutta, which was and still is a city with enormous contrast between its rich and poor. She waited two years for permission to do this, and eventually founded the order of the Missionaries of Charity. Several of her former pupils joined her in the order, giving up the chance of a comfortable life. Their vocation is to help the very poorest in any part of the world, living alongside them in poverty. Today the order works in many parts of the world, wherever there are poor people in need of help. Mother Teresa has also worked with Aids sufferers in New York and Washington. Several books have been written about her work (although she has never given permission for a biography), and more details can be found in these. A good example is *Something Beautiful for God*, by Malcolm Muggeridge (HarperCollins Fount).

Monks and Nuns

Christian and Buddhist monks and nuns do not own property in their own right. Christian monks and nuns are fed by the monastery or convent; Buddhist monks and nuns usually live on food which is given to them by lay Buddhists, who regard it as a privilege to give to monks and nuns. It is extremely offensive to Buddhists to describe monks and nuns as 'begging' for food or to refer to 'begging bowls'. The correct term is 'alms bowls'.

Unit 3

Sharing money

Purpose

- to introduce the idea that money earned is needed to contribute to the needs of the community as a whole
- to explain that many believe that money and possessions are something held in trust for God
- to explore the idea of giving away money

Ideas

★ Continuing the drama from Unit 1, where the children invented their own imaginary community, introduce an accident into the story. As a result of this accident one or more people in the community can no longer produce any food or other goods. *Who will look after them? Who will pay for their needs?*

★ Ask the children to list all the local services which are paid for out of central funds, e.g. roads, hospitals, schools, maintaining parks and collecting rubbish.

Where did the money come from to pay for these? What would happen if everyone kept their money to themselves? Why is it sometimes better to pay for a service as a group rather than as an individual? Who paid for these services before government took on this responsibility? What do you think used to happen to the poorer people when they were ill before the Government provided hospitals for everyone?

★ Find out about charities which operate in the local area, and look in detail at the work of one of them. This could include inviting someone in to talk to the class and letting the children make a display about the work. If you have chosen an overseas aid charity, this could be developed into a study of the area in which the agency works. Such a study would need to be done cautiously with a positive approach to the culture of the people concerned.

★ Hold a fund-raising event for the charity studied.

Muslims give away one fortieth of their wealth: this is one of the five pillars of Islam. *What do you think 'wealth' means? Is it everything you have, or everything you have except what you need for food and shelter, or is it everything you have except enough for food, your home, a colour TV, video, stereo and holidays abroad?* Make a chart of what

Muslim Zakat

Muslims are required to give one-fortieth of their wealth to the Muslim community to be used to relieve the poor. Wealth is generally regarded as anything that can be hoarded, e.g. silver and gold, money, merchandise. The exact rules governing the Zakat practice are fairly complex.

Tithes

The practice of tithing is laid down in the Bible (Numbers 18 : 21). Jews gave one tenth of their produce to the Temple for its upkeep and the support of the priests.

Early Christians gave spontaneous gifts in kind, but the practice became formalised and in England was made compulsory in the year 900 CE. Tithes of grain, animals and other produce were payable to the local church, or in some cases to the monastery which provided a priest for the parish. Barns were built close to the church or monastery to store this produce, and some of these tithe barns survive today.

Gradually the tithes were changed from produce to set sums of money, and in the 20th century were abolished as a legal requirement. Many Christians today make a voluntary donation of one tenth of their income to the church.

The different proportions laid down for Christians and Muslims cannot be directly compared, since they are given for different purposes, and one is a proportion of income and the other of wealth. Both Muslims and Christians, as well as individuals from other faiths, may well give away further sums of money.

are considered by the class to be luxury items. *Is your pocket money wealth?* (You don't need it to live, after all.)

★ Discuss the Christian traditions of giving (see Information Box) and discuss giving away things other than money.

★ Tell the story of the 'Widow's mite' (Mark 12 : 41-44). *Why was the money the widow gave worth more than the money the rich people gave?*

★ Other stories useful here are 'Zacchaeus' (*A Tapestry of Tales*); and 'Flags and Needles' (*A Tapestry of Tales*).

CROSS-CURRICULAR LINKS

Maths

Shopkeeper's difference and fraction work can be brought in here.

History

Trace the history of money from bartering to credit cards. *What has changed since your grandparents were at school?*

English

Discuss the idea of taxation. Debate whether charities are a good idea. Set up two groups who must present opposing views which the rest of the class can vote on.

Geography

Explore the currencies of different countries. *What must you do to your money when you go abroad?* Look in a newspaper to find out about the exchange rate. Find out about the names of the currencies of all the countries in Europe.

TIME

This chapter focuses on Judaism, Islam, Hinduism and Chinese religion. With particular reference to death, change, celebration and hope.

The theme of 'Time', which appears in the *REAL Infant Teacher's Handbook* too, is designed to take account of the child's gradual, widening perspective on time and its cycles. At the infant level the topic focused on daily and weekly cycles, at this level the focus is on the year.

This topic covers both cyclical and linear perceptions of time and the year as a regulator of festivals and anniversaries.

Unit 1
Measuring the year

Purpose

- to show that the year may be measured in a number of ways
- to show that festivals are often set by traditional calendars

Ideas

★ One starting point is to ask the children to work out how old they are in years, in months and in days. This would make them aware of the units with which time is measured.

★ From there you could introduce the notion of measuring time in other ways – such as by Christmases, school terms, winters ago, and by the moon. (You could tell the children that 'moons' are often used in fairy tales e.g. 'before the new moon' or 'two moons ago'.) Ask the children to measure the time since certain events in this way.

★ Children will appreciate the role the moon plays as a regulator of time, if they observe the changes in its appearance during the cycle. This could be started now and continued through the topic. Work in science about the relationship between the earth and the moon further enhances this understanding. It is particularly useful to look at the fact that the moon has a cycle of between twenty-nine and thirty days, and orbits the earth just over twelve times during the time that the earth takes to circle the sun. The children

Muslim calendar

The years are counted from the date of Muhammad's move to Medina (see 'Introduction to Islam' p.119). The year which begins in June 1993 according to western dating is 1414 according to Muslim dating. Years are based entirely on a lunar calendar of twelve months, alternately of twenty-nine and thirty days each. This gives a year approximately eleven days shorter than the solar year, but no adjustment is made, so that the relationship between the seasons and the months varies over time.

Jewish calendar

Years are counted from the creation of the world according to Jewish tradition. The year which begins in autumn 1993 according to western dating is 5754 according to Jewish dating. The calendar is based on lunar months of alternating twenty-nine and thirty days. It is adjusted to keep in line with the seasons by the addition of an extra month seven times in a nineteen year cycle, and of extra days in some months, according to fairly complicated rules.

Hindu calendar

The year is divided into twelve lunar months of thirty days each, and is kept in line with the solar year by the addition of an extra month every few years. Each month consists of a light fortnight, when the moon is waxing, and a dark fortnight when it is waning.

need to learn here that a year is the period of time it takes the earth to circle the sun. Use diaries and the newspaper for help with this and draw your own calendars showing the cycles to display in the classroom.

★ Demonstrate this ratio with a living model. One child who represents the earth walks around another who is the sun. A third child is the moon, and walks round 'the earth' twelve times while this child walks round the sun. (You could try spinning 'the earth' as well but you would end up with a very dizzy child!) This model would also serve to support a religious as well as scientific concept that the universe is in constant motion.

★ Look at some traditional religious calendars which are based on a lunar rather than a solar system of measurement. Try and find out the name of the current month in the Hindu, Jewish and Muslim calendars. These could be used to date the blackboard for the duration of the topic. SHAP calendars of religious festivals can be obtained from the address on p.135.

Unit 2
Naming the year

Purpose
● to think about the significance of the way the year is named
● to introduce a range of ways of naming the year

Ideas
★ You could start by asking the children what they think the year date signifies. *19— years since when?* Look with them at the meaning of AD and BC.

(Note: In discussing years in a multi-faith context, it is common to use the abbreviations CE (Common Era) and BCE (Before the Common Era), as we do in this handbook. The normal year numbers can then be used without specific religious reference.)

➡ *Why do you think people wanted to date the years from Jesus' birth?*

★ Look at other dating systems, such as Jewish and Muslim systems (see Information Box) and

discuss the reasons for the milestones used by these calendars.

➡ *Why do Jews and Muslims follow the BC and AD system in this country?*

★ Look at the Chinese system of naming years after twelve animals (see Information Box). Work out the animal representing the year the children were born or the year they began school.

★ The children could find out by asking adults, friends and family, what other events took place in the year they were born. If this information were then pooled it would be interesting to see whether there were any events in common.

★ Years can be known in other ways. Sometimes they are named to promote a special concern, e.g. Year of Peace, International Year of the Child, or to mark an anniversary. Find out how the current year is named. Ask the children to think of ways the previous year could be remembered. *What happened of significance that year?* Children may need help in 'placing' the year. One way of naming it would be something like 'When we were in Year 4', and this can serve as a guide to remembering what else happened that year. Some answers will be personal, e.g. 'The year I was bridesmaid to my sister'. Other answers will be from a common experience or knowledge, e.g. the year we went on a school trip to the sea, the

---

Chinese year names

The Chinese name the years after twelve animals, starting again with the first animal after twelve years. (There are other ways of identifying the year to prevent confusion.) The year names for twelve years are given below, and any other years can be worked out by calculating forwards and backwards from these.

1991	Ram
1992	Monkey
1993	Cock
1994	Dog
1995	Pig
1996	Rat
1997	Ox
1998	Tiger
1999	Rabbit
2000	Dragon
2001	Snake
2002	Horse

year the local team won the cup, etc. These events could be illustrated.

Unit 3
New Year festivals

See also the assembly called 'New School Year' in the *REAL Junior Assembly Book*.

Background work in science on the earth's orbit is valuable here, especially so that the children can see why there are seasonal variations.

The first part of the unit sets out to show that the day designated as New Year varies according to different traditions, and is imposed by people, not by any external logic.

Purpose

● to think about why New Year is celebrated

● to develop an understanding of the practices and customs associated with some New Year celebrations

Ideas

★ Give the children a circle which represents the year. Ask them to divide it into the four seasons, and colour them in appropriately. They can divide the year in any way they like, with horizontal and vertical lines, or with a diagonal cross, for instance. Now ask them to show where the year begins, and to justify their choice. You can show them where the Western New Year falls in relation to the seasons, and point out that the Jewish and Hindu New Years fall in the autumn, and Chinese New Year in the early spring.

★ You may wish to do some work on the equinoxes (when day and night are the same length in spring and autumn) and the solstices (the longest and shortest days at mid-winter and mid-summer). Find out the dates of these and

---

New Year festivals

Faiths differ in the importance given to new year celebrations. Chinese, Jewish and Hindu festivals are particularly important.

Chinese New Year

(Also see the topic on 'Chinese New Year' in the *REAL Infant Teacher's Handbook*)

The New Year falls in late January or February. Before New Year, homes are cleaned, because to sweep on New Year might sweep good luck out of the house. On New Year's Eve, the picture of the kitchen god, which is by the fire or stove all year, is burnt, ready for a new picture. The kitchen god goes to heaven to report on the family's behaviour over the last year, and sweet offerings are made before the picture is burnt, so that his report will be good.

The following day, the lion dance goes through the streets. There are fireworks, drums and cymbals as the lion (two people in an intricate costume) goes from house to house collecting lucky money bags and vegetables which have been hung outside. This brings luck to the house or business. Children also receive money in lucky red envelopes.

Jewish New Year

The new year starts on Rosh Hashanah, in September or October. This begins the 'nine days of awe' which culminate in Yom Kippur. The emphasis during this period is on reflection and repentance, and the shofar, the ram's horn, is blown during the synagogue service to call everyone to prayer for forgiveness. New Year cards are sent, and wishes for a good year exchanged. The period of repentance continues until Yom Kippur, and all must seek forgiveness from those they have harmed.

Hindu New Year

New Year's Day immediately follows Divali in October or November (see 'Introduction to Hinduism' p.113), so the festive period combines many themes. Before the festival, all account books for the year have to be closed, all debts paid, and all business finished. Any quarrels must also be made up before the festival. During the festival, offerings are made to Lakshmi, the goddess of good fortune and wealth.

find out if they fell on the same date as last year.

★ Make a class list of other New Years – e.g. the start of the different sporting seasons, the start of the school year, spring when things start to grow, and possibly autumn – the planting of bulbs at this time might signal the start of the growing year. Include birthdays in this record, as they indicate the start of another new year in the life of the child.

★ If the school has a collection of New Year cards this would be the time to show them. The children could make their own new year cards on a theme, e.g. the environment, sports, T.V.

★ Tell the children about some of the customs associated with New Year festivals. A common theme running through these very different celebrations is the idea of starting afresh in hope. There is the hope that the new year will be a kind one, but also the idea that all unfinished business must be complete before a new start can be made. This may be a case of getting accounts up to date, but as in the Jewish New Year there is an idea that all quarrels must be healed. Talk about these customs and provide the opportunity for discussion on themes of reconciliation, or being prepared to forgive.

★ Suggest that the children make their own New Year resolutions, not necessarily for public reading, but for themselves if they have private journals or diaries in class. They could also make a list of the New Year resolutions they think other people might make, e.g:

– the footballer at the start of the season
– the headteacher at the beginning of the school year
– the gardener in spring
– the Prime Minister at the start of the parliamentary year
– TV planners when they plan a new year's programmes.

Ideas

★ Ask the children to investigate why and when people celebrate. They could use some of the many books about festivals as a resource such as *Faiths and Festivals* by M. Palmer (Ward Lock) or the 'Celebrations' series by A&C Black. Different groups could make a circle diagram of the year for different faiths, marking in the festivals, perhaps with different colours for different types of festival (e.g. birthdays, sad times, happy times).

★ Make a class birthday book to which all could contribute over a period of time. This could contain the birthdays and brief biographies of people whose birthdays the children would like to remember. Some may be people in the family, in which case it is easy for the children to find out the necessary information. Other children may wish to write about a public figure, so a letter of enquiry will be needed.

★ Find out from the children what other anniversaries they keep or would like to keep and why? There is the opportunity here both for class discussion and for personal writing in journals. Here it will be up to the child whether they will show it to the teacher. Such writing may be intensely personal, such as wanting to keep the anniversary of the death or birthday of a recently deceased grandparent.

★ Create with the children a **Dance of the Year**, with the children divided into groups to work out a dance or mime for individual parts of the year. This could provoke a discussion about what would be included. At the simplest level it could be a series of mimes about the year. If you are able to spend more time and energy on it, it could include a selection of appropriate music to which the children dance, or even make up their own music with percussion instruments. This dance could be presented in an assembly as a climax to the topic.

Unit 4
Festivals of the year

Purpose
● to look at the way festivals mark out the year
● to see that some 'time' is specially significant

Unit 5
Cyclical and linear time

This unit and the following one are aimed at older juniors who will enjoy exploring the more difficult concepts tackled here.

In general the Western world operates with a

linear concept of time: everything has a beginning, a middle and an end, from the life of an amoeba to the life of the universe. In the Jewish, Christian and Islamic faiths the world is brought to a close at Judgement Day and there is a new beginning with a different sort of time. In contrast, Eastern faiths see time as a constant succession of cycles: the ant's life is one of many lives, our life is one of many, this universe is one of many; each life constantly changing in a process of creation, maintenance, destruction and re-creation (see Information Box).

Purpose

● to develop concepts of cyclical and linear time

Ideas

★ Ask the children to think of all the things which happened the previous year and which happen every year at the same time. Make a list of these then cut them out and ask the children to arrange these events round a circle e.g. seasons, festivals, start of the new year. Then ask them to mark on it things which were one-offs for that year, or extremely irregular occurrences e.g. 'I broke my leg'. Ask them to look for other daily or weekly cycles and to draw their linear counterparts.

★ Go on to explain to them that Hindus and Sikhs believe that this world and each life in it is

---

Life after death in Ancient Greece

The Ancient Greeks believed that in the afterlife, people retained only a shadow of their former selves, both physically and morally. They left the earth and went to live in the underworld, a shadowy place where very little happened. To get there they had to cross the river Styx (see topic on 'Water', p.27). Later on, the Greeks developed the idea that everyone received their just deserts in the afterlife. Those who had lived a good life and not offended the gods went to live in the Elysian fields, where life was pleasant. Those who had done wrong were condemned to endless torment, often by repeating pointless actions: Sisyphus was condemned to roll a stone endlessly up a hill; the Danaids had to go on filling a barrel which leaked the water out.

Life after death in Ancient Egypt

The Ancient Egyptians believed that life went on after death very much as it did in the Egypt they knew, but without any pains and troubles. That is why wealthy people were buried together with many useful everyday objects, and models of servants to wait on them in the next world. But it was important that the body should be preserved in order to reach this afterlife, so the bodies were carefully preserved and mummified.

Reincarnation

Hindus believe that the whole universe goes on endlessly being created, destroyed and re-created over millions of years, under the power of Brahma the creator, Vishnu the sustainer and Shiva the destroyer. But the role of destroyer is not seen as bad, but simply part of the endless cycle, just as the night has to be destroyed for day to come, or the seed destroyed for the plant to grow. In the same way people and animals are born, grow and die, and are then reborn in a different body.

Buddhists too see the world and all the creatures and plants in it as part of the cycle of birth and rebirth. The cycle will only come to an end when all creatures succeed in living according to the Buddha's teachings, and detach themselves from greed, love, anger, and all the emotions that tie them to this world.

---

like the year, or week, or month. It is one of many that go on repeating themselves. Different events may happen in each unit (rather as episodes of TV shows have the same format, but a different content each week) but they believe that after we die we will be reborn to live another life.

★ Contrast this with Jewish, Christian and Islamic beliefs that we have only one life on earth, and then the afterlife. Look too at secular beliefs that this life is the only one we have. It is not necessary to go into ideas about final judgement unless it arises spontaneously. Then you might find it useful to look at some of the Greek and Egyptian ideas about the afterlife (see Information Box).

★ Based on some of the Greek ideas about endless actions, discuss this with the children in a light tone. Ask them to write about something that they personally would not want to go on doing for ever. This may be irritating things such as waiting for your mother to finish talking to a friend after school, walking barefoot on a pebble beach, or pleasurable things such as sitting on a fairground ride or eating ice-cream.

Unit 6
Notions about time beyond time

Most religions have the notion that God is eternal – outside and beyond time. Again these are difficult ideas; we suggest them only so that children can begin to play with them, not in the expectation that they will be fully grasped.

Purpose
• to reflect on the subjective nature of time
• to begin to develop ideas about eternity by introducing the idea that time is a human measurement

Ideas
★ Ask the children to look silently at a particular point for one minute. Then sing or talk to each other for one minute. *Did they seem like the same amount of time?*
★ Compile lists of 'slow times' and 'fast times', preferably directly contrasting ones, e.g. waiting for the bus/running for the bus.
★ Refer to the 'Narnia' books by C.S. Lewis

(HarperCollins), or *Tom's Midnight Garden* by Philippa Pearce (OUP), if the class has read any of them. If they haven't this might be the time to read one, these books contain the idea that time passes at different speeds in different places.
★ Look at the idea of 'relativity of time' in space travel. Ask the children to write a story about space travellers returning to earth to find that 20 years have passed to their one.

CROSS-CURRICULAR LINKS

Science
Follow the life cycle of a bean from seed to fully grown plant with its own beans. Follow the life cycle of a frog from frogspawn to fully grown frog producing new spawn. Draw and display these. Plant your own beans in the classroom.

Investigate the planets. Make a model of the solar system particularly focusing on the Sun, moon and Earth.

Maths
Investigate time. Add and subtract time using clocks, write down the new times. Find out about the 24 hour clock, *Why is this used?* Add on time and give the answer as it would appear on a digital clock.

Geography
Find out about time zones. *If it is 10.00 am in Britain, what time is it in France, New York or Australia?* Look at a globe to explain this phenomenon.

JOURNEYS

Christianity, Hinduism, Judaism and Islam all focus on aspects of commitment and symbolic language which are the themes of this chapter.

'The journey' has often been used metaphorically to describe the progress of human beings through life, especially the spiritual life. Physical journeys are also part of many religions, in the form of pilgrimages to places regarded as holy because of their association with events or people important to that religion. A journey is associated with change – a change of scenery, a change of people, even a change in lifestyle or spiritual awareness.

To introduce this topic, or to run alongside it, you could read with the children one of the simplified versions of John Bunyan's *Pilgrim's Progress*, such as *The Family Pilgrim's Progress* (Scripture Union, 1983).

Unit 1
Going on a journey

Journeys can be exciting but also worrying. Through drama, children can look at their feelings about journeys without making themselves too vulnerable.

Purpose
• to introduce the theme of journeys
• to show that people go on journeys for different reasons

Ideas
★ Talk about journeys the children have made, and why. Some may have gone abroad or elsewhere in Britain for holidays, others to visit relatives. Some may have come on a long journey to reach Britain from another country, or moved house within Britain. Many will have gone on school outings. You could ask the children to write about their most memorable journeys for a class **Journeys we remember** book.

★ Act out a scene in a railway carriage in which several people are travelling for different reasons, and possibly to different destinations. Discuss what they might feel about the journey e.g. excited, bored, frightened, sad, happy. Decide what they might want to take with them. Perhaps they need presents for those they are visiting, a camera, holiday clothes, a favourite mascot (this can make the valuable point that even adults may have teddy bears or their equivalent). The actors can talk to each other about where they are going and why.

★ Plan and carry out an imaginary journey. With the children, decide where you are going, how you will travel, what you will take with you etc. Then write 'letters' and 'postcards' from different points on the journey, collect 'souvenirs', e.g. hotel bills, restaurant menus, brochures, carrier bags. This journey can take you into as many curriculum areas as you wish.

Unit 2
Places of pilgrimage

Pilgrimage has a long-established tradition in many religions. There is a feeling that certain places are endowed with special qualities because of their associations and are therefore spiritually rewarding to visit.

Also, look at the assembly 'The Assisi Pilgrimage' in the *REAL Junior Assembly Book*.

One of the 'five pillars of Islam' is that every Muslim who can afford it should at least once in his or her life make a pilgrimage to Mecca, the birthplace of the prophet Muhammad, and the place of the ka'ba. This is an oblong building with a black stone set into its N.E. corner said to be from paradise. The building is believed to be Adam's first house and was later rebuilt by Ibrahim (Abraham). According to Islamic tradition it is the first building built for the sole purpose of the worship of Allah. While there they perform certain ceremonies, and celebrate the festival of Eid ul-Adha.

The festival of Eid ul-Adha commemorates the willingness of the prophet Ibrahim (Abraham) to sacrifice his son Ishmael (Isaac in the Judaeo-Christian tradition) to God. Ultimately a sheep was sacrificed instead. It is still the custom, whether on hajj (pilgrimage) or at home, to share the meat of a sheep at this festival – often with the poor. See the 'Introduction to Islam' p.119 for more details.

In Christianity, Jerusalem is a favourite site for pilgrimage because it is the place where Jesus was crucified and rose again. The focus for pilgrimage differs slightly for certain groups. Thus, the Church of the Holy Sepulchre with the shrine of Golgotha and the shrine of the Tomb is central for Roman Catholics and many Orthodox Christians. For Ethiopians, the slab on which Jesus was laid for embalming is of tremendous significance. For many Protestants who find the Church too overpowering, the Garden Tomb (a simple stone tomb in the hillside) is the major focus, because some people feel it is more like the original tomb. The Via Dolorosa is walked by most pilgrims, being the supposed route Jesus took to the Cross.

Hindus regard the Ganges as a holy river throughout its length, but especially at Benares. Hindus go to Benares to pray and wash themselves in the river. When Hindus die, their relatives may arrange for their ashes to be taken to the Ganges and scattered there. Some other places of pilgrimage relate to the god Krishna, especially his birthplace, Vrindaban, where pilgrims walk all around the town on the festival of his birth.

Jews like to visit Israel, the 'promised land'. When there they go to pray at the Western Wall, which is all that remains of the temple destroyed by the Romans in 70 CE. People pray with their face to the wall, and may write prayers on paper and tuck them into cracks between the stones.

Purpose
● to look at the places of pilgrimage within different religions
● to appreciate the reasons for their importance

Ideas
★ Draw out the concept of pilgrimage by discussing secular 'pilgrimages' as well as religious ones – e.g. a visit to Wembley every year for the Cup Final, perhaps a return to the town or village where they or their parents formerly lived. *Are there any places which are special for you? Why is the place special? What happened there?* Make a class book of special places and their stories.

★ Look at places of pilgrimage for two or three religions. The children can find them on a map. Tell some of the stories associated with them. Examples from *A Tapestry of Tales* are 'Saint Bernadette of Lourdes'; 'Muhammad' and 'Hagar and Ishmael'.

★ On a world map, children could mark different places of pilgrimage, and different groups could plan the journey to reach them. *What means of transport would you use? How long might you be away from home? What clothes would you take?*

Unit 3
What happens on pilgrimage

The frame of mind of the person setting out on a pilgrimage is an important aspect of the ritual. Often special preparations for the journey are made.

Purpose
● to look at the way people prepare for pilgrimage
● to learn of their experiences on pilgrimage

Ideas

★ Find out from library books, such as the 'Celebrations' series by A&C Black, about the special preparations people make for pilgrimage. *Do they wear special clothes?* All Muslim men on hajj or pilgrimage to Mecca wear only two seamless sheets of white cotton, making them all appear equally dressed.

★ *What do they do when they get there? How does this relate to the story they are commemorating?* Christians at Lourdes may bathe in the waters of the spring which Bernadette found in the hope of being cured. Muslims run seven times between two hills to commemorate Hagar's running to find water. *Why do Jews mourn at the Western Wall in Jerusalem?* (They are recalling the story of the Temple and its destruction.)

★ Link this work with drama. Act out one of the stories you have read from *A Tapestry of Tales*. Explore how the characters are feeling.

★ Look on a map and find the places of pilgrimage. *How long would it take to get to them from your school? How much would it cost?*

Unit 4
Quest

Purpose

● to think about why people go on difficult journeys and struggle for some things which are important to them

Ideas

👁 *Can you imagine why people queue all night for: Cup Final tickets; pop concert tickets; 'the sales' at big shops?*

★ Develop the idea that some things are worth putting up with discomfort for – even suffering for. *How important are the above in comparison to: queuing at the doctor's; visiting someone in a hospital a long way away; going on hajj, or to Jerusalem?*

All these involve: inconvenience; giving up time; (maybe) discomfort.

★ Can you suggest any other situations which would cause you to endure the above voluntarily? *Why would you put up with these things?*

Unit 5
Your life as a journey

Using a stylized format to look at one's life is helpful in giving it perspective. The 'railway' is also used to express hopes, and perhaps fears, for the future.

Purpose

● to show the metaphorical use of the idea of journeying

Ideas

★ Ask the children to draw a plan of their lives so far as if it were a railway journey, with events which are important to them marked as railway stations. Some events may be major changes such as starting school, moving house, a new baby in the family. Others may be events which, though seemingly minor, are special to the child such as learning to ride a bicycle, getting a favourite toy, being allowed to stay up late for the first time, visiting the zoo or the airport.

★ Plan the rest of the journey. What 'stations' would you like to have in the rest of your life? These may include plans for the future, such as marriage, children, jobs, but may also include ambitions, such as learning to hang-glide, discovering a cure for cancer, playing football for England, becoming Prime Minister, the possibilities are endless!

★ Include some variations such as treating setbacks in life as obstacles on the line; combining the lines of several people which may intersect briefly or run parallel for part of their length; introducing junctions which are choices made at different times, leading to different sets of stations.

★ Make your own 'snakes and ladders' game with various setbacks and encouragements at each snake or ladder.

★ Other ways of representing a journey could be used: for example, walking along a road which branches and goes over hills and through valleys, or driving along a network of roads and motorways through towns and service stations. You could introduce a maverick or unplanned problem into the route: roadworks or a derailment of the train in front, or something to represent the ever-present possibility of having to change course. What might make you change course? *Has anything caused a big change to people in your family?* e.g. falling in love with someone from another country; going to war; winning a prize; illness; accidents; etc. Children could talk about this with older relatives and write a newspaper-style report of any notable changes of course.

For younger children a simpler version of this idea, using just ups and downs, could be used.

★ The railway or road format could also be used to record major events in the life of a religious figure which the class has been studying.

CROSS-CURRICULAR LINKS

Science

What makes things move? Look at forces at work and create your own vehicles. Work with batteries to produce a moving vehicle, with lights.

History

Investigate changes in transport. *What has changed since your grandparents were young?*

Geography

Look at a map of the local area. Find all the kinds of transport there are available locally. Compare the different ways to travel from your town to the next big town. Look at price, time and convenience.

CHANGE

The themes of hope and religious conversion are addressed here as well as a consideration of rites of passage. In particular the Jewish and Christian faiths are explored in this context.

Change is part of the fabric of the universe. Everything is constantly undergoing change though at times that change may be imperceptible to the human eye. Alongside these inevitable natural processes are changes in the circumstances of living: a house move, a new job or loss of a job, the death of a family member, a move to a new school or away from home for the first time. Such changes can be a source of great stress, indeed the thought of change can be the source of anxiety, e.g. many children harbour fears about the death of a parent and how it will affect them.

Positive experiences of change and a positive attitude towards it contribute to an ability to cope with change when it comes. This is particularly so for people facing bereavement.

Not all change is thrust on us. It is important that children learn that they can be authors of change. Things do not just happen to them; they can change themselves and change the world in which they live albeit in a small way.

Stories

There are many stories telling how conversion changed a person's life. These are perhaps best told during the time you spend on the topic. All the following stories can be found in *A Tapestry of Tales*: 'Stories of the Buddha' – born a rich prince, he was shocked when he eventually came into contact with suffering and death, and so became an ascetic. 'Holy week, Easter and Whitsun' – the fear and cowardice of the disciples was turned into courage after their experience of the resurrected Jesus. 'Saint Francis' – born into a rich family he became a saint known for the simplicity of his life-style. 'Zacchaeus' – who gave up cheating in his tax-collecting after his encounter with Jesus. The conversion of Saint Paul – the persecutor of Christians who became a major Christian teacher and missionary. Moses – whose experience of God's presence in the 'burning bush' turned him from a shepherd into a leader of the people.

Look, too, at the assemblies on 'Change' and on 'Dreams of Utopia' in the *REAL Junior Assembly Book*.

Unit 1
Everything is constantly changing

Most of these ideas could be done in a simple way, or developed further in science and history. Conversely, work in science and history could provide a foundation for this topic.

Purpose
- to acknowledge the amount of change taking place
- to realize that growth and decay are natural
- to introduce or develop the idea of cyclical change

Ideas

★ Make a chart recording in some detail how the sky, the position of the sun, and the weather change during the course of one day. Note the time and illustrate the weather conditions and the position of the sun.

★ Record, over a period of time, the changes which take place in plants in the classroom, a slice of bread, a glass of water, mustard and cress seeds, etc.

★ Look at how the natural world has changed since its beginning. Most children are fascinated by dinosaurs and the idea of evolution. Your school library will probably have books describing evolutionary stages, try in particular, *Dinosaur Bones* by Aliki and *Evolution* by J. Cole (A&C Black). Children could work in pairs to describe the evolution of particular animals, or the general stages of evolution.

★ Ask the children to find out some of the changes which have taken place in your area, by comparing present maps or photographs with those from the past. Your public library should be able to help with this or ask grandparents to recount the changes they have noticed.

★ Ask the children to find out how various ordinary items have changed in appearance in the past fifty or a hundred years. They could choose an item in which they are particularly interested, e.g. cars, clothing, prams, toys, aeroplanes, the way babies are dressed. Look at the 'History Mysteries' and the 'Turn of the Century' series by (A&C Black).

★ Ask the children to look for and describe clear examples of cyclical change, e.g. how a tree changes through the year, life cycles of frogs, butterflies, flowers, etc.

★ Ask the children to think of obvious examples where the end of one thing results in the creation of something new, e.g. tree into a boat, clay into a fired pot, balls of wool into a knitted garment.

Unit 2
What has changed in my life?

Purpose

● to create opportunities for children to talk about changes which have happened to them

● to talk about how they have been affected by these changes

● to help children think positively about such changes (this will not be possible in every circumstance)

Ideas

★ Begin a topic called 'How have I changed in a year?' You might be able to borrow a copy of the class photograph from the previous year. This can be used to stimulate discussion about what has changed in the intervening time – in the children personally, in the class, and in the school. Hairstyles may be different, where once there were gaps in the smile there may now be teeth and vice-versa, clothes worn in the photo may now be outgrown. The children may have acquired new skills, such as riding a bike, swimming a length, being able to do joined-up writing. The class probably has a different teacher, some children will have left for another school and others will have joined the class. The school may have had various staff changes, as well as some physical changes, e.g. a fresh coat of paint.

★ Ask the children to bring in photos of themselves when they were much younger. 'Guessing who the babies are' is always a popular game, especially when photos of teachers are included.

★ Use these baby pictures as the basis for a discussion. After commenting on the obvious physical changes, other questions could be tactfully raised by asking children to write for themselves, e.g.

– *How has my family changed since then?* Some children may have acquired a younger sibling, an older sibling or sadly a parent may have left home.

– *Am I living in the same place? Do I sleep in the same bedroom? Does my bedroom look different?*
– *Did I have my pets then?*
The children could make 'then and now' pictures, not only showing how they looked when they were younger but how their surroundings have changed.

Unit 3
Looking to the future

Here is an opportunity to teach upper junior children about the physical changes which may have already begun to take place in their bodies with the onset of puberty.

Another major change which many children will be facing is that of moving to a new school.

Purpose
● to encourage the children to look positively towards the future

Ideas
★ You may be able to obtain permission for a secondary school child to visit your class and answer questions about secondary schools.
★ Secondary school teachers may be willing to ask their students to prepare guides to the school for prospective new pupils.
★ Ask the children to draw pictures of what they will look like in five, fifteen and fifty years.
★ Ask them to make predictions of what they will be doing in five, fifteen and fifty years. After displaying them, these could be locked away, with some drama, only to be looked at in fifty years time!
(Also see the topics on 'Time' and 'Journeys' in this book.)

Unit 4
Taking on responsibility

Purpose
● to help the children think about what it means to be adult
● to look at the ceremonies of Bar Mitzvah, Baptism and Confirmation

Ideas
★ Ask the children to do their own research to find out the legal age when someone can drink alcohol, drive a car, get married, vote or join the army. *How old do you have to be to be grown up?*
★ The children could write stories about **A Day in the Life of Mum/Dad**. Encourage them to think of some of the responsibilities their parents have to fulfil during the day.
★ Look at the picture of Christian baptism in the Pictorial Charts display pictures, and talk about the promises being made, using the Information Box and the 'Introduction to Christianity, p.00. Go on to look at Confirmation. Ask the children to recall things they did not understand once, but now they do.
l *What is a confirmation candidate saying he or she wants to do? Is it simply a question of them being grown up and understanding more? What responsibilities do they have now they are confirmed?*
★ Similarly tell the children about Bar Mitzvah, making the point that this ceremony is related to a particular birthday (13th). Encourage the children to imagine what it must be like to be the Bar Mitzvah boy with all eyes on him. Draw out the privileges and responsibilities he now has as an adult member of the synagogue. (See 'Introduction to Judaism'.)
★ Note particularly how children are prepared both for Bar Mitzvah and Confirmation.

Baptism

Baptism can take place at any age, and is a sign of God's acceptance of the person as a Christian. Some Christians believe it is not right to undergo baptism until a person is old enough to make the decision that they want to follow Jesus Christ, for themselves. Others bring babies for baptism, with parents and godparents making promises on behalf of the baby. Adults are often baptised by complete immersion in water, while babies have a small amount poured on their heads. In both cases the water symbolises dying (drowning) and rising to new life in Christ. The promises made are the same for adults as they are for children.

The following responses are taken from the Anglican service, but differ very little from those used in other churches:

Do you turn to Christ?
I turn to Christ.
Do you repent of your sins?
I repent of my sins.
Do you renounce evil?
I renounce evil.

Confirmation

If someone has been baptised as a baby, the time comes when they have to decide, for themselves, whether they want to take on the promises which were made at birth on their behalf. Many churches run classes and dis-cussion groups for those considering confirmation, to make sure that they fully understand the Christian faith which they are promising to keep.

In the service, the candidates declare their belief in God: Father, Son, and Holy Spirit. A Bishop presides over a confirmation service, and each candidate for confirmation kneels in front of him. He lays a hand on their head, and prays for each person to be filled with the Holy Spirit.

Bar Mitzvah

When a Jewish boy is 13 years old, he becomes an adult as far as the Jewish faith is concerned. This means that he can be one of the ten adult males who must be present before the daily synagogue prayers can take place. He is also eligible to read the Torah aloud in synagogue services. The first time he does this is made the occasion of a family and synagogue celebration, focusing on the responsibilities the boy now has as an adult member of the faith.

Because the reading of the Torah in Hebrew is quite difficult (the Torah scroll is written without any vowels in it), the boy must spend some time preparing for the reading. He must also prepare for this new responsibility for his own actions and his own keeping of the Law. Preparation classes are usually held in the synagogue.

Unit 5

You can change, you can change the world

Purpose
● to discuss the difference that wanting something to change can make

Ideas
★ Draw together the stories about religious conversion (listed at the beginning of the topic) by asking children to recollect them. *What do all these stories have in common?*
★ Ask the children what changes for the better they would like to make: to the world, to the school, to themselves.

CROSS-CURRICULAR LINKS

History
Children can discuss change related to a topic they have studied in history work. *What changes did the Romans make to Britain?*

Discuss changes in the roles of men and women since the 1930s. Ask adults of different ages to come and visit the school to discuss these developments.

Science
Make cakes together and put them in the oven. When they are cooked write about everything that has happened to the mixture. Compare the taste, texture, colour, etc.

Geography
Look at pictures of different seasons. Describe all the changes that have taken place in the pictures. The children can write about how it would feel to be in the summertime picture, or the wintertime picture and try spring and autumn scenes, too. Describe the weather and what can be seen.

English
Read some favourite stories together and write different versions where the characters' personalities are completely different, so that a selfish person is kind, a naughty person well-behaved, a forgetful person remembers, etc.

LIGHT

This chapter focuses on the themes of celebration, holiness, and good and evil, as they appear in Christianity, Hinduism and Judaism.

There are few sights more magical than the glow of lights in the dark, whether they are candle flames, fireworks, bonfires or shining Christmas decorations in towns and cities at night. This almost mystical quality is one reason why light has always been an important symbol to human beings, in both social and religious contexts. But the magical and the mystical are only two aspects of the symbolism of light; there are others, much more powerful, which represent to people the presence of God.

Light overcomes darkness, as good overcomes evil; light is necessary for vision, just as God's light is necessary for real understanding; light can welcome and comfort, just as it is believed God can do; and light can also be as blinding and overwhelming as it is believed the full presence of God is.

Christmas is a festival of light, for Christians believe that Jesus is the light of the world. His birthday is celebrated at a time of year which is mid-winter for the northern hemisphere, because he came into the world in the depth of 'darkness' (see John 1).

It is not only Christians who have light as a symbol. Hindus have their own festival of lights, Divali, and Jews celebrate Hanukah. Both these festivals usually occur early in winter.

The main focus here is Christmas, but as Divali and Hanukah occur earlier in the year, details and suggestions for these are given first. You may wish to lay more emphasis on one of these, or use the idea of a 'festival of lights' to lead into Christmas preparations.

Refer to the 'Introduction to Hinduism' at the back of this book for more detail on Divali.

Unit 1
Light as a religious symbol

Purpose
• to encourage children to reflect on their experience of light
• to explore those properties of light that make it a central religious symbol

Ideas
★ If possible, visit a science exhibition featuring dramatic and curious aspects of light. Look at such things as the Aurora Borealis or laser beams.
★ In season, take the children to see decorative city illuminations.
★ In school, take opportunities to light birthday-cake candles. *What is nice about birthday candles?*
★ Talk with the children about the magical, mystical qualities of light. Then set the children some painting or imaginative writing. The firework theme is useful here.
★ Draw attention to the welcoming character of light by considering returning to an unlit home after a day out. Light as a comfort can be linked to a discussion about night-lights. In the same context, you might go on to discuss the effects of overwhelming light: *Could you sleep with a bright light shining on your face?*
★ If you have already done some work on the Jewish Sabbath, you could re-examine the welcome given to the Sabbath by the lighting of candles.

Unit 2
Lights at Divali

Purpose

- to familiarize children with one of the most important stories in Hinduism
- to explore how light is used in the festival of Divali, and thus develop children's understanding of light as a religious symbol

Ideas

★ Read the story of the Ramayana in *A Tapestry of Tales* and discuss it with the children. Then the class can make masks, either simple paper ones or more elaborate ones of papier mache, and mime or act out the story.

★ Individually, or in groups, the children can paint different events from the story. These can then be displayed in sequence as a frieze. Let the children decide which incidents would make good illustrations.

★ Discuss some of the ways that Hindus celebrate Divali, especially those ways that involve lights.

★ The children could make models of Divali lamps using modelling clay with a piece of yellow tissue paper for a flame, and place them

---

Divali, meaning 'row of lights', is a Hindu celebration which has many different aspects. The celebration combines festivals of lights, harvest and New Year. As a festival of lights it celebrates the victory of Rama over the demon king Ravana – the victory of good over evil. As a festival of harvest and New Year it focuses also on the worship of Lakshmi, the goddess of good fortune.

Before the festival, homes, shops and offices are cleaned and redecorated, and elaborate designs using chalks, sand and coloured foodstuffs may be made on the floor. All account books have to be closed and all debts settled, for this is a time for starting afresh, just as Rama did on his return.

Lights feature prominently at Divali. Windows are brightly lit with oil lamps so that Lakshmi can look in, and so that Rama and his wife Sita may be welcomed home from exile.

---

on window sills, just as Hindus do to welcome Rama and Sita. Using clay you could make one real lamp to light, with a cotton wick and olive oil or ghee for fuel.

★ Find out the date of Divali this year.

Unit 3
Lights at Hanukah

Purpose

- to make more explicit the idea of light as a symbol of the presence of God
- to show how and why Hanukah is celebrated by Jews

Ideas

★ Tell the children the story of Hanukah from *A Tapestry of Tales*. Talk about it with them, so that they understand why the menorah is for Jews a symbol of freedom and truth, and of God's presence.

★ Learn a Hanukah song: see J. Gilbert, *Topic Anthologies for young children 3: Festivals*, OUP (Teacher's Book and audio cassette).

★ As a class, the children could paint, or make models of eight menorahs, the first with one candle lit, the second with two lit, and so on.

★ Find out when Hanukah is celebrated this year. If it falls within the school term, make a simple menorah with a row of candles and light the appropriate number each day.

Unit 4
Lights at Christmas

See the notes on Christmas in the 'Introduction to Christianity' at the back of this book. The Christmas story is given in full in *A Tapestry of Tales*.

Purpose

- to remind children of the Christmas story and focus on a central Christian belief
- to help children to understand symbolism e.g. the light of the star as a symbol of guidance; light itself as a symbol of holiness; the symbolic timing of the celebration of the nativity of Jesus in mid-

The festival of **Hanukah** lasts for eight days. The focus of each day is the lighting of the candles. Each evening one candle is lit, this is burnt down and replaced for the next day when two candles are lit, and so on until, on the eighth day, all are alight. Parties are held during the festival, and at these the spinning of the dreidel takes place. The dreidel is a small top with Hebrew letters on each edge. Depending on which letter the top falls, you can either take from a 'bank' of sweets or nuts, or you must contribute to the 'bank'.

Making a dreidel

Traditional dreidels are cubic in shape, with a shaft stuck through to make it spin like a top. A simpler version can be made from a square of cardboard, with a matchstick or pencil stub pushed through.

The four sides are each labelled with a Hebrew character. These stand for Hebrew words meaning 'a great miracle happened here'. The game is played as follows:

Everyone starts with 10-15 sweets, nuts, or whatever you are playing with.
Each player puts one of these in the bank.
Players take turns to spin the dreidel. If the result is 'Nun' the player does nothing.
If it is 'Gimmel' the player takes everything in the bank.
If it is 'Heh' the player takes half of what is in the bank.

If it is 'Shin' the player puts two into the bank.
Whenever the bank is down to one or nothing, everyone puts in one.
The game is over when one player has won everything.

There are variations in these rules, and you could adjust them to suit the circumstances.

Festival food

The importance of the oil in the Temple is remembered by the traditional food of Hanukah, which is latkes or levitot – potato pancakes fried in oil.

Recipe
3 large potatoes
1 onion
2 eggs
2 tablespoons of flour
1tsp. salt
oil for frying

Grate the potatoes and onion. Mix in the eggs, flour and salt. Drain off any excess liquid. Drop a spoonful at a time into a well-oiled frying pan. Fry on both sides until deep brown.

Latkes can be eaten with almost anything savoury, and are particularly good with soured cream.

winter, showing what he is believed to be rather than the actual day of his birth
• to help children to understand what is meant by 'holy'
• to give children a chance to experience a candle-lit procession

Ideas

★ Read the story of the birth of Jesus, including how the shepherds were visited by an angel and the wise men were guided by the light of a star.
★ Look at Christmas cards, postcards and other reproductions of paintings depicting holy people with haloes. Explain that haloes are still pictured around the heads of holy people as a sign that God is with them. *What do you think a holy person would be like?*

★ Discuss the use of candles at birthdays. *What sort of lights do we use to celebrate Christmas?*
★ Talk about celebrating birthdays, and how we can celebrate someone's birthday although we do not know the exact day on which they were born. Explain that Jesus' birth is celebrated in the dark months of the year because he came to us as light into darkness – the light of the world. The timing of Christmas was established in the northern hemisphere, where December is a winter month. (For expansion of this point, see 'Birthdays' in the *REAL Infant Teacher's Handbook*, p.47).
★ Collect Christmas cards and scraps of wrapping paper to make a display on the theme of light at Christmas.
★ Help the children to make mosaic pictures of the holy family using small pieces of shiny paper.

The Christingle

The people of Moravia, in Czechoslovakia, were the first to make christingles. This custom is now popular in Britain. Some Christians use them in a procession in church, some use them to decorate the home at Christmas. The practice has been made more popular in recent years by the Church of England Children's Society, who help churches to plan Christingle services where the children bring donations for the Society. You could contact your local branch for more details.

The orange stands for the world and all that is in it.

The candle stands for Jesus who Christians believe is the light of the world.

The red ribbon stands for blood. It reminds Christians that Jesus died on a cross.

The dried fruit stand for all the good things in the world, like kindness and love.

To make a christingle you need:

> an orange (larger ones are easier to handle)
> a length of red ribbon
> a small candle
> some cocktail sticks
> dried fruit – large raisins are easiest
> peanuts in their shells
> a sharp knife

Stand the orange on the table and make a small hole in the top. Insert the candle into this so that the orange holds it firmly. Put the ribbon horizontally round the orange, and secure with one or two cocktail sticks. On the end of these fasten dried fruit and nuts.

The christingle has a tendency to overbalance unless the candle is quite small. You can improve its stability by putting more cocktail sticks lower down, with more fruit and nuts on. However, it is meant mainly for holding rather than standing.

★ Make a christingle candle and explain its symbolism to the children. Better still, let the children make their own christingles and use them in a procession in the dark, perhaps accompanied by the singing of a carol.

★ The christingle procession is an activity which could be part of an assembly. Perhaps you could make it a feature of a celebration of light. This is a good way for the children to share with other classes what they have learnt about light as a symbol in different faiths.

CROSS-CURRICULAR LINKS

Science

Investigate the properties of light. Find out about reflection and shadows.

Make a collection of bulbs, batteries, wires and foil and try to make the bulb light up.

Shine a torch on to different materials such as black paper, tin foil, fluorescent paper, reflective arm bands, a brick, metal objects, a mirror, jewellery with sparkling stones and bicycle reflectors.

Experiment to find out which are the most visible colours to wear in the dark.

History

Find out about different sources of light. *How was your grandparents' house lit? What about their parents and grandparents?*

Geography

Draw a diagram mapping all the lights and switches in your house. Extend this to show all the street lights in the local area.

What is the weather like in Australia at Christmas time? What about in Norway? Find these countries on a globe and talk about why the weather is so different in these two places.

CHRISTMAS CUSTOMS

Most of the customs associated with Christmas have a religious significance, though many people who observe them are often unaware of this. This topic looks at some Christmas customs to draw out their religious significance, and with it increase understanding of Christian belief. Customs from other countries are also described to throw light on British practices.

Unit 1
The Christmas crib

Purpose
● to look at the idea that the story of Jesus can speak to each age

Ideas
★ Tell the children the story of St. Francis and the first Christmas crib (see Information Box). Stress to the children that the figures were dressed as

St. Francis and the nativity scene

St. Francis lived in Italy in the twelfth century. He is known even today for his love of animals, but his greatest concern was to tell people about the love of Jesus, and help them to understand it better. People saw lots of pictures of Jesus showing him to be a king. How could they learn that Jesus had been as poor as they were and therefore understood their troubles?

One Christmas Eve while everyone else was in church at midnight mass he collected wood and built a humble stable next to his church. In it he placed simple carved figures of Mary, Joseph and the baby Jesus. He brought in live animals to stand round the crib. When people came out of church after hearing the story of the birth of Jesus, the story seemed to be actually happening before their eyes.

From that day to this all over the world Christians have made Christmas cribs. There are cribs in churches and lots of Christians make a small crib scene at home.

Italian peasants not as first century Jews. Francis was not interested in historical detail but in the relevance of the story to the people of his own age.

★ Make a crib scene for the classroom with the figures dressed in modern dress.

★ Make up with the children a nativity play with a contemporary setting, e.g. a homeless couple in London, having to stay at a run-down bed and breakfast or sleep under railway arches.

★ Make a class collection of Christmas cards and postcards depicting the Nativity. Try to get as wide a selection as possible and look with the children at the historical setting of them. One of the most moving but simple paintings is Rembrandt's Nativity in the National Gallery which depicts a humble peasant cottage.

★ Encourage the children to design Christmas cards with contemporary settings, they could use drawing, painting or collage.

Unit 2
Christmas tree

Purpose
● to understand the Christmas tree as a symbol of everlasting life
● to further develop the notion that by sharing with others you are giving to God

Ideas
★ Tell children about the Christmas tree in Britain, and its long-standing tradition in Europe (see Information Box).

➥ *Why do people buy a fir tree at Christmas?*

★ Go on to tell the children about the Polish

custom of hanging home-made decorations on the tree as a way of making presents for God's tree.

★ Ask the children to make simple decorations to take home to put on their trees, or to hang on the school's tree.

★ Make a Christmas tree for the birds, or show the children how to make one, by hanging nuts, fruit, etc. from the branches of a bush or tree.

There is more than one story about how the Christmas tree came to be. In Medieval Britain it was customary to bring greenery into the home at Christmas, symbolising life continuing even in the dead of winter.

In German medieval plays, Adam and Eve are portrayed being expelled from paradise. Paradise was represented by a fir tree hung with apples (apples are a very common German Christmas tree decoration).

There is a story that Martin Luther, the initiator of the Reformation, was so struck one evening by the beauty of the night sky full of stars that he put candles on a fir tree in an effort to re-create the effect for his children.

Christmas trees were common in Europe, but unknown in Britain until the nineteenth century, when the custom was introduced by Prince Albert, Queen Victoria's husband, and rapidly became very popular.

Unit 3
St. Nicholas/Father Christmas

The giving of gifts at Christmas has a double meaning. First, it mirrors God's giving of himself to the world in the incarnation of Jesus. Secondly, Jesus's parable of the sheep and goats on judgement day (Matthew 25 : 31-46) has given rise to many legends on the theme that giving to the poor and needy is the same as giving to Christ himself.

Purpose
• to look at the background to Father Christmas
• to show the way one belief may be illustrated in different ways

• to develop the idea that giving to the poor is like giving to God

Ideas
★ Tell the children about St. Nicholas, and discuss the different names he is called, and the different customs associated with him.
★ Tell 'The Story of Baboushka' the Russian gift bringer (*A Tapestry of Tales*), as this brings out very clearly how giving to every child is like giving to Jesus. The Christmas story 'Papa Panov' (*A Tapestry of Tales*) also illustrates this vividly. These stories lend themselves to artwork, drama and story-writing.

St. Nicholas

Virtually nothing is known about the historical Saint Nicholas. He was Bishop of Myra at the end of the third century. Many legends have grown up about his goodness and kindness, especially to children, and he is known as the patron saint of children and of sailors.

One story tells how he took pity on three daughters of a poor man, who had no dowry and were in danger of being sold into slavery. He threw three golden balls or sacks of gold through their window at night to provide their dowries. Giving at night, or in secret, is one of the characteristics of the St. Nicholas tradition.

Another story tells of a famine in Myra, when there was no grain for the people to eat. When grain ships came into Myra on their way to other cities, Nicholas begged a little grain from each one, promising that when they reached their destination, none would be found to be missing. Some of the grain he kept as seed, and some of it he ground and cooked himself to make bread for the children of Myra.

German children clean their shoes on December 5th and leave them out for St. Nicholas. If they have been good the shoes are filled with sweets and other delicacies. If not the shoes are filled with sticks for beating. (Needless to say, the latter never happens).

In Holland, on December 6th Santa Claus, also known as Bishop Nicholas, drives through the streets of Amsterdam in a carriage, with his assistant Black Peter distributing presents.

Unit 4
Christmas lights

Also see the topic on 'Light', p.82.

Purpose

● to demonstrate the effects of light, particularly at Christmastime

Christmas lights

Celebrating Christmas in the middle of winter is a sign of the belief that the coming of Jesus was like a light coming into a dark world. The winter was cold and dark so Christians began to celebrate Jesus's birthday right in the middle of winter. And they celebrated it with lights.

Christmas tree lights

Many people now put up their Christmas trees long before Christmas. But the old custom was to put up the tree on Christmas Eve. Then the lights would be lit as a sign that Jesus, the light of the world, was born.

Advent candles

Some Advent candles are marked off so a little bit is burnt each day. Other Advent candles are in a ring of four candles, sometimes with a fifth in the middle. On the first Sunday of Advent one candle is lit, on the second Sunday two candles are lit, on the third Sunday three candles are lit so that on the fourth Sunday all four candles are burning. On Christmas day the centre candle is lit as well.

Advent candles are not only a way of looking forward to Christmas. Sometimes it is easy for Christians to be so busy preparing for Christmas they forget why they are celebrating. When they light the Advent candles it is a time for being quiet and thinking about Jesus coming to the world.

You can make an Advent wreath by making the ring out of wire mesh or florist's foam covered with greenery, and arranging the candles round the ring.

Ideas

★ Ask children to make a list, or a collection of pictures, of different lights at Christmas, e.g. lights in shopping streets, Christmas tree lights or candles, candle-lit services. Use wrapping paper, Christmas cards or gift brochures for resources.

★ Ask the children to illustrate scenes from the nativity story, paying special attention to the light – e.g. the star that the wise men followed, the 'glory of the Lord' which the shepherds saw, perhaps the light from the inn before the door is closed. You could use gold and silver foil for the light.

★ Make an Advent wreath with the children (see Information Box). But do not anticipate Christmas by lighting all the candles before Christmas day. Instead of lighting the candles on a Sunday as is normally done in the home, you could light them on a Friday afternoon, anticipating the following Sunday. At the end of term, give the wreath to someone the class has chosen. (Perhaps a classmate who is ill, or the lollipop person who is a 'beacon' for them on dark mornings, or the headteacher who is a 'shining example' to them!)

CROSS-CURRICULAR LINKS

Science

Study pictures of the different seasons and notice particularly how some trees lose their leaves in winter. Collect leaves from deciduous and evergreen trees and look at them with a hand lens. Write about the differences between the various leaves, particularly notice size, colour and texture differences.

History

Invite an older person into school to tell the children about how they celebrated Christmas when they were a child. *What sort of presents did you have? How was the tree decorated? What did you eat for Christmas dinner?*

Geography

Find out about Christmas customs in other countries.

PASSOVER

The festival of Pesach (Passover) is one of the central festivals of the Jewish faith.

For many Jews Passover is the highlight of the year. It is a time when all the family tries to gather together for at least the first night. It lasts seven or eight days depending on the particular tradition of Judaism followed. Like all festivals it links the present community of faith with their forebears and with those who are to come.

It celebrates the Exodus of the Israelites from Egypt and the formation of a covenant relationship with God. It is also a Spring Festival of cleansing and renewal, and the house is thoroughly cleaned before the holiday to remove all traces of leaven (yeast), which is forbidden during the festival (see Information Box).

During the festival Jews are exhorted to attend synagogue but the central event is the Seder meal which takes place on the first, and sometimes the second night of the festival. It is a time of festivity but also a religious service which follows a set order ('Seder' means order). The service is set out in a book called the 'Haggadah' or 'Telling' (see Information Box 5). It includes prayers, blessings, discussions of the significance of the day, and the ritual actions with the symbolic food.

The service expands the central theme of the Passover: that of deliverance from slavery into freedom. The story is told of how God brought the Israelites out of slavery in Egypt to serve him as a free people. This story is known as the Exodus.

The basic format for the Seder meal was established in the early centuries CE, although it built on a traditional meal which had been celebrated for many centuries. There are inevitably minor variations in tradition and practice (see Information Boxes).

A study of the festival in the classroom can deepen children's understanding of the Jewish faith, especially as it highlights the way Jews see the physical world as being part of the spiritual world. It also provides the children with the opportunity to explore the important theme of what it means to behave as a 'free' person.

The fundamental purpose in looking at the festival is to increase the children's understanding of Judaism. But note that the story of Exodus is also a key one in the Christian faith.

Unit 1

The story behind the festival of Passover

The story behind the festival is found in the opening chapters of the book of Exodus in the Bible. Many Jews and Christians do hold firm to a belief in the historical accuracy of the account, but whether one believes in its literal truth or not, the important point is the part this story plays in the Jews understanding of their relationship with God.

Purpose
● to familiarize the children with the story and connect it with the festival

Unleavened bread

The festival is known as the Festival of Unleavened Bread, because when the Israelites left Egypt they were in such a hurry there was no time for their bread to rise. Leavening also became a symbol of pollution and passion and so during the festival no leavened grain is permitted. Cakes, bread, biscuits, etc. are made without yeast from matzah flour. This is flour which has been prepared under supervision so that it has had no chance to begin fermentation. Everything made from matzah flour must still be cooked within 18 minutes of water being added so no natural fermentation has had a chance to begin. Although matzah bread is eaten all year round, traditionally it is not eaten for a month before the festival. The bread is referred to as matzah, plural matzot.

Ideas

★ Explain to the children about the Passover celebrations and then tell the story in as dramatic a way as possible. A version of the story is given in *A Tapestry of Tales*, but it may be more powerful to use your own words. Encourage the children to join in with the encounter with Pharaoh. You may find it easier to tell the story in three or four sessions rather than one. Two points need emphasising:

● that the Israelites were taken from slavery into freedom

● that this freedom was for forty years a life in the desert, and that some of the Israelites grumbled that they would be better off in Egypt.

You may need to tell children that Israelites is another name for Jews. It refers to someone who is a descendant of Jacob, whose name was changed to Israel.

★ Use the story as a basis for extemporary mime or drama. If you are skilled in this area you could extend this to dance/mime e.g. dance of slaves, dance of the plague animals.

★ Divide the children into pairs or groups to illustrate and write about one section of the story. These stories can then be displayed in sequence, or made into a simple book for the class library. The story lends itself to telling in a strip cartoon form.

Unit 2
Preparation for the festival

Purpose

● to help children become aware of the need for preparation for special events

● to broaden an understanding that Passover is the 'Festival of Unleavened Bread'

Ideas

➥ Talk with the children about spring cleaning or the need to get ready for special visitors. *What happens in your house if a special guest is coming? How do you help to get the house ready?* It is good for the children to acknowledge differences. This discussion can be used to lead into the need to prepare a house for Passover and especially to rid the house of all leavened or yeasted foods. Talk about the reason behind this practice (see Information Box).

★ Make some leavened and unleavened bread with the children so they can see the difference. (See Information Box for recipe for unleavened bread. Recipes for bread with yeast can be found in many cookery books.) Use fresh yeast if you can obtain it so that the children can see the change in the water when the yeast is activated.

★ Take the opportunity to spring clean the classroom and then tell children about the 'inspection game' (see Information Box) with candle and feather, and play it with them. Perhaps you could

Preparation for the festival

Beforehand the whole house is thoroughly spring cleaned, and all leavened food removed. (This includes all flour based foods). Many Jewish households have two sets of cutlery and china reserved only for the festival. (Two sets because meat and milk must be kept separate.) A final search for leavened food takes place the night before Passover. Traditionally a candle, feather and bag are used for this search. The children often hide pieces of bread, usually 10 pieces, around the house beforehand and make it into a game. The blessing is said, the candle lit, and the search begins.

invite in the head teacher to take the role of the head of the household and search for the hidden pieces.

Unit 3
The Passover service

In the chapter on 'Festivals' at the beginning of this handbook we put the case against 'celebrating' a festival of a faith which does not have a number of followers in the class. What is suggested here is not a celebration, but an 'acting-out' in order to gain an insight into the ceremony.

Purpose

• to bring the Passover to life for children
• to demonstrate that religious rituals can take place in the home
• to develop an understanding of the use of food in ritual

Ideas

Information about the service is given on the following pages.
★ Bring the Seder meal to life by telling the children about it in a vivid way. Set the scene by demonstrating how the table is laid going through the significance of each item as you lay it.
★ If you have been able to obtain a copy of the 'Haggadah' look at it with the children.
★ Try and evoke a sense of family and an air of celebration. Emphasize that the occasion is a mixture of set ritual foods and a festive meal, of set prayers and general chat and that it ends up with a fairly raucous sing-song.
★ The following could be given special attention:
– the recitation of prayers of blessing
– giving the children a chance to taste the horse-radish and haroset
– the spilling of the wine
– the youngest child asking about the 'leaning'.
★ Alternatively if you have a Jewish friend or are able to contact a local rabbi invite them to talk to the class from personal experience or you may be able to do so yourself. They may be willing to help you stage a simplified Seder service.

The Haggadah

This book gives the 'order of service' for the Passover meal. It is written in Hebrew, but there are many editions available with a parallel text in English. A Haggadah is often illustrated for children. You may be able to borrow one from a Jewish family or from the local library. The book *A Feast of History* by Chaim Raphael (Weidenfeld & Nicolson, London, 1972) includes a Haggadah as well as much other information about Passover. Remember that as Hebrew is written from right to left, the book starts at the right hand end, and the pages turn from left to right.

As the meal starts the leader pronounces the blessing over wine:

> 'Blessed art thou, O Lord our God, King of the universe, who has created the fruit of the vine.'

Before the matzah is eaten, the leader uncovers the dish and raises it, saying:

> 'The bread of our affliction which our forefathers ate in the land of Egypt. Let all who are hungry come and eat, let all who are in need come and celebrate the Passover. This year here and next year in Israel. This year as bondsmen, next year as free men.'

At one point in the service the leader dips his little finger into the wine and drips a drop from it on to the table as each plague is mentioned. This recalls sorrowfully the ten plagues sent to Egypt and the suffering of the Egyptians.
During the service the youngest child asks four questions, which draw out the significance of the occasion. One is,

> 'Why is it that on all other nights we eat and drink either sitting or leaning but on this night we lean?'

The answer is that on this night they remember that they are free people and not slaves. In the ancient Roman world free people ate lying on couches by low tables, which would result in a leaning position.

Seder table

A white cloth covers the table. The room is lit by candles.

Everyone has a wine glass for even the children must sip from 4 cups of wine during the meal. One extra cup, usually a special, large goblet, is set out for Elijah. It is said that Elijah visits every household on Seder night.

There is matzah for everyone, and bowls of salt water.

In addition, in front of the head of the household are two plates. On one are three matzot covered with a plate or cloth.

The other plate is the Seder Plate, on which these items are arranged in the following manner:

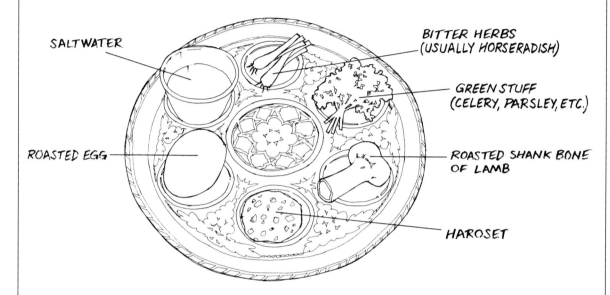

SALT WATER

BITTER HERBS (USUALLY HORSERADISH)

GREEN STUFF (CELERY, PARSLEY, ETC.)

ROASTED EGG

ROASTED SHANK BONE OF LAMB

HAROSET

The shankbone (lower leg of lamb) stands for the roasted lamb which was the Passover sacrifice. (The blood of the lamb was sprinkled on the doorpost to identify the home of an Israelite to the Angel of Death – see 'The Israelites escape from Egypt' *A Tapestry of Tales*).
Raw beetroot is sometimes used as a substitute by vegetarian Jews. Others draw a cutout picture of a shankbone.

The roasted egg is in memory of a festival sacrifice offered in the days of the Temple in Jerusalem.
Hard-boil, shell, and singe over a flame.

The bitter herbs are usually horseradish, a reminder of the bitter lives in Egypt.

The haroset is a sweet mixture which looks like the mortar used by the Israelite brickmakers in Egypt. It serves as a reminder of that labour but also of the sweet things God gives.
Each household has its own recipe, but it is basically a thick mixture of pureed apple,

ground nuts and sweet red wine. Blackcurrant juice or grape juice can be a substitute for wine in the classroom.

The greenstuff comprises greens dipped in salt water, a dish popular with free men in ancient times. It is also a sign of spring and new life.

Matzah – Proper kosher matzah is made from flour which has been supervised from reaping to milling, and there are strict rules for its production. The following is a recipe to convey taste rather than comply with these rules.

Mix flour and water in a ratio of $3\frac{1}{4} : 1$.
Divide into pieces about the size of the palm of your hand.
Each piece should be kneaded thoroughly and continuously (to prevent it from rising) for about 1 minute.
Roll out the dough into very thin circles, and prick with a fork.
Bake in a hot oven for 2 to 3 minutes.

The session could be concluded with learning one of the popular passover songs. See *The Seder Handbook* by Clive Lawton published by the Board of Deputies of British Jews (see Useful Addresses p.135).

At Passover, Jews sing many songs, one is a mnemonic song similar in format to 'Green Grow the Rushes O':
> Who knows one?
> I know one.
> One is God in heaven and Earth.
> and so on, adding verses until:
> Who knows thirteen?
> I know thirteen.
> Thirteen God's attributes
> Twelve the tribes
> Eleven the stars for Joseph
> Ten Commandments
> Nine months to bear
> Eight days to circumcise
> Seventh day for Sabbath
> Six books of Mishnah
> Five books of Torah
> Four the Mothers
> Three the Fathers
> Two the Tablets
> One is God in Heaven and earth.

Unit 4
Ways of remembering

Purpose
• to enhance an understanding of Passover
• to think about what is important and how it may be remembered

Ideas
★ Ask the children to remember days which are important to them and why. See if you can encourage them to go beyond Christmas and birthdays to think about events which may have changed their lives e.g. the day they moved house or started school. You might also raise with them the question of which events they think have been of national or global significance. You will need to link this back to the Exodus being a significant historical event for the Jewish people. You could extend the conversation to why the children think these events are so important, how they have changed their lives or that of the world. (Even if your class has done little history in school, some will have picked up information from news programmes, newspapers, etc.)
★ Discuss with the children the facts they think are the most important to know. Ask them why.
★ Refer the children back to the Seder service, to recall all the things which are aids to memory such as food, song, actions.
★ Look at the Passover number song. Make up a number song with the class,
e.g. 1 is for the headmistress,
    2 for the school secretaries,
    3 for the school gates, etc.
★ Make a collage of food which has associations for the children. Ask what certain foods remind them of and talk about other ways to recall certain events.

Unit 5
Slavery into freedom

Purpose
• to explore further the idea of slavery into freedom in a personal sense
• to enhance an understanding of Passover

Ideas
★ Recall with the children that the festival celebrates liberation from slavery into freedom and remember all the things that emphasized this in the Seder meal, discuss children's concepts of their own freedom. *Why do you need to obey your parents? Do you always need to obey another child? Do you sometimes feel as though you are doing things 'because you can't help it'?*, e.g. throwing a tantrum, being horrid to someone.
★ Divide the children into groups to make up mini dramas, in which a person wants to do the right things but is under pressure to behave differently e.g. agreeing to a dare they know to be stupid. Make up alternative endings to the same stories.

RAMADAN AND EID UL-FITR

Fasting during Ramadan is one of the five pillars of Islam. The month of Ramadan is a time for Muslims to remind themselves of the values of self-control and submission to Allah, as well as remembering the plight of those who are hungry in the world. At the end of this time, Muslims rejoice in the festival of Eid ul-Fitr, thanking Allah for enabling them to observe fasting.

Unit 1
Obedience

Purpose
- to discuss the role of obedience in religious life

Ideas

➡ *Who are you obedient to? What do they ask of you? Why do you obey them?* Discuss whether it is easier to obey through love than through fear.

★ Use the Pictorial Charts display pictures to introduce Islam if the children have not studied Islam before. Talk about the mosque, wudu and the Qur'an and how Muslims obey Allah: the word Islam means 'submission'. Explain that there are five main areas in which Muslims obey Allah – the 'five pillars of Islam' – and one of them is fasting.

Unit 2
Ramadan

Purpose
- to look at the fast of Ramadan and the reasons behind it

Ideas

★ Find out what the children ate yesterday. Each child can draw and cut out the foods he or she ate, and the drawings can be placed on a class collage.

★ Write down the times when the children ate yesterday, or the times when they would eat during a typical day. *What is the longest period you would normally go without food?*

★ Talk about hunger. *Have you ever been hungry?* Perhaps some children have taken part in a sponsored fast. *How does it feel to be hungry?* Explain that Muslims do not eat or drink between dawn and sunset for the whole month of Ramadan.

★ Some children may be willing to try giving up some luxury foods e.g. sweets, for a week. Ask the children to describe what it feels like.

★ Estimate the times of sunrise and sunset today. *Was it light when you got up this morning? Will it be dark when you have tea? When you go to bed?* Check the estimates against the published times of sunrise and sunset in the newspaper. *For how many hours would you be fasting, if you were a Muslim?*

★ Find out the times of sunrise and sunset at different times of the year.

Fasting during Ramadan lasts from dawn to sunset each day, and neither food nor drink are taken during this time. Muslims believe this fulfils several purposes. It enables Muslims to control their desire for worldly pleasure, teaching them self-restraint. It is a reminder that many in the world are hungry, through necessity not choice. Finally, it is an expression of obedience to Allah, who has commanded that Muslims should fast during Ramadan.

The Muslim calendar does not coincide with the Western calendar. There is a difference of nine days each year. Because of this, Ramadan may fall in the short days of winter or at mid-summer, as well as at any time between.

☞ *Would it be easy not to eat or drink during the day in winter? What about in the summer?* Explore the difficulties of hunger and thirst. *Does this help you to understand how it feels to be hungry all the time? How do you feel now about people who go hungry? Do you feel differently now?*

★ You will need to explain that not every Muslim is expected to fast during Ramadan. Discuss who is excused and why (the sick, the elderly, young children, pregnant women and travellers). Some of these groups are expected to make up for missed days later.

Unit 3
Controlling yourself

Self-control is a difficult skill. Even for adults it may need reinforcement. It is particularly difficult for children, since they spend much of their lives being controlled by others. Ramadan is, for Muslims, a time for special self-control in all areas of their lives.

Purpose

● to explore the idea of self-control as demonstrated at Ramadan

Ideas

★ Can the children think of anything people find it difficult not to do, even though they know they shouldn't do it? Examples may be over-eating, smoking, lying, fighting, nailbiting.

☞ *What would be the hardest thing for you to give up for a whole day?* Make a class collage illustrating the different activities.

☞ *How do people avoid doing something they are trying to give up?* Discuss the different ways: some may involve outside intervention, others may involve avoidance tactics, such as walking away from a situation where a fight may develop. *If someone else helps the person, what happens when that person isn't there?*

☞ *Do you think that having a time (like Ramadan) when you were expected to try particularly hard would be helpful?*

★ Try a sponsored silence. *For how long can you give up talking?*

Unit 4
Eid ul-Fitr

Purpose

● to discuss the celebration of Eid ul-Fitr

Ideas

★ Explain that the festival, coming as it does at the end of a long time of fasting, is the occasion for great rejoicing.

☞ If the children tried a sponsored silence, or some other form of self-discipline, ask them how they felt when it ended?

☞ *How would you feel after a fast like Ramadan?*

★ The first thing Muslims do after Ramadan, is to pray at the mosque, at dawn. Talk about how the fast of Ramadan helps to bring Muslims closer to Allah.

★ At Eid, people wear their best clothes to go to the mosque. Make a list of other times people might wear their best clothes – e.g. a party, wedding, job interview, Easter service. *How do you feel when you wear your best clothes? What clothes would you wear for a special occasion?* Draw a picture of them.

★ Eid cards are given (see illustration). Children can design an Eid card using geometric patterns.

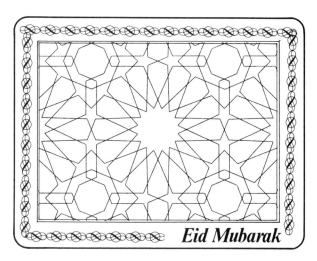

Eid card

★ Money is given to charity by Muslims at this time. *How does Ramadan encourage people to be generous to those less well off than themselves?* Ramadan makes you appreciate what it is like to be hungry. *Who do you know of in the world who is hungry? What organisations try to help them?* This might be a time to organise a collection for one of the famine relief organisations.

★ Sweets are a major treat at Eid ul-Fitr. *What favourite foods would the children like to eat after a fast?*

★ If there are a substantial number of Muslims in the school, you could organise an Eid party, but while it is possible to join members of a faith as they celebrate, it is not possible to 'celebrate' a festival which is not your own, so we would not advise an Eid party in a school where there are no Muslims. If you are having a party, the school could be decorated with Islamic geometric patterns (see illustration in the *REAL Infant Teacher's Handbook* p.43), and any sort of party food is suitable, especially sweets (providing, of course, that it does not contain pork or other pig products). Muslim families in the school might be asked to provide recipes for dishes that they normally have at home.

EASTER

In many parts of the world it is the custom for Christians to greet each other on Easter morning with the triumphal words, 'Christ is risen', which evoke the response, 'He is risen indeed'. It is on Easter Sunday, in particular, that Christians celebrate their belief that God raised Jesus, the Christ, from the dead. It reinforces their assertion that good will overcome evil, and their hope that they will experience life after death. The death and resurrection of Jesus are central events in the Christian faith. Christians, however, vary in their interpretations of the significance of these events, and ultimately the meaning of them is a mystery. If the children ask awkward questions don't worry about saying that you do not understand – you are in the company of many.

The topic is designed to give children some insight into Easter and the response of Christians, and to explore ways the festival is celebrated. The Easter story is central to this festival and to the way it is celebrated, so this unit differs from most of the others in this book, because it follows the story in detail. As the topic focuses on the person of Jesus, this might also be the time to read the children some of the parables he told, and other stories from his life.

Unit 1
Lent – the preparation for Easter

Purpose
● to introduce children to Lent and the practices associated with it
● to develop an understanding of the need for preparation, including preparation for a festival

Ideas
★ Ask the children to make a list of the things which must be done before:
– a birthday party
– going on a hike with their cub or Brownie pack
– going away on holiday
– the start of the new school year.
➪ Discuss the idea of preparation and being ready.
★ Ask the children how they get themselves ready for a spelling test or a party. Look at the ways we consciously try and put ourselves in the appropriate mood.

★ As an introduction to Easter and Lent, pay special attention to the person of Jesus. You may need to make the link for the children between the baby Jesus of Christmas and the adult man of Easter.
★ The children could write a profile of Jesus as an exercise to find out what they know. You may then need to fill in the gaps. Points which might be included are that Jesus:
– was a storyteller
– was a teacher
– was a miracle-worker
– was born in impoverished circumstances
– died on a cross (but see Information Box on the Muslim view of Jesus)
– had a mother called Mary
– taught about love
– had followers called disciples
– is followed by Christians
– is believed by Christians to be the son of God.
★ Tell children about Lent as a time of preparation for Easter. Discuss why Christians want to prepare themselves for Easter, as well as baking cakes, buying Easter eggs, etc. *What would the children give up for Lent?* Some may even want to

try a period of abstinence from something they enjoy.

INFORMATION BOX

The period of Lent is the period of 40 days (excluding Sundays) which immediately precedes Easter. For many Christians it is a time of reflection on their faith, and especially the sufferings of Jesus. Part of the spiritual preparation for Easter is often the self-denial of something pleasurable, e.g. biscuits, sweets, alcohol, watching television. Once it was a common practice to abstain from all animal products during Lent. Hence the tradition of eating pancakes on Shrove Tuesday, the day before Lent starts so that all eggs, butter and milk could be used up. In some countries vegetarianism is still practised during Lent.

INFORMATION BOX

Muslim view of Jesus

Muslims believe that Jesus was a prophet, and give him great honour, but do not worship him and do not believe that he was the son of God. Accounts of Jesus' death in the Qur'an are open to different interpretations, but it is generally believed by Muslims that Jesus did not die on the cross. Muslim pupils may therefore give different accounts of Jesus, and if this arises you will need to point out the different views of Jesus in the two faiths.

Jewish view of Jesus

Jesus was born a Jew, and he and the first Christians lived according to the Jewish Law. But Jesus' claims to be the Son of God and the Messiah, gave deep offence to Jews. Jews still await the coming of the Messiah.

Hindu view of Jesus

The Hindu pantheon is large and varied, and many Hindus give honour to holy men who have lived at different times. Some include Jesus in this, and honour him as a great religious teacher. But since they see the one Godhead as being expressed in a variety of forms of gods, the idea of Jesus as the only one to be followed is foreign to Hindu thinking.

Unit 2
Palm Sunday

Purpose
● to familiarize the children with the story of Palm Sunday

Ideas
★ Tell the story of Palm Sunday. Note that in the retelling of the story in 'Holy Week, Easter and Whitsun' (*A Tapestry of Tales*) we have included the religious leaders' discussion about Jesus, in order to set the scene for the trial and crucifixion. In the Church year Palm Sunday is the Sunday before Easter, but there is no implication in the Gospels that Jesus' entry into Jerusalem was just five days before his crucifixion.

★ Make palm crosses with the children. Many churches make and distribute palm crosses on Palm Sunday to commemorate the palm branches waved by the crowd. Palm leaves, both straight and ready formed into crosses, can be obtained from SPCK (see Useful Addresses p.135), who can also provide instructions for making the crosses.

★ The story would make a dramatic subject for a class mural.

INFORMATION BOX

Palm Sunday is a celebration of Jesus' entry into Jerusalem. (Matthew 21 : 1-10). A tradition from the prophet Zechariah predicted that the promised Messiah would ride into Jerusalem on an ass. Messiah (Christos in Greek) means 'the anointed one of God'. His coming was eagerly anticipated because it was believed that he would bring in a new age of God's rule on earth. There have always been debates within Judaism as to how this rule would be manifested. Christians believe that Jesus was this promised Messiah, hence the title 'the Christ'. Jews still look forward to the Messiah's coming.

Unit 3
Maundy Thursday: the Last Supper and the garden of Gethsemane

The Last Supper refers to the last meal that Jesus ate with his disciples before his crucifixion, and it is generally held to have been a Passover meal (see the topic on Passover p.89). The Passover at that time would not be the same as that celebrated by Jews today, as the present form dates from the centuries after Jesus.

The story as it is retold in *A Tapestry of Tales* includes the arrest of Jesus in the garden of Gethsemane and Peter's subsequent denial of Jesus.

Purpose
• to familiarize children with the story
• to look at ways these events are marked today
• to explore the themes of service and betrayal that lie within the story

Ideas
Tell the story see 'Holy Week, Easter and Whitsun' (*A Tapestry of Tales*).
★ Talk about Jesus washing the feet of the disciples. This would usually be performed by slaves, servants or disciples for their masters. Here the roles are reversed. Today it is the practice in some churches for the bishop or priest to wash the feet of members of the congregation on Maundy Thursday. The stole worn by the celebrant in a communion service had its origin in a towel which showed the priest to be the servant of the congregation. Discuss with the children what it means to be a servant. Ask them to think of ways that people, including themselves, can voluntarily serve each other.
☙ *How do you think Peter felt when he heard the cock crow?* (See also Ideas in the 'Friends' topic, p.30).
★ On Maundy Thursday some churches hold an 'agape' meal (pronounced a-ga-pay), re-enacting the Last Supper. (Agape means love.) The congregation share a simple meal together and throughout the evening the story of the Last Supper is told. At one point bread is broken and shared by all present, and a cup of wine is passed from one to the other. You could imitate this with

the class, using blackcurrant juice instead of wine. (If the bread is a loaf baked by the class, so much the better – see topic on 'Food', p.32.)

Note that you are not re-enacting the Last Supper as such, so no-one is being asked to portray Jesus.

★ Encourage the children to find out how Christians have followed Jesus' command to 'do this in remembrance of me' (see suggestions in the 'Food' topic, p.32). Encourage children who have been to communion services to talk about their experiences and observations with the class (bearing in mind that these may not always be favourable impressions).

Unit 4
Good Friday and Easter Sunday

It is part of Christian belief 'That Christ died for our sins in accordance with the Scriptures', but it is understood in different ways both by individuals and officially by different sections of the Church. That Jesus was crucified is a historical statement about which there is little dispute in the western world. His resurrection from the dead is a matter of belief, because it was a miracle. Although there are stories about sacrifice for the good of others in a number of traditions and children's novels, it is perhaps best to tell these stories throughout the year, and let the Easter story stand on its own at this time, without having any such parallels drawn with it.

Purpose
• to familiarize children with the story of Easter and enable children to gain some insight into its significance for Christians
• to help the children become aware of the role of drama and art in worship

Ideas
★ Read or tell the story from 'Holy Week, Easter and Whitsun' (*A Tapestry of Tales*). Use a collection of pictures showing different types of crucifix and different people wearing crucifixes to

CELEBRATING EASTER

When the story of the crucifixion has been read on Good Friday in an Orthodox church, an icon or holy picture of Jesus is laid on a stand in the centre of the church, and people stand round with lighted candles as they would at a funeral. The icon is then taken around the church with the worshippers following like mourners, the bells are tolled before it is brought back and laid in the centre of the church.

At midnight, just as Easter Sunday is about to begin, all the congregation and the priests meet outside the door of the church, holding candles. They hear and shout back the announcement 'Christ is risen from the dead: by death he has trampled down death: and to those who are in the grave he has given life'. Bells are rung and in some countries there are sirens, guns and fireworks. The doors open and everyone goes in to the church, where the icon of Jesus has already been returned to the altar.

In some Orthodox churches, people bring a decorated basket of food to the Easter service, which begins before midnight on Saturday, and lasts until 3 or 4 am on Easter morning. As the final act in the service, the baskets of food are brought forward, and a candle is lit on each. The priest blesses the baskets, which are then taken home for Easter breakfast. The baskets contain eggs and sugary loaves and other items that have not been eaten during Lent.

In some Christian churches, all the lights and candles are put out just before midnight on Easter Saturday, and a fire is lit outside the church. At midnight, when it becomes Sunday, a special candle called the Paschal candle is lit from the fire and brought into the church. It is lifted up and the priest sings 'The light of Christ' then everyone lights a candle from it.

Many churches strip all the pictures, decorations and flowers from the church on Good Friday, and keep the church bare until Easter Sunday, when it is decorated especially with flowers and candles.

Easter Eggs

While eggs are probably associated with the pagan spring festivals which took place around Easter-time, they are often given by Christians at Easter as a reminder both of the resurrection of Jesus and of the new life which Christians believe they have received through his sacrifice.

In some places, such as the Ukraine, Easter eggs are highly decorated. Children can decorate hard boiled eggs by drawing designs on them in wax, dipping them in food dye and gently melting off the wax.

Many of the traditional designs incorporate symbols such as the cross, the open tomb, the nails, the crown of thorns, etc.

Stations of the Cross

In many churches, particularly Catholic ones, it is the custom to follow the stations of the Cross. These are pictures or, more simply, points round the church marked in some way, which represent fourteen key events from the arrest of Jesus to his burial. During the week before Easter, or sometimes more frequently during the year, the priest leads the congregation to each station, where they meditate upon and pray about the particular event in the story, and more generally on the sufferings of Jesus.

Easter gardens

Children often make miniature gardens representing the garden where Jesus' tomb was, showing the tomb with the stone rolled away.

THE DATE OF EASTER

The dating of Easter was a matter of controversy for many centuries, and is still a cause of confusion. The problem arises because the events of Easter took place around the Jewish festival of Passover, which is fixed according to the Jewish lunar calendar. However Easter is always celebrated on a Sunday, and the Western solar calendar has since been developed over the centuries. The present system of dating Easter was fixed in the seventh century. The formula is complicated but some children may find it interesting to research and calculate Easter in different years.

draw out how the story is significant for people throughout the world.

★ Explain to the children the Stations of the Cross. Make stations with them round the classroom. We suggest that rather than following the traditional fourteen stations, children extract for themselves the salient points of the story, perhaps five or six, and make stations about these.

★ Make hot cross buns with the class. *Why is there a cross on top?* Tell them about the practice of fasting on Good Friday until 3 pm – the hour that Jesus died – and breaking the fast with a hot cross bun.

★ Tell the children about the ways the Easter story is dramatized by some traditions. You could perhaps make your own classroom bare and solemn one Friday in the way that some churches do on Good Friday. Then in contrast you could decorate the room with Easter flowers and decorations for the following Monday.

★ Tell children about the Easter vigil and the lighting of the Paschal candle (see the Information Box). If you have one to show them, even better.

★ Make an Easter garden.

★ Decorate Easter eggs, and discuss with the children why these and other symbols of new life are used at Easter.

BAISAKHI

On April 13th each year Sikhs commemorate the formation of the Sikh brotherhood, the Khalsa. The Sikh holy book, the Guru Granth Sahib is read from beginning to end over a period of three days in the gurdwara. At the end of this there is a large communal meal in the langar, the Sikh kitchen at the gurdwara.

In the classroom, the main focus of this topic will probably be the story and its significance for Sikhs, rather than the celebrations. Generally, the benefit of studying this festival is to draw together the children's knowledge of Sikhism.

Also look at the assembly 'Baisakhi – Against Injustice' in the *REAL Junior Assembly Book*.

Unit 1
The Sikh Gurus

Purpose
• to introduce or develop an understanding of what the Gurus mean to Sikhs
• to familiarize the children with some of the stories of the Gurus

Ideas
★ Introduce the topic by explaining that Sikhs are celebrating at this time.
★ Look at a picture of a Sikh man, one of the Pictorial Charts display pictures would be suitable. Explain to the children that one reason why Sikhs wear a turban is so that they will look like their Gurus (see Introduction to Sikhism p.130).
☞ *Why do people sometimes imitate someone else in their clothing? Is it just because they like the clothes? Might it also be that they admire the person? Which people do you admire and why?*
★ Tell one or two stories about the founder of Sikhism, Guru Nanak, from *A Tapestry of Tales*. Ask the children to identify what they think is admirable about him.

Unit 2
Choosing a successor

Purpose
• to extend an understanding of Sikh notions of Guruship
• to consider what are worthy qualities in a person

Ideas
★ Discuss with the children how successors are chosen: the new king or queen, the new Prime Minister, the new school head, a new member of Parliament. *What qualities would you look for in a person to do these jobs?*
★ Tell the story found in *A Tapestry of Tales* called 'Guru Nanak chooses his successor'. What qualities did he look for?

Unit 3
The formation of the Khalsa

Purpose
• to familiarize children with the story
• to think about what it means to take care of the weak and the needy in our society

Ideas

★ Tell the story from 'The Khalsa' (*A Tapestry of Tales*).

☞ Draw out the idea that the Khalsa Sikhs were ready to give up their life to combat injustice. *What do the children think is unfair in our society? What sort of people are easily hurt by others? Is it always easy to stand up for someone who is being teased?*

★ Tell the children about the Sikh tradition of service to others (see 'Introduction to Sikhism', p.130). Many Sikh communities organise lunch clubs for old people, youth clubs, outings for inner city children, etc. Talk to the children about the Sikh community in Britain who pledge themselves to take care of the environment. This is an example of Sikhs applying the principle of service to others today.

Unit 4
Joining the Khalsa

Purpose

● to appreciate that Sikhs still join the Khalsa today

● to reflect on what it means to have a commitment to an organisation

Ideas

★ Describe to the children the way Sikhs join the Khalsa (see Information Box) and remind them of the 5 Ks.

☞ Ask the class to describe what clubs they belong to. *What are the rules? What are the uniforms?* But stress that the Khalsa is a lifelong commitment and taken very seriously.

☞ *Why do organisations have rules and often uniforms as well?*

★ Ask the children to make up an organisation, committed to something they think is important and to describe its rules, uniforms, etc.

INFORMATION BOX

Joining the Khalsa

Sikhs are often initiated into the Khalsa at the festival of Baisakhi, but it can happen at any time. Because it is a very serious commitment, many Sikhs do not join the Khalsa until quite late in life, when they know that they are ready. It involves a great commitment to live according to the teachings of the Gurus: to serve others humbly, to avoid all intoxicants and drugs, except medicinal ones, and to be willing to commit everything, even life and liberty, to the struggle against injustice and oppression, and to uphold the Sikh faith.

Any five Sikhs who are members of the Khalsa can carry out the ceremony. These five represent the *panj pyares*, the faithful five who were the first members of the Khalsa. The Guru Granth Sahib must also be present, as it is for any Sikh ceremony.

The candidates drink some of a special sweet drink called *amrit*, which has been stirred with a sword. Some of the amrit is sprinkled on their eyes and hair. Then the *granthi* (the reader of the Guru Granth Sahib, who acts as a religious teacher) talks about the commitment they have taken on, and how they must live their lives as Khalsa Sikhs. At the end of the ceremony the sweet food Karah Parshad is distributed (see topic on 'Food', p.37).

INTRODUCTION TO BUDDHISM

There are about 121,000 Buddhists in Britain at present. This number has increased rapidly over the last ten years, largely due to conversions. As well as western-born converts, there are Buddhists in Britain from China, Sri Lanka, Japan, Vietnam and Thailand, as well as smaller numbers from other countries. It is difficult to give a firm figure for Buddhists worldwide, but it is probably in the region of 500 million, with the largest numbers in Sri Lanka, Burma, Thailand, Cambodia, China, Japan and Tibet. However, over half the world's population live in areas where at one time or another Buddhism has been the dominant religious force.

Strictly speaking Buddhism is an non-theistic religion, as there is no belief in a transcendent God. Nevertheless all forms of Buddhism have always recognized the existence of numerous 'supernatural' and god-like beings, though not everyone who would call themselves a Buddhist would believe in their existence. Nor is there belief in a permanent unchanging soul; everything is changing and after death comes rebirth unless enlightenment has been achieved (see below).

THE BUDDHA

Buddha means 'the Awakened'. A Buddha is not a god, but a human being who has awoken from the sleep of greed, hatred and confusion in which it is believed all creatures usually live. Because he has developed perfect wisdom and compassion he can help others to awaken. Buddhists believe that there may have been many such people. In particular, the title Buddha is given to the founder of Buddhism who lived in the 6th and 5th centuries BCE.

Siddhattha Gotama (Siddhartha Gautama) was born near the border of Nepal with India in about 560 BCE. According to tradition, he was brought up in luxury as the son of the local ruler. However, he was deeply troubled about old age, sickness and death, and eventually left home to become a wandering monk. He went to the most famous of religious teachers but none of them had the answer to human suffering. Then he tried extreme methods of self-deprivation but these turned out to be as useless as his former life of luxury. So he developed his own method of practice called the Middle Way because it avoids both extremes. He ate enough to live in a healthy way and discovered how to calm the mind by a form of meditation based on breathing.

He found what he was looking for on the full moon night in May when he was 35 years of age.

He sat under the sacred bodhi tree and, stilling his mind, looked within and saw truth. From this experience, called 'Awakening' or 'Enlightenment', he became the Buddha. He spent the rest of his life travelling on foot, teaching and helping people. He taught a way of life based on giving, morality, and the development of calmness of mind. A person who follows his teaching can experience the qualities of love, joy and compassion which are shared with all beings, and develop a mind that cannot be thrown off balance by pleasant or unpleasant things, thus leading to perfect happiness and freedom; known as nibbana (nirvana). When the Buddha died, aged 80, he left his teaching, the Dhamma, as a guide, and the order of monks and nuns, the Sangha, to carry on his work.

THE SPREAD OF BUDDHISM

Buddhism eventually spread far beyond India. It has helped to shape the life of many countries in Asia and has now begun to have a following in the West. One of the people who helped the spread of Buddhism was the emperor Asoka, who ruled in India from about 268-233 BCE. He is still respected in India as one of the greatest rulers in its history. In keeping with the Buddha's teachings he respected monks and priests of all religions but particularly honoured the Buddhist Sangha. He supported them in their efforts to spread the knowledge of the Buddha's teachings. He called the Third Council of the Sangha to make sure that the Buddha's teachings were remembered and handed on correctly. He sent out missionaries to neighbouring kingdoms, among them his own son and daughter who are believed to have taken Buddhism to Sri Lanka. By these actions, Asoka encouraged the spread of Buddhism through India and beyond.

Buddhism has also become wedded to some local folk religions. For example, Chinese Buddhism is quite distinctive having within it aspects of Taoism, as well as local folk features.

SCRIPTURES – THE PALI CANON

There are two major sub-divisions of Buddhism: the Northern school called the Mahayana and the Southern School known as the Theravada. The term 'Theravada' means 'teachings of the elders'; this arises from the traditional belief that the holy books of the Theravada Buddhists are the oldest and the ones closest to the actual words of the historical Buddha, Prince Siddhattha Gotama. These sacred texts are known as the Pali Canon and have shaped the growth of Buddhism in Sri Lanka, Burma, Thailand, Laos, Cambodia and Vietnam, as well as profoundly affecting the religious life of other areas of South East Asia.

The Pali Canon is so-called because of the language in which it is written – Pali, an ancient North Indian language which was in use when the historical Buddha was alive. The other great language of Buddhism, the language of the Mahayana school, is Sanskrit. Sanskrit words such as 'nirvana' and 'dharma' are softened in Pali to 'nibbana' and 'dhamma'; hence the different versions of the same words.

The Pali Canon evolved over a long time. At first the stories and sayings of the Buddha were passed down by oral tradition, by the telling of stories and the memorising of the Buddha's words. Buddhism, in its Theravada form, has always stressed that the Buddha taught the path to be followed, and gave clear indications as to how to follow it. These are summed up in the Four Noble Truths and the Eightfold Path (see below). In forming the community of monks (the Sangha) Buddha created the perfect instrument for the survival of his message. The teaching is

known as the dhamma (ultimate reality). These three elements come together in the the traditional Theravada Buddhist invocation: 'I seek refuge in the Buddha, in the Dhamma and in the Sangha'.

As time passed, and particularly as divisions grew in the interpretation of what the Buddha taught, it became necessary to write down the oral traditions. The Pali Canon is vast. In the complete Thai edition, it fills 45 large volumes, not including any of the commentaries, some of which are of great antiquity. It is therefore impossible to give a date when the Pali Canon was written down, but the text of the Canon was fixed, according to tradition, at the Third Buddhist Council in 253 BCE. It was not until the first century CE that the first Buddhist scriptures were written down.

The Canon is sub-divided into three major sections or pitakas (baskets). The Vinaya Pitaka (discipline basket), contains rules and regulations for the Sangha, as well as a brief biography of the Buddha, relating where and when he gave certain rules. The Sutta Pitaka (instruction basket) contains sermons and discussions of the Buddha and the monks, as well as descriptive sections telling the life story of the Buddha. The third section, the Abhidhamma Pitaka, (the great teaching basket), is seen as being the most important as it is felt to be the most profound. Indeed, unlike the rest of the material, which was given on earth, tradition has it that the Abhidhamma was given by the Buddha when he ascended to heaven, to preach to the gods.

The Pali Canon is traditionally written on palm leaves and bound in the customary Asian way, of placing the leaves between two boards and fastening them through the middle with string. In Buddhist countries, such books are presented to the monasteries by lay people for the monks to study. It is still customary for monks to learn sections of the scriptures by heart and then to recite them at festivals or other special occasions.

THE FOUR NOBLE TRUTHS

The major teachings of the Buddha, which he delivered in his first sermon, known as 'setting in motion the Wheel of Truth', are called the Four Noble Truths.

The First Noble Truth maintains that all existence is suffering; the Second that the cause of suffering is desire which fuels actions and leads to rebirth; the Third that the extinction of desire puts an end to suffering and leads to enlightenment and the escape from rebirth; the Fourth that the path to enlightenment is open to all people. This path is called the Eightfold Path.

THE EIGHTFOLD PATH

This is the path to enlightenment, and consists of: 1. right knowledge, 2. right thought, 3. right speech, 4. right actions, 5. right livelihood, 6. right effort, 7. right mindfulness, 8. right concentration.

The consequence of enlightenment is the extinguishing of all passions and desires; it is like the candle of a flame being blown out. When someone attains enlightenment they lose the sense of self which keeps us attached to rebirth in this world of suffering. This state is called nibbana, which is the final cessation of all craving and attachment. Thus the Buddhist must ultimately give up even the desire for nibbana, since the desire for nirvana is itself an obstacle to its attainment.

The principle of kamma is believed to affect everyone's lives. Whatever an individual thinks or does brings consequences, whether in this life or the next. Thus misfortune in the present life is often attributed to misdeed in the former. However as one perfects Buddhist practice and teachings, turning from desire and the sense of self, the effects of kamma dissipate.

THE SANGHA

The Sangha was established by the Buddha. It is a community of monks and nuns who keep alive the knowledge of the teachings of the Buddha (the dhamma). They have chosen to live as closely as possible to the Buddha's teachings. Monks and nuns rely on gifts from the lay community for their food and clothing. In many countries the monks and nuns often provide medical care. Some are itinerant but most live in monasteries. People come to the monasteries to meditate, listen to the teachings or ask advice.

BUDDHIST DEVOTION

Buddhists prefer the word devotion to worship. Buddhist devotional acts (pujas) take place in both home and temple, though these are essentially individual rather than communal. Puja is often offered in the morning and evening, and particularly at full and half moon. Artefacts and images are the focus for devotion to the Buddha; there is often a small shrine in the home. Bowing as a mark of respect, the offering of gifts such as flowers, and chanting contribute to the devotion. Sweet incense is often used.

DAILY LIFE

Buddhists try to follow the Eightfold Path in their daily lives. Many Buddhist homes have statues of the Buddha which may be a focus for daily meditation. Piety is expressed in giving to monks and nuns. There are no rules on dress or food though many Buddhists are vegetarian. Monks and nuns wear saffron coloured robes and shave their heads.

RITES OF PASSAGE
Birth

There are no pure Buddhist ceremonies, customs owe more to neighbours or pre-Buddhist beliefs, as birth itself is of no great significance in the teachings of the faith. Thai Buddhists, for example, in customs which have their origins in Hinduism, cut the baby's hair at one month old, and tie sacred threads around the baby's wrists. There is a belief in Thailand, that everyone has a 'khwan' or guardian spirit and the sacred thread helps the guardian spirit feel at home.

Ordination

The initiation into the Sangha is marked by a special ceremony; in Burma it includes re-enacting the story of how Prince Siddhattha became the Buddha. Becoming a monk or nun is not necessarily a life long commitment; in Thailand and Burma many boys enter the Sangha for a period between the age of ten and twenty.

Marriage

Marriage is not regarded as 'sacred' but a contracted partnership (divorce is acceptable). Although monks and nuns are often invited to join in the celebrations, and to preach and recite the scriptures their presence is not, strictly speaking, necessary. The ceremony does not take place in a religious building. Simple vows are sometimes taken, e.g. in Sri Lanka the vows are:

'Towards my wife I undertake to love and respect her, to be kind and considerate, be faithful, delegate domestic management, provide gifts to please her.' Chastity is also highly valued as a way of life, because of the importance of the Sangha.

Death

A 'good' death is important and it is the duty of the relatives to help the dying person obtain it, so that he or she may have the best possible rebirth within the restrictions of kamma (karma) (see above). A calm, joyful state of mind, positively recollecting the good deeds in life, is encouraged. Devotion is made so that 'merit' may be shared with the deceased. Grief is not common unless the death is an untimely one. Funerals are usually by cremation. Northern Buddhist belief is that there are 49 days between lives so that it is customary to read the Tibetan Book of the Dead, to the dying or recently deceased to guide them through those days.

FESTIVALS

Wesak (Nisakha)

This festival is usually in May or June. The major events of the Buddha's life, his birth, enlightenment and death all happened on the same day in different years. Wesak celebrates his life and teaching. It is marked by acts of worship and the decoration of homes and temples with flowers and lanterns, extra hospitality is given to the monks. Themes: the life of the Buddha.

Dhammacakka

Takes place around July and commemorates the Buddha-to-be's conception and his leaving home and celebrates the Buddha's first sermon after gaining enlightenment. It also marks the beginning of the 'Rains', the three months when Buddhist monks should remain in one residence and which is traditionally a time of increased contact between monks and laity. People visit monks to take them gifts of food and to hear them preach and read the scripture. Theme: the Buddhist community.

CHINESE BUDDHISM (CHINESE FOLK RELIGION)

Popular Chinese religion as it is practised by many of the Chinese immigrants to Britain is a fusion of Buddhism with Taoism, Confucianist and local folk beliefs. It combines a belief in rebirth with ancestor worship, and in some instances belief in a series of hells which act as purifying stages before rebirth. Honour of the ancestors reflects the idea that we are what we are, because of decisions and acts made by our ancestors.

It is believed that the forces of Yin (female) and Yang (male) must be kept in proper balance. Suffering and pain come when one is greater than the other. This balance also applies to the human body; illness is a result of imbalance of forces.

FESTIVALS

Chinese New Year

An increasingly popular festival in this country, in mid-January to early February. Accounts are made up, families should effect reconciliation where there has been argument. The festival is concerned with keeping away as much bad luck as possible, and bringing in good luck. Thus in a sense it says that the past should be left behind and one should face the future with hope. There are gongs, drums and fireworks to keep away the bad luck of the previous year; and much red, a lucky colour. Red door banners with good luck symbols are put by doorways, and a 'lion' visits restaurants and businesses to bring good luck. Where there is a large Chinese community, such as in Manchester, there may be a dragon dance through the streets. In the home a paper cut out of the kitchen god, has his lips smeared with honey and he is burnt, to be sent to the next world to report on the family's behaviour during the year. As the years are named after animals, the animal of the year will be part of the theme of the festival. Everyone has a birthday at Chinese New Year rather than an individual one though this practice is changing among Chinese in Britain. Themes: new start, reconciliation, hopes, good wishes, luck.

Moon festival

This an autumnal harvest festival at the time of the brightest moon in September. There is a procession of coloured lanterns in fish and animal shapes. Moon cakes are the main food. These are small pastry cakes filled with a sweet mixture of lotus or melon and egg. Theme: harvest.

INTRODUCTION TO CHRISTIANITY

Christianity is a world religion with over 1,000 million followers in many countries. At the heart of Christianity is the belief that Jesus of Nazareth was God's anointed one, the Messiah, indeed that he was God himself.

Christianity began, with the followers of Jesus, as a sect of Judaism in approx 33 CE. Soon it was seen as a new religion and spread throughout the world as Christians sought to convert others to their faith. Christianity came to this country with the Roman invasions and is the main faith in modern Britain. The Church of England is the established Church and the largest denomination. It has close ties with the state, the Queen being its official head. The main area of growth in the Christian Church today is among the Black Protestant churches.

JESUS CHRIST

The dates of Jesus' life are not known precisely, but are generally accepted to be approximately 4 BCE–29 CE. He was born a Jew in Palestine, which was then occupied by the Romans. His mother, Mary, is said to have been a virgin when she conceived. The Bible, the Christian holy book, tells how his birth was attended by visitations of angels (messengers of God) and that his humble birthplace was visited not only by shepherds but by wise men from a far-off country.

According to the gospels, the accounts in the Bible of his life, he grew up in Nazareth, a town to the north of Jerusalem. At thirty he left his home to become an itinerant healer, teacher and preacher, proclaiming that the kingdom of God was near. He taught using parables or illustrative stories. At the heart of his message was the imminence of god's kingdom, a kingdom characterized by hope, love and forgiveness between people, and between humanity and God. Three years later he was put to death on a cross by the Roman rulers, at the instigation of some Jewish leaders.

However, Jesus' followers believed that Jesus was raised from the dead, and proclaimed him as the Messiah (the Christ), God's chosen one. Christians believe that Jesus was God incarnate, God present in physical form on earth. Jesus is described as Saviour, but what this signifies varies. For some Christians this means that Jesus died as an innocent bearer of the punishment that humanity deserves; for others it shows that God was willing to go out to meet humanity, sharing the pain of being human, in an act of reconciliation.

The Trinity

Christianity is a monotheistic religion, teaching that God has three ways of being: a transcendent creator (father), the incarnate Jesus and the Spirit working in the world. While most Christians use male language about God, there is a growing movement for female as well as male metaphors to be used.

THE BIBLE

The Christian holy book, the Bible, is divided into two main sections, the Old Testament and the New Testament.

The Old Testament was developed over a period of more than a thousand years. Much of it began as oral tales which were then written down. The earliest written accounts are generally thought to date from 900 BCE and these were later merged with other stories. It is the same collection of books as the Hebrew Bible (see Introduction to Judaism), but is interpreted in different ways by Christians. For example, Christians see the writings of the prophets as predicting the coming of Jesus.

The New Testament is written in Greek and contains the Gospels, which are accounts of the life and teachings of Jesus; the Acts of the Apostles, which record the progress of the early Christian church; the letters addressing pastoral and theological concerns from early Christian leaders, including St Paul (the best-known early missionary, who was converted to Christianity after being an opponent of the early church) and the mystical Revelation of St John. Most of the New Testament was written within the first seventy years after the death of Jesus. Both Old and New Testament are used as part of worship but the New Testament is the part of the Bible which Christians use most frequently to guide them in their daily lives. They see it as speaking of a new agreement between God and humanity, one which extends to the whole world and is not confined to the Jews.

Some Christians believe that the whole of the Bible is divinely inspired and literally true. At the other end of the spectrum are those who regard the Bible as a testimony of faith and an exploration of meaning in narrative form. In the middle are those who declare that the Bible contains spiritual truths but makes no claim to be a book of accurate history.

Many translations of the Bible into English have been made, the most commonly used being the Authorised or King James version of 1611, the Revised Standard Version of 1885, the Jerusalem Bible of 1965 (Roman Catholic translation) and the Good News Bible of 1966/75 (Evangelical). The Bible has also been translated into hundreds of languages for use throughout the world. While there are some very beautiful editions of the Bible which are well cared for there are no rites associated with it and copies are usually treated like any other book. Study of the scriptures is particularly important in Protestant churches.

CHRISTIAN DENOMINATIONS

The Christian Church is divided into many different bodies – usually called denominations. The first major division came between the Churches associated with Rome and those associated with Constantinople. In 1054 the Church divided into the Western, Catholic Church and the Eastern, Orthodox Church. From then on the vast majority of new denominations came from the Western Catholic Church. In the Orthodox Church, each Church is self-governing and thus the tensions between groups is considerably less.

Small denominations grew up in the late Middle Ages such as the Waldenses. However, it was with the coming of the Protestant Reformation that a major division occurred within the Christian Church. In 1517 Martin Luther nailed his 95 Theses on the Church to the door of Wittenberg Cathedral in Germany. Soon, the German Princes were establishing 'Lutheran' or 'protesting' churches (hence the name 'Protestant') all over Germany. The Lutheran Church is now found in Germany and Scandinavia and also in places with large German or Scandinavian populations such as America and Australia. In 1948 they came together to form the Lutheran World Federation.

In England, Henry VIII's break with Rome formed the Anglican Church in the 1530s. This is now one of the world's largest Christian bodies with member churches in many parts of the world. They are linked through the key figure of the Archbishop of Canterbury.

From the Church of England came many other denominations. The Baptists, who believe in adult, not child baptism, arose in England and Holland in the early decades of the 17th century. In the 18th century, Anglican hostility to the evangelical reform movement of John Wesley led him to form the Methodist Church. It is believed they were so called because of their methods of Bible study and fellowship.

The Quakers, most renowned for their silent worship, arose in the mid 17th century – a period of intense religious debate. This period also saw the rise of Congregationalism and Presbyterianism. The Congregationalists believe that everyone is an equal part of the Church and all have responsibilities to act as priests. Presbyterians base their structure on elders (called 'presbyters') who govern the Church, on the pattern they see as being present in the New Testament. These two Churches have united in Britain to form the United Reform Church. In this century the growth of Pentecostal churches has been quite phenomenal. Started in the first decade of this century, they are marked by openness to the action of the Holy Spirit – just as the disciples were at the first Pentecost (see below).

There are many other small churches which are too numerous to mention. In recent years a number of churches have united to present a common front. In Britain the British Council of

Churches works for church unity. On a world wide basis the World Council of Churches strives for the same end.

The main theological differences between Roman Catholic and Protestant churches are to do with authority. In Protestant churches all authority is in the Bible and divisions within Protestantism have tended to come from different interpretations of it. The Roman Catholic church also holds the Bible to be authoritative, but as it has been interpreted by the Church in its synods (decision-making councils). The leader of the Church, the Pope, speaks authoritatively on behalf of the whole Church. Mary, the mother of Jesus, has a much higher status in both Roman Catholic and Orthodox churches than in the Protestant traditions.

Beliefs

There are some differences in teaching between the various Christian denominations, but the basic beliefs of the Christian church are the same throughout. Christians believe that Jesus is both God and man, the second person of the Holy Trinity of God the Father, God the Son and God the Holy Spirit. They believe that there is only one God, who created everything that exists, and who cares for his creation. In Jesus Christ, God showed his love and compassion for all creation and in the raising to life of Jesus after his crucifixion, God has shown that there is life after death; that love overcomes evil. Christians believe that they should try to show God's love through their lives and that at death, believers will go to be with God.

WORSHIP

Christian worship can be congregational or individual. Congregational worship may take place anywhere, since the Church is not, strictly speaking, a building but a community of believers. When a building is set apart for worship, its form is largely determined by the denomination of the worshippers. It may be a big sumptuous cathedral or a small wooden building. Some denominations have a tradition of art and image; others of stark simplicity. Services may be highly ritualized with a written liturgy, which is sung, or at the other extreme they may be entirely spontaneous. The prayer Jesus taught his disciples, known as the Lord's Prayer, is said in most acts

of worship. There is usually, but not always, a minister or priest who leads the services and provides spiritual guidance for the congregation. In Orthodox, Anglican and Catholic churches there are rites which only the priest can perform.

Most churches have a ritual which celebrates the death and resurrection of Jesus by the sharing of bread and wine. This is known variously as the Eucharist, Lord's Supper, Communion or Mass. It dates back to the very early church when the first Christians re-enacted the meal known as the Last Supper which took place just prior to the crucifixion and at which Jesus instructed his disciples to remember him by sharing bread and drinking wine. The main day of worship for Christians is Sunday, the day of the Resurrection.

DAILY LIFE

Practising Christians try to live out their faith in their relationship with others in their daily lives. They may pray privately or with their families. In many Christian families and communities grace is said before meals to ask God's blessing on the food and bedtime prayers are also said. Christians often devote some time each day to studying the Bible and thinking about God. Roman Catholic and Orthodox homes often have pictures (icons) or statues which are a focus for worship. Some Protestant homes have verses from the Bible or short prayers around the home, on the walls.

RITES OF PASSAGE

Baptism and Confirmation

Baptism is the ceremony through which a person becomes a member of the church. According to the denomination it may be performed while the person is a baby, or when he or she is an adult, and may involve total immersion or sprinkling with water. In churches where infant baptism is practised, the child is given a Christian name at this time and often godparents are present who promise to ensure that the child is brought up in the Christian faith. Churches which practise adult baptism believe that membership of the Church should be the result of an active and informed decision by the individual. They sometimes hold thanksgiving services for a child. Those who join a church which practises infant baptism may be baptised as adults. The ceremony of baptism, however performed, symbolises death and rebirth, and purification.

Confirmation is a ceremony which follows infant baptism and signifies the coming of the Holy Spirit in the life of the believer. In Orthodoxy it immediately follows Baptism for it confirms the presence of the Holy Spirit in the life of the believer. In other churches it is seen as a confirmation by the individual of vows they could not make for themselves because they were too young at baptism. Adults are often confirmed, but for the majority the ceremony takes place earlier: at around the age of seven in the Roman Catholic church or in early adolescence in others. It serves to mark a new stage of life and presents are often given and a party held.

Marriage

In the Roman Catholic church marriage is for life, a union created by God which can only be broken by death. All Christian churches regard it as a serious commitment not to be taken lightly and divorce is discouraged. During the marriage ceremony the couple make public vows of commitment to each other and often exchange rings.

Marriage is not regarded as necessary for all Christians, and celibacy is seen as an equally valid option. Roman Catholic clergy, as well as monks and nuns, take a vow of celibacy. Communal life in a convent or monastery is also valued by much of the church.

Death

Christians believe that death is not the end of existence. There is belief, as it is expressed in the creeds, that there will be a day of resurrection. However, popular Christian belief is that the soul lives on and goes to be with God immediately after death. Some Christians believe in a literal hell for those who have not followed Jesus as Saviour or the teachings of the church. Others believe that God is loving and forgiving to all. Others are agnostic about the situation. Christians may be buried or cremated after a church service which commits the body to the grave, commemorates the deceased and offers comfort to the bereaved.

FESTIVALS

The main Christian festivals are Christmas, Easter and Pentecost (sometimes called Whitsun).

Christmas

This festival, which celebrates the birth of Jesus, falls on 25th December. (Because the Eastern Orthodox calendar is different from the Western, their December 25th falls in the Western early January.) The date was chosen in the fourth century CE to replace the pagan mid-winter festivals, and many of the customs of these festivals are now associated with Christmas. Theologically, the mid-winter when the world is dark, was seen as the appropriate time to celebrate the coming of Jesus, who is spoken of as the light of the world. It is seen as a time particularly for family celebration and gift-giving. Churches and homes will often have a representation of the Nativity scene as a reminder of the birth of Jesus in a stable with a manger as his bed. There are a wide variety of different local Christmas customs throughout the world. Special songs called carols are sung and greetings cards sent.
Themes: the incarnation, light, giving and childhood.

Easter

This is a time when Christians remember the death and resurrection of Jesus. The period of 40 days before Easter is known as Lent, and is a time for prayer and self-discipline; Christians often give up some pleasurable activity or food during this time. The week leading up to Easter is known as Holy Week, the Thursday of Holy Week commemorates the Last Supper which Jesus shared with his disciples and the Friday, Good Friday, the crucifixion of Jesus. The resurrection is celebrated on Easter Sunday. Easter, though a movable festival, always occurs in the spring, a time of new life. Eggs, which are a symbol of new life, are exchanged.
Themes: new life, hope, triumph of good over evil.

Pentecost or Whitsun

This celebrates the coming of the Holy Spirit on the disciples after the resurrection and Ascension of Jesus and commemorates the beginning of the Church itself. When the Holy Spirit came, the disciples were filled with a new sense of power, spoke foreign languages that they had never learnt, healed the sick, and spoke about God with enthusiasm and power.

Saints' days

In the very early church all Christians were called saints. However it soon arose that some Christians were recognized by the Church as being particularly holy and the term saint came to be applied to them. Every day of the year has a saint associated with it; their lives are remembered and celebrated on this day usually in quite a quiet way. Celebration of these days is less common in Protestant communities. Among the major Saints' festivals are Lady Day (the Virgin Mary), Martinmas (St. Martin), St. Luke, St. Swithin, Michaelmas (St. Michael and all angels), St. Nicholas, John the Baptist – and, of course, St. Valentines Day! All the Saints are commemorated on All Saints' Day and the following day is All Souls' Day when the souls of all the departed, good or bad, are prayed for. In central Europe it was common for people to celebrate as their own special day, the day of the saint after whom they had been named, rather than their birthdays.

Other special days

Probably the most commonly celebrated festival is Harvest Festival – the thanksgiving for God's providence. Other festivals recall special events or stories of the Christian faith. For instance, Holy Innocents' Day recalls the story of Herod's soldiers killing all the baby boys in Bethlehem in an attempt to kill Jesus himself. Ascension Day commemorates Jesus' ascension into heaven. Candlemas stands as the day when Jesus was taken to the Temple in Jerusalem as a baby and was greeted by the priest as the 'Light of the World'.

Mothering Sunday

The fourth Sunday in Lent for Western Christianity, is celebrated, nowadays, by people visiting their mothers and giving them presents or cards. In medieval times it also included a celebration in which congregations of small, dependent churches and chapels visited their 'mother' church.

CHRISTIAN PILGRIMAGES AND HOLY PLACES

While there are no prescribed sites for pilgrimage many Christians like to visit places associated with the Bible, such as Israel and the area of the Mediterranean, or an area associated with saints. Following the Via Dolorosa in the old city of Jerusalem, said to be the route Jesus walked to the cross, is one way that Christians recall his suffering. Other sites which are popular with Roman Catholics are places where there have been visions of Mary, the mother of Jesus, e.g. Lourdes in France which is a place of healing.

INTRODUCTION TO HINDUISM

The term 'Hinduism' can give a misleading impression of an organised, homogeneous body of believers. In fact Hindus vary considerably both in belief and practice, and their faith, in contrast with many other religions, has no founder. 'Hindus' was the name given to the inhabitants of the area of India round the river Indus. Thus Hinduism is simply 'the religion of the Indus valley'. It is a faith that has emerged out of many local practices.

It is estimated that there are about 705 million Hindus world-wide, with about 500,000 in Britain. Hindus began to visit Britain or study here in the 19th century, and after the First World War some settled as merchants and businessmen. Many Hindus in this country are from families who came from India in the 1950s and 60s, but the majority arrived from East Africa somewhat later, having gone to East Africa during the period of British rule and later been expelled.

One important characteristic of Hinduism is its acceptance and inclusion of many varying beliefs and ways of worship, thus allowing for enormous variety, and making it impossible to give a full, or indeed any single account of practices and beliefs.

GODS AND GODDESSES

A passage from the Rig Veda (one of the sacred books) sums up the Hindu attitude to God:

'That which is one, the wise call by many names.'

Hindus believe in one central Godhead, who is essentially unknowable, and has many manifestations. Everything in the universe embodies something of God for God is operating within creation rather than separate from it. However, sometimes Hindus speak of a central trinity of gods: Brahma (the creator), Vishnu (the sustainer of the created order) and Shiva (the destroyer, though this destroying function is not seen as something necessarily bad, and Shiva is also called the recreator and is connected with potency and fertility).

There are many other manifestations of God, and all have their female counterparts. These include Vishnu's wife, Lakshmi (the goddess of wealth), Shiva's wife, Parvati (who also has a fiercer aspect as Durga) and the elephant-headed god, Ganesha (patron of learning, good beginnings and the remover of obstacles).

In addition it is believed that Vishnu has manifested himself on earth, in animal and human form, in order to fight evil and restore the balance between good and evil. These manifestations are called avatars. Two of the avatars in human form are Rama, the perfect man (see Ramayana, below), and Krishna, who is worshipped with particular devotion. As well as his appearance in the Bhagavad Gita (see below) there are many stories about Krishna as a boy and young man. He is often pictured and worshipped as a baby, and his mischievous nature as a boy is celebrated, including apparently reprehensible acts, like stealing butter. As a young man, he fought evil in many forms in order to restore the world to good. He also came to restore the true knowledge of God. Many stories are told of his life, including the occasion when he played tricks on the cow-girls (gopis). Their love for him is a symbol of spiritual devotion. Krishna is usually represented with a blue skin, symbolising pure spirit, and he inspires great devotion.

For some Hindus the gods have a separate literal existence. For others the gods are symbols representing aspects of the universe: for example, the central trinity described above, symbolizes the constant cycle of change which is a part of all aspects of life from the smallest to the largest i.e. everything is in a process of creation (Brahma), growth and sustenance (Vishnu), decay and death (Shiva) and rebirth to something new (Brahma). In Hindu thought the universe itself is part of this cycle – ours is thought to be one of many universes which will exist for a while, but will end, and then change to something new.

Since all embody something of God, a particularly good and respected person may be worshipped. For instance, some Hindus include Gandhi or Jesus among those worshipped.

SCRIPTURES

The oldest Hindu scriptures are the Vedas, written in the ancient language Sanskrit (reputedly around 1200 BCE). These four books are mainly philosophical and technical, giving detailed instructions for the conduct of sacrifices and other ceremonies.

The Upanishads, (reputedly written about 800 BCE), consider the fundamental nature of humanity and its place in the universe. Most are written in verse, and hymns from the Vedas and the Upanishads are used in worship.

From these there developed literature to bring religious thought within the reach of ordinary people. Best known are the epics, the Ramayana, dating from about the 9th century BCE, and the Mahabharata, from the 6th century BCE.

Ramayana

The Ramayana tells the story of Rama, a prince who was banished by the machinations of one of his father's wives from the kingdom that should have been his, to live in exile in the forest. With him went his wife Sita and his brother Lakshmana.

When Sita was kidnapped by the demon king Ravana and taken to Lanka (modern Sri Lanka), Rama and Lakshmana, with the help of the monkey god Hanuman and his army, eventually overcame Ravana and rescued Sita, then returned rejoicing to their kingdom.

Rama and Sita are regarded as the perfect models of manhood and womanhood, and Lakshmana's brotherly love and loyalty are also celebrated.

Mahabharata

This tells the story of the wars between two families of cousins, the Pandavas and Kauravas, over a disputed section of land.

The most celebrated part of the Mahabharata is the Bhagavad Gita, the Song of the Lord. At the beginning of this, Arjuna, a Pandava nobleman, is beset by qualms about the numbers of people bound to be killed in the battle, and is reluctant to fight. His charioteer is Krishna, an incarnation of the god Vishnu, and in the Bhagavad Gita he urges Arjuna to fight, with an exploration of humanity's duty and relationship to God, and the meaning of life. God's care for humanity and humanity's duty of devotion to God are movingly described, and the Bhagavad Gita has become the heart of the Hindu scriptures, inspiring great devotion.

WORSHIP

The variety of the Hindu faith is reflected in the ways of worshipping. The aim of worship is to realise the oneness of the individual with the divine, and the Bhagavad Gita, one of the most influential Hindu scriptures, gives several paths for this, all of equal merit:
– there is the path of knowledge through understanding the relationship between atman (the soul) and Brahma (the godhead)
– there is the path of yoga or discipline, and right action according to one's dharma (one's duty according to position in life). Good rebirth or karma will result from right actions
– there is the path of bhakti, loving devotion to one's particular deity.
These paths can be combined but the specific emphasis is left to the individual. In fact, all religious observance is an individual or family matter and there is no minimum requirement below which one ceases to be a 'proper' Hindu.

Religious observance is largely home-based, and most Hindu homes will have a shrine to honour their own particular choice of deities. A cupboard, shelf, or corner of the room may be specially set aside, and it is here that Hindus place pictures, statues or symbols of those worshipped.

The representation of God, in whatever form, is treated with great respect. A statue may be dressed in clothing suitable for the season, and decorated with flowers, and might be put to bed at night and 'woken' in the morning. Statues are regularly bathed and anointed, and offerings of food and drink may be made during worship. This is a way of making concrete the respect and devotion to God.

In a devout Hindu home, worship (puja) is made three times a day, morning, noon and night, and the form this takes may vary. Before offering puja, a Hindu should wash all over, preferably in running water, so in this country showers rather than baths are popular. Worship may take many forms, but usually involves lighting the arti lamp, a sacred flame using ghee or oil, and incense.

In the temple

Attendance at a temple is not regarded as a necessary part of a Hindu's religious duties, but rather one of many ways of helping the individual to grow closer to God. In this country temples serve as both social and religious focal points for the Hindu community.

Services are often held every evening, but many people will attend on Sunday when the main service of the week takes place in Britain. The choice of Sunday is mainly based on convenience, as Hinduism has no special day of the week. Before entering, people remove their shoes as a mark of respect. As they enter, people offer their own devotion to pictures or statues of deities, placing gifts of fruit or sweets before them. An important part of the service is the arti ceremony, where a sacred fire is lit in a special dish, and offerings are made to symbolize the offering of devotion to the Lord. Before worship a bell is rung to announce one's presence to the god. The arti fire, having been offered to the deities, is then passed amongst the worshippers. The blessings of the deities are shared by passing one's hands over the flame and then over the face and head.

At the end of the service a prayer for peace is said: 'Aum shanti, shanti, shanti' ('Oh God, let there be peace, peace, peace'). Everyone present is then given a gift of the food which has been blessed and offered to the gods, as a sign that God is in everyone.

HINDU DAILY LIFE

Much worship takes place in the home (see above).

The Caste system

The caste system originated as a way of clarifying the rights and duties of people in different walks of life. The four main divisions of caste are: Brahmins (priestly class), Kshatriyas (soldiers), Vaishyas (farmers and merchants), Shudras (manual labourers).

The first three are known as the twice-born castes, and are permitted to study the Vedas. Over the last 4,000 years more than 3,000 subdivisions of the castes have arisen. In addition there are the Untouchables or Harijans. (This name, meaning Children of God, was given by Gandhi in his efforts to improve their lot.) These do work which is polluting, such as leather work, involving the dead bodies of animals. The system has come under criticism because of its rigidity, and in some areas is now relaxing somewhat, particularly in Britain.

Food

There are no particular rules for Hindus, but because of the principle of ahimsa, non-violence, many Hindus are vegetarians, but this is not universal. Furthermore, since cows are often regarded as sacred, beef is not eaten, though milk products are taken freely. Some Hindu festivals and phases of the moon involve abstaining from certain foods for a given period, but again this is up to the individual. Before eating a small portion of food is offered before the shrine for a blessing from the god. This is then mixed with the rest of the food so that all the food is blessed.

Dress

There are no rules of dress for Hindus. In Britain most men wear western dress, and where women continue to wear the sari this is a matter of personal choice and has no religious significance. Sometimes Hindus wear simple robes and shave their heads (e.g. many members of the Hare Krishna movement).

RITES OF PASSAGE

Reincarnation

Many aspects of Hindu life, and particularly the ceremonies relating to birth and death, are shaped by the Hindu belief in reincarnation. The individual soul is destined to be reborn many times, in different bodies, whether human or animal, the circumstances of each rebirth being affected by the deeds in previous lives, known as karma. The aim is to live life as well as possible, in accordance with the situation one is placed in, so that the next rebirth will be a better one. A series of ceremonies throughout life, called *samskaras*, contribute to this.

A Hindu's life is divided into four distinct stages. The first begins with the initiation ceremony (see below) and marks the student stage. The second is the stage of the married householder. The third means literally the 'forest-dweller' stage and comes when a man has fulfilled his religious and social duties to his family. He hands over his duties to his household and spends his time reading holy books or he may devote himself to a cause e.g. building a new temple. Few women enter this stage though some hand over the running of the house to the daughter-in-law. The final stage, though it is much respected, is entered by a very few men and no women. Here they become wandering holy men independent of any ties.

Birth

The religious care of a baby and his preparation for a good life begin in the mother's womb, as the pregnant woman reads the scriptures to her baby. As soon as the baby is born, the father recites prayers, and the baby is given a taste of honey. Since a person's horoscope is extremely important throughout life, careful note is taken of the exact time of birth. The name of the child may be chosen according to what the horoscope reveals. Naming takes place on the twelfth day after birth. The baby is placed in a swinging cot, lamps are lit, and the priest announces the name. Other ceremonies take place later – when the baby's head is shaved to remove any bad karma carried over from the previous life; when the ears are pierced; when the child first sees the sun, and when it takes its first solid food.

Thread ceremony

This is a ceremony for boys of the three upper castes at the age of seven or older. It is performed more frequently in India than in Britain.

At this ceremony the boy is given a thread of three strands which he must always wear. Vows are taken accepting the duties of being a man. It is a family ceremony, conducted in the presence of a priest and the sacred fire. It is followed by a feast, and the exchange of presents between parents and guests – presents may be given to the boy in a separate ceremony. The whole ceremony ends with a benediction for the boy:

'Oh son, growing in strength and vigour, may you live a hundred autumns. May you become long-lived, brilliant, radiant.'

Marriage

A Hindu marriage is an alliance of two families, and it is often the case that the married sons continue to live in their father's house. Parents usually choose a marriage partner for their child, although either bride or groom can refuse. Generally, the marriage partner comes from the same caste, for traditional reasons, but also because it is recognized that the couple will be more compatible if they come from the same background. The horoscope is important in choosing a marriage partner, too.

The families exchange presents when the betrothal is made. A Hindu wedding is a very long and elaborate ceremony, at which different relatives of the bride and groom have specific roles to play. The bride spends a long time preparing for the wedding with the women of her family. She is given several beautiful saris, and her hands are decorated with henna patterns. The women guests usually wear saris given them on their own wedding day, usually red, the colour of rejoicing.

The wedding may take place in the home, or in the temple, or in a hall hired for the purpose. A canopy is set up, with seats for the bride and groom, and the sacred fire. At first a curtain is held between them so that they cannot see each other. This is then taken away and their right hands are tied to each other, and they walk round the sacred fire hand in hand. Different fruits and sweets are eaten during the ceremony, and food is offered to the gods. After the wedding there is a feast.

Following the wedding, the bride and groom are expected to live with the groom's parents, at least for a time, while the bride gets to know her new family.

Death

The Hindu treatment of death is closely bound up with the belief in reincarnation. The body is always cremated, which should be done as soon as possible after death. In India this is done on a funeral pyre of wood, in Britain at a crematorium. The family of the dead person are considered polluted by the death, so they do not go out of the house.

On the thirteenth day after the death, the family make an offering of rice balls, after which they are no longer polluted and can resume normal activities. The soul is believed to have been reborn in a new body by this time. At the funeral ceremony, lines from the Bhagavad Gita are said, consoling mourners with the assurance that the loved one will be reborn.

The ashes are collected and scattered in a river, particularly the river Ganges. Hindus in Britain often arrange to have the ashes of their loved ones flown to India and scattered in the Ganges.

FESTIVALS

In India there is great variation in what festivals are celebrated and how, depending on local tradition and which gods are particularly worshipped. However, some festivals are universally celebrated, and it is mainly these that are celebrated in this country. The dates vary slightly each year, as most Hindu festivals are based on a lunar calendar of twelve months. Every fourth year a thirteenth month is added. Some of the most commonly celebrated festivals are:

Mahashivaratri
This festival occurs in February-March. It is the festival of the god Shiva, celebrated by devout Hindus by fasting and offering a meal to a Brahmin (priest of the highest caste).

Holi
In March-April Holi is celebrated. This festival combines elements of a spring festival with celebration of the pranks that Krishna played as a young man. Also involved is a story about a demon goddess called Holika, from whom the name Holi comes. It is celebrated with bonfires and by squirting coloured water at each other, and general tricks and good fun.
Themes: spring, laughter.

Rama Naumi
This celebrates the birthday of Rama in March-April. A model of the baby Rama in a cradle is set up in the temple, and those coming bring offerings to the cradle.

Raksha Bandhan
This takes place in August. The main ceremony is the tying of a silk thread, with a flower, to the wrists of others. In some places this is done for friends and relatives by the head of the house, others celebrate the day as sisters' day, and sisters tie the threads to their brothers' wrists.
Themes: friendship, loyalty, family.

Janmashtami
In August-September this festival celebrates the birth of Krishna and his miraculous delivery from the demon Kansa who wished to kill him. A feature of the worship at this festival is a picture or statue of the child Krishna on a swing, which people take turns to push, to keep him amused.
Themes: childhood, birthdays.

Dusshera
This is also known as Durga puja, or Navaratri and occurs in September or October. It celebrates the most important female deity, Devi (consort of Shiva), who has many forms about whom many stories are told. As Kali she destroys time, as Parvati she is the faithful wife of Shiva, as Durga she is the destroyer of evil demons. The festival lasts ten days, during which time different manifestations of the goddess are honoured, and stories told. On the last day the statue of Durga is taken in procession to be washed, accompanied by dancing and plays.
Themes: conquest of evil, women's power.

Divali
This, in October, is the most widely celebrated Hindu festival. It is celebrated in many different ways, and combines many elements – the most important of which is the New Year, when traders close their old accounts and open new account books and pray to Lakshmi, goddess of wealth. At this time, also, is the celebration of the return from exile of Rama and Sita (see Ramayana, above), symbolizing the triumph of good over evil. Arti lamps are lit in every window, and paper effigies of the demon Ravana are burnt.
Themes: light, renewal, love, harvest.

There are countless local and regional festivals celebrating particular deities, shrines or events.

HOLY PLACES, PILGRIMAGE

Throughout India there are places which are particularly associated with certain deities, and others which are more generally holy. The river Ganges is holy throughout its length, and particularly so in certain places such as Benares. Pilgrimage to holy places is recognised as being one means for the individual to grow closer to God, but there is no duty of pilgrimage. It is undertaken only if the individual feels it will help him in his religious quest.

ATTITUDES TO OTHER FAITHS

As Hinduism believes that each must find their own path, they are very tolerant of other faiths, except when they come into social and political conflict as with the Sikhs and Muslims in modern India. Practices and figures from other faiths are absorbed into it easily. They will attend a Sikh gurdwara or a church and marriage between Sikhs and Hindus is not unusual.

INTRODUCTION TO ISLAM

Islam is the faith practised by Muslims. Its birthplace was in Arabia in the 7th century. Today it is followed by over 1,000 million people throughout the world and it is estimated that there is a growing population of ten million Muslims in Europe. Countries with pre-dominant Muslim populations Bangladesh, Indonesia, Iran, Malaysia, Pakistan, Turkey, all the countries in the Middle East and North Sahara. There are substantial Muslim populations in West Africa and what was Yugoslavia and in the C.I.S and Albania. The word Islam means 'submission to the will of God (Allah in Arabic) in all things'.

There are two main divisions in Islam, Sunni (the larger) and Shi'a. Sufi'ism is the mystical tradition within Islam.

The earliest Muslims to immigrate to Britain were ex-seamen from various Muslim countries who settled in ports such as Cardiff and Liverpool. The main immigration took place in the 1950s and 60s when many workers from the Indian sub-continent arrived in Britain. However, while the majority of Muslim children in schools are from Pakistani and Bangladeshi backgrounds, there are also those from the African continent, from the Middle East and from the Far East.

THE PROPHET MUHAMMAD

All Muslims accept that Muhammad was the final and most important of the prophets of whom the first was Adam, and who include Moses and Jesus. When they speak of Muham-mad they say, 'Peace be Upon Him' as a mark of the respect he is shown. They do not make images of him, of any kind, and he is not worshipped for worship belongs only to God.

Muhammad was a trader in Arabia in the 7th century. He was an honest upright man, reflec-tive in character. When he was 40, in 610 CE, while in a cave at Hira, outside the city of Mecca where he lived, he had a vision of the angel Jibra'eel (Gabriel) who instructed him to memo-rise and recite words given to him; words which called people to worship one true God. Muham-mad began to teach this message of the oneness of God, in the city of Mecca, which at that time practised a polytheistic religion. He met with stiff opposition and eventually he and his followers journeyed to Medina where the first Islamic community was founded. Muslim dates are all calculated from this journey (the Hijrah) in 622 CE. A period of missionary, political and military activity followed so that by the time of the Prophet's death in 632 CE Islam was established in most of the Arabian peninsular, including Mecca itself.

THE QUR'AN

Muhammad continued to receive revelations until he died aged 62. He memorized these himself and taught them word for word to his followers, and finally they were committed to writing. They were collected into one volume soon after his death. As the words are regarded as the direct transmission from God himself, the Qur'an is read and studied in the original Arabic and translations are never used in worship. The book contains teachings about God, daily life and disputes, as well as Islamic versions of stories also found in the Bible and other Christian sources. It does not contain stories about the life of Muhammad. Muslims consider the Qur'an to be the foundation of all other knowledge.

Reading of the Qur'an is an important part of Muslim faith. Passages from the Qur'an are also used to adorn buildings and artefacts, calligraphy being a highly prized art form. Copies of the Qur'an are always treated with great care. It is usually wrapped in a clean cloth and kept on a high shelf. A special stand is used to hold the book for reading. Before handling the book, Muslims always make sure that they themselves are clean. The book is not venerated as a physical object but is respected as the word of God.

Children often attend after school classes in the local mosque so that they can learn to read

Arabic and recite the Qur'an. A Muslim school-child will often be learning three languages: the mother tongue of the home (e.g. Urdu), English and Arabic.

HADITH

Muhammad is believed to have interpreted the word of God by his actions (sunna). Stories of his life and his sayings which were outside the Qu'ranic revelations were handed down and collected over a period of more than two hundred years. They were carefully examined by scholars for their authenticity, by checking the reliability of the line of transmission, and are known as Hadith. Hadith are a source of guidance for Muslims where there is no specific guidance in the Qur'an and the combination of the Qur'an and Hadith forms the basis of Islamic law (Fiqh).

THE FIVE PILLARS OF ISLAM

Muslims express and uphold their faith in their daily lives by practising the five pillars of faith:

The declaration of faith

'There is no God but God and Muhammad is his prophet.'

Islam is a strictly monotheistic religion. There is great stress on the unity and transcendence of God. The Qur'an forbids the worship of idols and no images are made of God or the Prophet (thus one should not ask a Muslim child to draw their idea of God or to illustrate a story with Muhammad in it). While there is some Muslim pictorial art, especially from the period of the Moguls and the Ottomans, many Muslims object to any pictures of humans. Most do not mind primary age children drawing figures.

In the Qur'an Allah is spoken of with 99 names each one saying something of his character (e.g. Revealer, Sustainer, Judge, the All-wise, the All-Compassionate). Muslims often think about God by reciting these names with the help of prayer beads.

Prayer (salah)

Five daily prayer times are laid down, at dawn, after midday, late afternoon, after sunset and at night time. In Muslim countries these prayer times are announced by a muezzin making the

call to prayer from the minaret, a tall tower at the side of the mosque. A translation of the call is:

'God is most great (four times)
I bear witness that there is no god but God (twice)
I bear witness that Muhammad is the messenger of God (twice)
Hasten to Prayer (twice)
Hasten to success (twice)
God is most great (twice)
There is no god but God.'

Prayers should be preceded by wudu (ritual washing) in a specified order. The worshipper washes hands, mouth, nose, face, arms, passes wet hands over his hair, cleans ears and washes feet. This is a preparation for prayer so that the person moves away from the things of the world to the things of God.

The prayers consist of a series of set words, accompanied by set postures. They are gradually learnt by Muslim children as soon as they start to speak. Prayers are normally performed at home, or wherever the Muslim happens to be, on any clean surface (this may be a prayer mat but need not be) and facing in the direction of Mecca. This direction is known as the Qiblah.

On Fridays, Muslims are expected to perform the after midday prayer in the mosque, in congregation. But Friday is not a 'holy day' in a Jewish or Christian sense. Business may go on before and afterwards. Women may attend prayers in the mosque but sit in a separate area, often in a gallery upstairs. When prayers are held congregationally people stand in rows shoulder to shoulder with no gaps. At Friday prayers a sermon (Kutbah) is often given by the imam, the leader of the community; political as well as specifically religious issues may be addressed. The imam is not a priest, there are no rites which only he can perform. He is chosen for his wisdom and qualities of leadership.

At the end of set prayers, the worshipper adds his or her own prayers silently, maybe asking God for forgiveness, for guidance or giving thanks for particular blessings.

Fasting (sawm)

The ninth Muslim month, Ramadan, is laid down as a month of fasting: an adult Muslim refrains from eating, drinking, smoking and conjugal relations from dawn to sunset. This is in obedience to the Qur'an and is regarded as a time to learn discipline and identify with the poor. Children under the age of puberty are exempt from the fast but may undertake a more limited one. For example, some junior age children will miss one meal or fast on alternate days. Women who are menstruating, travellers, and the sick are also exempt but must make up the time later. Since the Islamic calendar is lunar, Ramadan occurs gradually earlier each Western year.

Welfare tax (zakat)

Zakat is the right a community of Muslims has on all the surplus wealth of an individual. It is frequently calculated at an annual rate of 2.5% and is usually distributed among the needy.

Pilgrimage (hajj)

If they can afford it, all Muslims are expected to perform the pilgrimage to Mecca during the month of pilgrimage at least once in a lifetime. There they will set aside their normal clothes and wear a simple white garment as a mark of equality with others and humility before God. One of the many acts a pilgrim is expected to perform in Mecca, is to make seven circuits round the Ka'ba, touching or kissing the black stone in the Ka'ba wall, if it is possible to do so in the vast throng of pilgrims. The Ka'ba itself is a simple cuboid building and is believed to stand on the site of Abraham's first shrine.

The pilgrims also perform other ceremonies at different sites near Mecca associated with the prophet Ibrahim (Abraham) and his wife and son, Hagar and Ishmael.

THE MOSQUE

A mosque in Britain may be purpose-built or may be a converted house or a former church. Purpose-built mosques usually have domes and minarets. Inside there is little furniture since Muslims sit or kneel on the floor for prayer. A niche in the wall called the mihrab, marks the direction of Mecca. A small set of steps, called a minbar, is used by the imam for the Friday sermon. A series of clock faces show the prayer times for that day. There is a separate section for women. The mosque may be decorated with abstract patterns, words from the Qur'an and sometimes pictures of the Ka'ba. Outside the main room of the mosque are facilities for ritual

washing (wudu), and there are often also school and meeting rooms. There is usually a place to prepare the dead for burial.

DAILY LIFE

Many details of daily life are laid down in the Qur'an or the Hadith.

Food

Any meat eaten must be slaughtered in the correct way including invoking the name of God. This is called halal meat. Pig meat is very strictly forbidden and is regarded with revulsion by most Muslims. The Qur'an also outlaws alcohol. Before eating, or beginning any task, Muslims should say Bismillah, in the name of God. Only the right hand is used for eating, as the left is reserved for dirty or polluting tasks.

Dress

There is no specific Islamic dress and Muslims from different countries will dress quite differently. However, both men and women are required to dress modestly. For women this means covering the whole body in public, except for the face and hands. (Some very strict Muslim women cover the face as well.) Clothing should be loose and not reveal the shape of the body. Not all but many women cover their hair in public. Although this is not required until puberty some junior school girls do keep their heads covered. Some Muslim girls are embarrassed by uncovering their arms and legs in public and may be better doing PE in a tracksuit.

RITES OF PASSAGE

Birth

As far as possible, the first thing a baby hears should be the call to prayer, whispered in each ear. Customs vary according to the country of origin. All boys must be circumcised; in Pakistan this is usually at seven days; in Turkey at seven years. Other popular but not strictly speaking Islamic customs from the Indian sub-continent include shaving the child's head and giving the weight of the hair in silver to the poor, and putting a sweet in the child's mouth when it is brought home as a symbol that its nature will be sweet.

Marriage

Parents have the responsibility of choosing a marriage partner for their children, as marriage is regarded as linking two families not just two people. However the Qur'an decrees that the girl must give her consent and not be forced to marry. The imam usually performs the ceremony but this is not strictly necessary. It is essentially a contract between the two people. Brides from the Indian sub-continent usually wear red for rejoicing and gold jewellery and have their hands decorated with henna. There is an elaborate exchange of gifts between the two families and as big a party as the family can afford. The bride and groom don't see each other during the actual ceremony. Divorce is permitted but vigorously discouraged.

Death

One of the articles of faith of a Muslim is that there will be a Day of Judgement on which all the dead will be raised and judged by God. Those whose good outweighs the bad will go to Paradise and the others to the Fire.

After death the body is ritually washed and wrapped in a white shroud, and should be buried as soon as possible. Prayers are said by the community, affirming God's power over life and death. Excessive grief is discouraged as it is presumed that someone who dies as a practising Muslim will go to Paradise.

FESTIVALS

There are two main festivals in Islam:

Eid ul-Fitr

This celebrates the end of the month of fasting. It is heralded by the sight of the new moon. Congregational prayers are offered and special foods prepared. New clothes are often bought for the festival and presents may be given. Sending cards wishing Eid Mubarak (a happy or blessed festival) is a growing custom.
Themes: obedience, self-discipline.

Eid ul-Adha

This celebrates the willingness of the prophet Ibrahim (Abraham) to sacrifice his son Ishmael when God asked it of him. A lamb was sacrificed instead of Ishmael on Gods's command, so the sacrifice of a lamb or goat is an important part of the festival. There is also the culmination of the Hajj.
Themes: obedience, self-discipline.

HOLY PLACES

Mecca is the holiest place in Islam and is now visited every year by about 3,000 million Muslims performing the fifth pillar of the faith. It is also the direction (Qiblah) all Muslims face when they pray no matter where they are. The second holiest place is Medina, situated north of Mecca where Muhammad is buried. The third holiest place is Jerusalem (Alquds) which was originally the direction which Muslims faced when they prayed.

MUSLIM ATTITUDES TO OTHER FAITHS

Muslims believe that every child is born a Muslim but wander or are led from the true path of obedience to Allah, as it is laid down in the Qur'an. Therefore they seek to win others back to the faith. There is respect shown for Christians and Jews as 'people of the book' and because prophets who were the predecessors of Muhammad are honoured in these faiths. However the teaching of the Qur'an is deemed to have superseded earlier teachings so that its stories and beliefs abut Jesus are the correct ones. (Indeed they set out to correct what they see as Christian misunderstandings on issues such as the divinity of Jesus.)

Additionally, Muslims also believe that God sent prophets to all people no matter where they were in time or space; and in this sense consider Islam to be the natural, primal religion.

INTRODUCTION TO JUDAISM

Because the Jewish religion is specifically the religion of a particular people (a Jew is defined as the child of a Jewish mother) there is a particular difficulty for observers. The close connection between religion, culture and nationality makes it impossible to define what is, in the Western way of thinking, specifically 'religious'. This introduction is concerned with Judaism as a religion rather than an ethnic definition.

(Note: A Jew can also be someone who has converted under Jewish law though this is not encouraged in the modern era.)

HISTORY

The biblical account of the Jewish religion traces its origin back to the special relationship of Abraham with God, and the covenant made by God with Abraham, that states, 'I will be your God, and you will be my people'. The story tells that this promise was renewed with succeeding generations, down to Jacob and his twelve sons. Jacob was renamed Israel, and the descendants of his sons, the twelve tribes of Israel, were led out of oppression in Egypt by Moses (c1300 BCE), with whom the covenant was re-affirmed and consolidated by God's giving laws by which the Israelites were to live.

The resettlement of the Israelites around the river Jordan was followed by the first 'golden age' of the Jews, the reigns of David (c1000 BCE) and then of Solomon (c950 BCE), who built the first Temple in Jerusalem.

From c900 BCE Israel split into two – Judah in the south and Israel in the north. It was a period of petty wars and great risk of religious compromise with the other peoples of the area. In this setting many prophets arose (e.g. Micah, Isaiah and Jeremiah) trying to call the Israelites back to the One God. In 587 BCE the last free part of Judah fell to invaders, and the Jewish leaders were carried off to Babylon. This is the Exile. It ended around 540 BCE. By 450 BCE the Temple at Jerusalem had been rebuilt and a new, post-Exile form of Judaism had arisen under Ezra the Scribe. It is at this time that the Torah (see below) and other books began to take the form in which they now exist.

It was not until c160 BCE that the Jews regained full independence through the military successes of the Maccabees. By 60 BCE, the Romans had taken command of Palestine. In 66 CE the Jews rose in revolt and nearly succeeded in throwing out the Romans. However the revolt failed, ending with the mass suicide of the defenders of the rock fortress Masada in 73 CE and with the destruction of the Temple in Jerusalem by the Romans. From then on until 1948 the Jews were unable to rule their homeland and the Diaspora (dispersion), begun with the Exile in 587 BCE, now spread to all parts of the Roman world and beyond. During this period, especially from 70 CE–300 CE, the structure of present day Rabbinic Judaism was laid.

The history of the Jews from 70 CE is marked by periods of tolerance alternating with terrible oppression. There have been Jews in Britain since at least the Norman conquest and, as in the rest of Europe, they were alternately accepted and persecuted or expelled.

Many Jews arrived in Britain and the USA in the 19th century, escaping oppression in Eastern Europe. Others arrived this century, as a result of the Nazi persecution of the Jews. Some other Jews in Britain are descended from those who flourished in the Mediterranean world, particularly Spain, under Muslim rule in the Middle Ages. When later expelled from Spain, they settled in various countries, and have preserved different traditions from the Jews of Northern Europe. These are known as Sephardis, and may still refer to themselves as 'Spanish and Portuguese', for instance in the names of synagogues.

Northern European Jews are known as Ashkenazis.

In 1948 after the holocaust under the Nazis the State of Israel was established. The period between the final fall of the temple and 1948 is also seen as an Exile.

Thus there are differing traditions among Jews in Britain. At present there are an estimated 330,000 practising Jews in Britain.

DIVISIONS WITHIN JUDAISM

The majority of Jews in Britain are Orthodox, resisting change and following the traditions closely. Within Orthodoxy there is the Hasidic movement whose origins were in 18th century Poland. Hasidic men are distinguished by their long side curls, beards and gaberdine coats.

In the nineteenth and early twentieth century various trends in Europe and America moved away from from traditional, or 'Orthodox' observance, giving rise to Conservative, Liberal and Reform Judaism which in varying degrees believe that Jewish practice must adapt to changing circumstances, and so have introduced changes such as use of the vernacular as well as Hebrew in services and a more liberal interpretation of the Law.

SCRIPTURES AND OTHER RELIGIOUS WRITINGS

The Hebrew Bible

This is the collection of books known to Christians as the Old Testament, but this term, implying its being superseded by the New Testament, is not used by Jews. The Hebrew Bible is regarded as containing three different types of book.

The most important section is the Pentateuch, the first five books of the Bible, regarded by traditional Jews as having been directly revealed by God to Moses. These five books are known collectively as the Torah but the term may also be more loosely applied to the whole Hebrew Bible. These books contain stories of the Creation, the Patriarchs, the Exodus from Egypt and the Jewish law.

Then there are the Prophets, e.g. Amos, Hosea, Isaiah, as well as the histories such as Joshua, I and II Samuel, I and II Kings.

Holy writings, consist of the Psalms, as well as such books as Ruth, Esther and Jonah and other poetic writings such as the Song of Songs.

The language of the Torah is Hebrew, and it is read in worship in the original Hebrew in Orthodox synagogues. Many Jews learn Hebrew in order to understand the readings and prayers, but many follow them in a parallel text giving both Hebrew and their native language. Every synagogue has a set of parchment scrolls on which the Torah is written. This is an extremely skilled and laborious job, performed as an act of devotion itself and done by a specialist scribe. It often takes a year to write a full Torah.

The Torah scrolls are treated with great respect, and kept in a special cupboard or alcove (called the Ark) in the eastern wall of the synagogue (the wall which faces Jerusalem). The scrolls are 'dressed' in velvet coverings and silver ornaments, recalling some of the ritual clothing worn by priests in temple times. Each scroll has a belt to hold the two sides together when rolled, a breast plate, and a crown, together with a silver pointer used when reading to avoid touching the parchment – both as a sign of respect and a measure to preserve a very costly item for as long as possible.

Mishnah and Talmud

All Jewish life and practice is based on the Torah and its commandments, but since these were given thousands of years ago for a very different world, learned teachers have discussed and passed down orally a series of interpretations and judgements based on the Torah. Many of these have been collected in two works, the Mishnah (second century CE) and Talmud (sixth century CE) and these are used to help Rabbis make decisions on new cases.

THE SYNAGOGUE

The synagogue is the centre of Jewish community life. It fulfils three main functions: as a house of assembly, where the Jewish community can meet for any purpose; as a house of study where the Torah and Talmud are studied, and children learn Hebrew etc.; and a house of prayer, where services are held on Sabbaths and festivals, and prayers are said every day (see worship).

Each synagogue is independent, run and supported by its members, but usually belongs also to a synagogal group. No Rabbi (literally 'teacher') or other qualified person is necessary for its existence, but in practice there will usually be a Rabbi employed by the congregation to have authority over the running of the synagogue and to attend to the religious needs of the congregation. He may also be called upon to settle matters of dispute about interpretations of the law, especially in Orthodox synagogues.

As well as the ark for the Torah already mentioned, most synagogues have a raised platform, the bimah near the centre of the room where the Torah and prayers are read, and a sermon may be preached. In Orthodox and traditional synagogues, men and women sit separately, women usually at the back or upstairs, since they do not take an active part in the services. In most Reform synagogues men and women may sit together.

Synagogues may be decorated but have no images of people or animals as the law forbids the making of images.

BELIEFS

At the heart of Jewish belief is the Shema, found in Deuteronomy 6:4-7:

> Hear, O Israel: the Lord our God, the Lord is One.
> And thou shalt love the Lord, thy God with all thy heart and with all thy soul, and with all thy might. And these words, which I command thee this day, shall be upon thy heart, and thou shalt teach them diligently unto thy children, and thou shalt talk of them when thou sittest in thy house, and when thou walkest by the way, and when thou liest down and when thou risest up.

God is creator, and Lord of all the universe with a special relationship with the Jewish people who have a vocation to be His people. (Images of God are forbidden and many Jews will not write the word, putting G-d instead.) The people's part of this covenant is to keep God's laws as faithfully as possible: the law that was given to Moses at Mount Sinai. Its main headings are given as the Ten Commandments, but more detailed laws are given elsewhere in the five books of Moses, and these are worked out in further detail for changing circumstances in the Talmud (see above). Although Reform and Orthodox Jews (see above) may differ as to how literally the Law is to be interpreted, they agree that a Jew's first duty is to obey God's law.

The Law

To the Jew, the law is God's merciful provision of guidelines, without which it would not be possible to do God's will and remain in the covenant relationship with him. While some laws have obvious ethical and practical reasons, others cannot be understood in those terms, and are an indication of God's 'otherness' from humanity. Study of the law is an important part of Jewish life.

DAILY LIFE

Jewish daily life follows the laws found in the Torah (see above) and much of the practice of the faith takes place in the home. On the doorposts of the home are small boxes (mezuzah) containing the words of the Shema (see above) in obedience to the command to write the words on the doorposts and acting as a reminder to love God in one's comings and goings. Many Jews will not have paintings or statues of living creatures in the home. There are some set prayers but there are also prayers for many occasions, such as seeing a new moon, or the sea for the first time after a long period or setting out on a journey, as well as for food and drink. Thus the life of faith is believed to permeate the whole of one's life. Study and learning are highly prized and many Jewish young people in this country go to study in Israel.

Food

Jewish food laws (called kashrut) relate to what is eaten, how it is slaughtered, how prepared and cooked, and how eaten. Jews are allowed to eat animals which both chew the cud and have a cloven hoof. All others are forbidden. As well as the well-known prohibition of pig products, this includes rabbit and some other animals, but not many which are commonly eaten in Britain. Animals and birds must be ritually slaughtered in the correct manner by an adult Jew, and certain parts of the animal may not be eaten. Meat must be drained of blood before being cooked. Jews eat fish so long as it has both fins and scales. Fruit, vegetables and grain products are checked to make sure they contain no insects.

Meat products and dairy products may not be eaten together or at the same meal, and great care is taken in Orthodox Jewish households to keep them separate at all stages of preparation, using a completely different set of utensils for the two types of food, and different refrigerators or different shelves of the refrigerator, different washing-up bowls, etc. Other Jews have a more liberal interpretation of the food laws. Food which fulfils the requirements of kashrut is known as kasher, ritually correct (commonly rendered as 'kosher'). Many observant Orthodox Jews will usually not eat in restaurants or non-Jewish homes so as to ensure that kosher is strictly kept.

A blessing is said before and after food.

Dress

All Jews wear head coverings for services, with the exception of liberal Jews. Orthodox Jews also wear head coverings at other times to show their submission to God. In the case of men these are usually small caps called yarmulkas. Some Orthodox women wear wigs.

During the daily recitation of the Shema at home Jewish men also tie small boxes to their left arm and forehead (tefillin). These contain the shema (see above) and are worn in obedience to a command to write these words on mind, heart and hand.

Daily prayer

Public congregational prayers are said at the synagogue every weekday, but this can only take place if ten adult Jewish males are present. It is therefore every Jewish man's duty to attend prayers as often as possible to help form a minyan, or quorum.

Shabbat (day of rest)

The observance of Shabbat (anglicised to Sabbath) is laid down in the Law, but it is also regarded as a privilege and celebration by devout Jews.

Jewish reckoning of days starts at nightfall, so the Sabbath begins on Friday evening. It is very much a home and family based celebration. During the Sabbath no work is done, no money is carried or business transacted. This is in celebration of the account of Creation in the Bible, where God rests on the seventh day. Everything is done to make the day special – best clothes, the best food that the family can afford, and families spend time together. The day has been described as a queen, and as a bride, and the family welcomes it into the home with great joy.

On the Friday evening, some members of the family often go to the synagogue though the women often stay behind to prepare the Sabbath meal. The meal will have been cooked before nightfall, as well as a meal for Saturday midday, as it is forbidden to light a fire on the Sabbath.

The table is prepared with a white cloth, and on it are placed two special loaves, hallot, covered with a cloth, a cup of wine (the kiddush cup), and candles. The Sabbath begins with the mother lighting the Sabbath candles while saying a blessing. This may occur while some family members are still at the synagogue. When all are seated round the table, the father recalls the institution of the Sabbath by reciting the opening verses of Genesis 2. Then comes the ceremony of Kiddush: he blesses and shares a cup of wine, and blesses, breaks and shares the two loaves.

After the meal, grace is said and table songs in praise of the Sabbath are sung. It should be a joyful time of celebration.

On Saturday the whole family usually attends synagogue service in the morning, and may spend the afternoon visiting friends or relatives, or relaxing as a family. On Saturday evening a ceremony called havdalah (separation) marks the end of the Sabbath. The family gathers round, a special candle is lit, and a box is passed round filled with sweet-smelling spices.

RITES OF PASSAGE

Birth

As a sign of the covenant between God and the Jews, the Torah lays down that every boy baby must be circumcised. This operation is performed at home by a specially trained person (a mohel) on the eighth day after birth. Family and friends attend, and there is a tradition that the prophet Elijah attends every circumcision, so an empty chair is placed for him, called the Throne of Elijah. The baby is placed briefly on this chair, then handed to the sandek (the godfather) who holds the baby while the mohel recalls the covenant, and recites a blessing while cutting off the foreskin. Blessings and good wishes are said, and wine is shared by all. The baby's name is announced at this time. After the ceremony there is a meal, the 'feast of the fulfilment of a commandment'. Blessings take place for girls in the synagogue and there will usually also be a meal. In some synagogues boys will also have a blessing there. Children are usually given a religious name as well as a secular one and are often named after recently deceased relatives. Traditions vary according to background.

Bar Mitzvah

When a Jewish boy is thirteen years old, he is regarded as being old enough to take responsibility for himself and his observance of the Law. He is in religious terms an adult, a 'son of the commandment', bar mitzvah in Hebrew, and can take an active part in services and be counted in the minyan, the quorum for public prayer. One of the privileges and duties of a Jewish man is to be called to read a passage of the Torah in Hebrew in a synagogue service, so a special occasion is made when he does this for the first time. Friends and relatives attend the synagogue to hear the boy read, after saying a prayer promising to keep God's commandments. The Rabbi preaches a sermon about the boy's new responsibilities and recites the blessing from Numbers 6 : 24-26.

Refreshments are served at the synagogue, and the parents usually give a big party, at which the boy receives presents, some of which symbolize his move into adulthood, such as a briefcase or prayer book. At this age, too, the boy may put on the tefillin for the first time. In progressive Jewish congregations girls, too, celebrate their coming of age at twelve years with a Bat Mitzvah (daughter of the commandment) ceremony.

Orthodox Jews have a Bat Hayil service for girls, aged twelve, on a Sunday afternoon. This is because they believe that girls/women cannot take part in a mixed service.

Marriage

A Jewish wedding takes place (often on a Sunday, since it cannot be held on the Sabbath or festivals) under a canopy, the hupah, which is decorated with flowers, and symbolizes the new home the bride and groom will make together. The celebration is usually in a synagogue but this is not a necessity, and in many countries, including Israel, is often in the open air. The bridegroom places a gold ring on the bride's forefinger. The marriage contract is read out, and the Rabbi recites seven marriage blessings. At the end of the ceremony, the bridegroom breaks a

wineglass under his foot. Different accounts of this are given – some say it is recalling, even at a time of joy, the destruction of the Temple in Jerusalem; others that it is to warn off Lilith who according to legend spurned marriage. Marriage is encouraged and celibacy frowned on.

Death

Jews believe in the resurrection of the dead, but there are different beliefs about what happens to the body, and consequently about burial or cremation. Orthodox Jews do not cremate their dead, seeing this as a denial of belief in bodily resurrection, but non-orthodox may do so.

The body must be buried as soon as possible after death, and is washed, anointed with spices and wrapped in a white sheet. Burial must be in Jewish consecrated ground.

For a week after the death, close relatives sit at home, wearing a torn or cut upper garment, taking no part in ordinary life. Friends and relatives have a duty to visit, bringing food and other help to the mourner. For eleven months after the death a special prayer is recited every day at the synagogue, and every year the anniversary of the death is remembered. The whole process of mourning and its gradual lessening as the mourner is permitted to resume certain aspects of everyday life, is formalized, and many believe this is an emotional support to the mourner.

FESTIVALS AND HOLY DAYS

Jews follow a lunar calendar with a thirteenth month being added every third year of a nineteen year cycle. Thus the festivals fall in approximately the same Western month each year but the date varies. The new day begins at nightfall so festivals begin in the evening. The years are counted from the traditional Jewish dating of the creation of the world (1993 is the year 5753).

Rosh Hashanah and Yom Kippur

These festivals take place in September. Rosh Hashanah is the Jewish New Year, and begins a period of repentance leading up to Yom Kippur. Jews prepare for Rosh Hashanah during the month before, with reflection and self-examination. Before the evening service the shofar, a ram's horn, is blown to call the people to repentance and to start the New Year afresh. The food eaten on this day is symbolic of wishes for a good year ahead – bread dipped in honey, apple dipped in honey. Rosh Hashanah is followed by ten days of repentance, leading up to Yom Kippur, the Day of Atonement. This is a fast day, when Jews must seek the forgiveness of those they have wronged. At the evening service, the kol nidrei is sung, where the worshippers ask for absolution from religious vows they have taken in the past year and failed to keep.

Themes: creation, new start, repentance and reconciliation.

Sukkot

The seven day festival of Sukkot in September-October time, also known as Tabernacles, or booths, commemorates the time when the Israelites lived in temporary shelters in the desert in their wanderings from Egypt to the Promised Land. Families build temporary shelters in the garden or leaning against the house. These are filled with greenery and must be partly open to the sky. The family eat there, and some may sleep there. Synagogues often have their own sukkah, where refreshments are served after the service. It is also a harvest festival; children often make lulavs which are sheaths of palm branches, myrtle, willow and etrogs (a lemon-like fruit) bound together.

Themes: God's provision, fertility, harvest.

Simhat Torah

Falling two days after Sukkot in September-October, this festival celebrates God's mercy in giving the Torah, and marks the end of the annual reading of the whole Torah, week by week. The Torah scrolls are carried in procession round the synagogue, with singing and dancing, and the children may follow waving flags.

Themes: the Scriptures, the Law.

Hanukah

Hanukah is celebrated in December. The story of the festival is told in *A Tapestry of Tales*. It arose in the second century BCE when Judah Maccabee defeated the Greek tyrant who had forced the Jews to abandon their religion. When the temple was re-dedicated after the victory there was only enough oil for the temple lamp to last one day, and it would take eight days to prepare a fresh supply. The lamp was lit and, instead of lasting only one day, it kept burning for eight days.

The festival of Hanukah celebrates the survival of the Jewish faith in adversity. At its heart is the lighting of candles in a special eight-branched candlestick, one on the first day, two on the second, and so on. Hanukah parties are often held, with special games and songs.

Hanukah is a particularly popular festival with Jews in Europe and the United States as it is near Christmas and it has become more of a children's festival than it probably was in its origins.

Themes: commitment, light in the darkness.

Purim

This festival in February-March, celebrates the story of Esther, the Jewish queen of the Persian king Xerxes, who saved her people from destruction by the king's minister Haman. The festival is a very light-hearted and noisy one, with people dressing up in odd clothes for the synagogue service. In this service the scroll of Esther is read, and every time the villain's name, 'Haman' is spoken, the congregation try to drown the sound by making noises as loudly as they can – booing, waving football rattles, banging tin trays, etc. A special three cornered biscuit, filled with poppy seeds, is often baked which is said to look like Haman's hat.

Themes: deliverance, survival in adversity.

Pesach or Passover

This festival in March-April, celebrates the whole story of God's deliverance of the Israelites from captivity in Egypt, as told in Exodus. The Israelites had to depart so quickly from Egypt that they had no time to bake ordinary bread, but made unleavened bread to take with them.

Jews are commanded to commemorate this by eating unleavened bread (matzah) during the eight days of the festival. Before Pesach all yeast or even flour and water mixtures which might ferment are cleared out, the house is cleaned, and a ceremonial search is made with candles on the eve of the festival for any remaining scraps, which are then burnt.

The high point of the festival is the Seder meal eaten in the home on the first evening of the festival. (Seder means order: the meal progresses in a set order.) Families try to assemble to eat the meal together, and may invite those who have no family to join them. The meal recalls in words and symbols the Israelites' departure from Egypt. The youngest child present asks a series of questions which are answered telling the story of the Exodus. Questions and answers are in a book called the Haggadah. The meal will include a roasted lamb shank bone to recall the lamb killed by the Israelites, bitter herbs (usually horse-radish) to recall their suffering, and saltwater for their tears. A green vegetable, usually parsley, and an egg are also eaten. This special Pesach food is arranged on a seder plate, which is often a very beautiful and treasured family possession. At the meal four cups of wine are drunk by all present to remember God's four acts of salvation (see Exodus 6.7), but a little of each is spilt to recall the suffering caused to the Egyptians by these acts.

Orthodox Jews, outside Israel, usually keep two Seder nights. This is because the festival begins with the rising of the new moon in Israel, and outside its boundaries, before modern communications, it was not always easy to tell when this occurred.

Themes: redemption, liberty (in physical and moral sense), spring.

Shavuot

This festival takes place in May-June. Also known as Pentecost or the Feast of Weeks, this festival combines elements of a festival for the wheat harvest in Israel, with the main emphasis of commemorating the giving of the Torah to Moses on Mount Sinai. It celebrates the consecra-tion of the people to the Torah and the book of Ruth is read aloud as Ruth was willing to take on the Torah. Often young boys begin their study of the Torah at this festival.

Themes: commitment, dedication, the law.

HOLY PLACES AND PILGRIMAGE

The land of Israel has a special status for Jews. The story of their prophet Abraham says that the land was given to Abraham and his descendants. However there is a diversity of opinion across the religious spectrum about the rights of Jews in the region. Some Orthodox Jews believes that Jews are entitled to own the land within the old Biblical boundaries even if it displaces other peoples. Others are more concerned that after many centuries of persecution Jews should have a state of their own but are less concerned about claims based on the Bible. A few Orthodox Jews are opposed to the political state of Israel, believing that the Messiah should come first. Although there is no injunction to travel to Israel many Jews do like to visit as often as they can afford it.

Within Israel, the Western Wall in the old city of Jerusalem is of particular importance. This is the only wall which remains of the 2nd Temple which was destroyed in 70 CE. People come there to pray and to celebrate festivals or Bar Mitz-vahs.

INTRODUCTION TO SIKHISM

The Sikh religion began in the Punjab region of North West India with the teachings of Guru Nanak who was born in 1469.

There are now about 16 million Sikhs, mainly in the Punjab, in India but also in America, Canada, Southern Africa, Hong Kong and Britain, where the Sikh community is estimated at half a million. Sikh immigration to Britain began in the early 20th century; but most Sikhs arrived after the Second World War. There are now Sikh communities in most major British cities.

THE SIKH GURUS

In the Sikh religion a 'guru' denotes one who leads one to the light/truth. God himself is the true Guru. (One of the Sikh names of God is Waheguru – Wonderful Lord.) However, the title Guru is also given to the ten successive spiritual leaders of the Sikh community.

Guru Nanak was the first human Guru. He was born into a Hindu home in the town of Talwandi in North West India, now Pakistan, at a time of tension between Hindu and Muslim. There are many stories told of his early life, his wisdom, his devotion to truth, honesty, his concern for the poor, and his rejection of empty ritual. Above all, he taught that the light of God is in everyone and all are equal. He was opposed to the caste system (see Introduction to Hinduism p.113). He spent much of his life as an itinerant teacher passing on his message by his example, and in his many hymns. In the final stage of his life he established a Sikh community, in which labour was not divided according to caste or status, and all ate together as equals.

At the end of his life, he appointed as successor a man noted for his deep humility. This practice of each Guru naming who should succeed him continued for approximately 200 years, until the tenth Guru, Guru Gobind Singh, named instead the Sikh holy book and the Sikh community, the Panth, to lead after him (see below, the story of the Khalsa). Meanwhile the Sikh movement had become increasingly militaristic, with defence of religious freedom for all being a cause for which many Sikhs (including two of the Gurus) were martyred. There was also a great concern for social justice. Sikhs believe that God has never taken human form so although highly respected, the Gurus are not worshipped.

THE SIKH HOLY BOOK – THE GURU GRANTH SAHIB

Granth means book, and Sahib is a title of respect, so Guru Granth Sahib means something like 'the highly respected book, God's messenger'. It is regarded as a living Guru, and is treated in many ways in accordance with this. For instance, when the Guru Granth Sahib is moved, it must be accompanied by the Panj Pyare (the five beloved, any five Khalsa Sikhs – see below) who correspond to the attendants who would accompany an honoured person. The Guru Granth Sahib is taken into a separate room at night, and must always be approached with respect, and with clean hands. Decisions regarding the community must be made in its presence. However, Sikhs are not worshipping the book, they are giving it what they regard as proper respect.

It is a collection of nearly 6000 hymns by the Gurus, and also includes the writings of some non-Sikhs, Hindus and Muslims. The first Gurus taught their hymns to their followers and they were also written down. Guru Arjan, the fifth Guru, first collected them together into one volume, known as the Adi Granth. In the 19th century the page length and numbering were standardised so that every copy is identical – 1430 pages long. It is written in Gurmurkhi, the correct name for written Punjabi. Guru Gobind Singh instructed that Sikhs were to look upon it as their guide, a symbolic representation of all the Gurus.

The Guru Granth Sahib teaches that there is one God and all people are equal. It accepts the concepts of reincarnation and the laws of karma, i.e. that the consequences of one's actions are carried through into following lives. It prohibits the use of intoxicants and rejects both idol worship and formal priesthood.

Central to the teachings of the Guru is the belief that the purpose of life is self realization; on knowing the self a person meets God, thus peace and harmony are achieved. Prayer and the singing of hymns are seen as important disciplines to help a person focus on God and realize God within. Service to others is also fundamental.

The original copy of the Guru Granth Sahib is kept in the Golden Temple in Amritsar in the Punjab which was built especially to house it. Amritsar has been a place of pilgrimage for Sikhs since the fifth Guru.

THE KHALSA

In the late 16th and throughout the 17th centuries the persecution, which the Sikhs had always faced, intensified. In order to give a sense of solidarity as well as create a means of protection for Sikhs, Guru Gobind Singh in 1699 founded the Khalsa, a brotherhood of committed Sikhs who would uphold the Sikh faith as well as fight when necessary against persecution.

Becoming a member of the Khalsa is a voluntary step which all Sikhs have to consider carefully since it involves a more disciplined way of life, both spiritually and physically. For instance, some particular prayers must be said daily, and a strict diet must be followed. They must wear certain clothing (see below).

Initiation into the Khalsa usually takes place at Baisakhi (see below), but it can be at any time. Five members of the Khalsa perform the ceremony, at which a special sweet liquid, amrit, is drunk and sprinkled on the candidates, and they are reminded of the duties and responsibilities of Khalsa Sikhs. The ceremony is sometimes referred to in English as 'baptism'.

THE PLACE OF WORSHIP – THE GURD-WARA

The gurdwara (meaning house of the Guru) acquires its sanctity from the presence of the Guru Granth Sahib which is installed in a prayer room under a rich canopy on a raised platform, resting on cushions. It is covered with a special cloth, the rumala. Before entering the room where it is, Sikhs remove their shoes and cover their heads and then they bow before it as a sign of respect. They will also give money or food which is placed before the sacred book. The Guru Granth Sahib is at the centre of all services. Many of its hymns are set to music and sung by the congregation or by a group of musicians, since music forms an important part of Sikh worship. The Guru Granth Sahib is read by the Granthi (who is a reader, not a priest) and interpretations are often given by the Granthi, but any member of the congregation, male or female, may speak. During the service one member of the congregation sits behind the Guru Granth Sahib and at intervals waves the chauri over it. This is made of long hairs embedded in a handle, and recalls the personal care of a living Guru in a hot country.

At the end of a service, everyone stands for the final prayer, (ardas) and a sweet food, karah parshad, is served. During the service, people come and go informally, and children are allowed to move about, but the atmosphere in the prayer room remains reverent and peaceful. Services in Britain are held on Sundays as a matter of convenience. There is no set day of worship. After a service, everyone shares a communal meal, a langar or free kitchen to which all are welcome, no matter what their status or religion. Vegetarian food is served so that people of every faith may participate.

DAILY LIFE

Because of the need for the Guru Granth Sahib to have its own room, just as a living Guru would, few Sikhs have their own copies of the Guru Granth Sahib (and obviously no Sikh child could bring a copy to school). However, many Sikhs have a copy of certain excerpts, known as the Gutkha, and set prayers from it are said every morning and evening. Sometimes they are said over the dishes; or while the children are dressing; or in the car with the prayers on a cassette; or the whole family might meet together before or after a meal. There are 39 'steps' in the morning prayer, which are obligatory to members of the Khalsa, but many families recite just the first five. Meditation with the aid of prayer beads is also encouraged but is usually only practised by older women.

The opening verse of the Guru Granth Sahib, which is said in the morning and evening prayers and indeed repeated throughout the Holy Book is as follows:

'There is one God, Eternal Truth is his name, maker of all and present in all. Fearing nothing and hating nothing; timeless is his image; not born and not dying, by the grace of the Guru made known.'

This is known as the Mool Mantra.

Diet

Sikhs may eat meat, but they will not eat meat slaughtered according to the rules of Islam or Judaism. They see those methods of killing as unnecessarily cruel. Furthermore animals should not be killed wantonly, but only out of need. Out of respect for Hindu views, beef is rarely, if at all, eaten. The Sikh faith discourages the use of any drugs (except medicinally), including tobacco and alcohol. Members of the Khalsa are expected to refrain from these altogether.

Dress

Members of the Khalsa are required to wear the five Ks and other Sikhs are encouraged to do so too. The five Ks are symbols which mark them out as Sikhs and are as follows:

the kanga: this is the comb which keeps the hair tidy and is a symbol of discipline.
the kara: this is a bangle to symbolize that there is one God, one brotherhood, and that truth is eternal. It is nowadays usually made of stainless steel to symbolize strength and resistance.
the kacchera: these are long, above the knee, breeches, worn to show that a Sikh was always ready to ride to battle in defence of just causes. The dhoti, the garb worn at the time of Guru Gobind Singh, was not suitable for horseback riding.
the kirpan: this is a sword, similarly a sign of the Sikhs' willingness to fight injustice. British Sikhs usually carry or wear a miniature kirpan.
the kesh: this refers to long uncut hair (which in Indian tradition is a sign of wisdom) which must be kept very neat.

The turban is not one of the five Ks, but is worn to keep the hair tidy. It is not worn by primary school age children and boys' long hair is gathered together and tied up in a handkerchief on the top of their heads. The long hair rule is not observed rigorously by all Sikhs in Britain.

RITES OF PASSAGE

Birth and Naming

When a baby is first born, the words of the Mool Mantra may be whispered in its ear, and a drop of honey placed on its tongue to symbolize good and pure words. Later on the baby is taken to the Gurdwara for the first time, when its name is given. Every male Sikh has the last name 'Singh' meaning lion, and every female, 'Kaur' meaning Princess. This was another practice instituted by Guru Gobind Singh to show that all are equal. (In Britain some Sikhs take Singh as a family name to conform with European practice.) The naming of a child takes place at an ordinary weekly service, or the child may be taken to the Gurdwara as soon as he or she comes out of hospital. The parents bring gifts of food for the langar, and of butter, sugar and flour for karah parshad. They also, present a new cloth (rumala) to cover the Guru Granth Sahib. Hymns are sung expressing gratitude for the birth of a baby. When the random reading is taken for the day, the Granthi or reader announces the first letter of the reading. The family then chooses a name for their child which begins with that letter, so the family must come prepared with a whole alphabet of names.

Marriage

The family assists in the choosing of a partner and while the couple will probably have met before the wedding they will have been chaperoned. Great care is given to the choice and no-one is made to marry against their will. The ceremony follows the usual form of service but hymns are sung which are appropriate to the occasion. The couple are given advice on marriage and a hymn called the Lavan is sung. After each of the four verses the couple walk round the Guru Granth Sahib, with their families in attendance, to show their support for the couple. The bride usually wears a red khameez (red for festivity) and her hands may be decorated with henna (a social custom, not a religious requirement). She wears gold bangles and a wedding ring and often her husband will have given her jewellery. Marriage is important in Sikhism which has no monastic movement.

At a birth or marriage, the family may pay for the langar, the free kitchen, to be open for three days so that the Guru Granth Sahib is read in its entirety. A private wedding feast is usually held after the langar.

Death

Sikhs believe in a cycle of reincarnation, similar to Hindu beliefs, so they teach that it is wrong to mourn excessively for someone who has died, since they live on in another body.

A dying person tries to say 'Waheguru' just before death, and family and friends may read hymns from the Guru Granth Sahib. After death, the body is washed and dressed in the five Ks, if the person was a member of the Khalsa. If not, not all of the five Ks are necessary. Then the body is taken to be cremated – in India on a funeral pyre, in Britain at a crematorium. A prayer for the peace of the soul is said, followed by the evening or bedtime prayer. The ashes, and the metal kirpan and kara, which will not burn, will be scattered on running water, a stream or a river. There is a service at the Gurdwara, where a speech is given about the dead person, and karah parshad is shared. A meal is served in the langar, and the Guru Granth Sahib is often read through during the period following. The family often give gifts to charity.

FESTIVALS

There are two groups of festivals:

Gurpurb: commemorating events in the lives of the Gurus. One of the best known is Guru Nanak's birthday.

Some Sikh festivals are held on the same dates as Hindu festivals, but have a totally different religious content: these are Baisakhi, Divali and Hola Mohalla which corresponds with Hindu Holi.

Baisakhi

This is the festival when Sikhs celebrate the foundation of the Khalsa.

Themes: commitment, discipline, religious freedom, equality.

Divali

At Divali lamps are lit in the home, to commemorate the release from prison of Guru Hargobind. Friends visit one another and it is generally a home-based festival.
Theme: religious freedom.

Hola Mohalla

While Hindus celebrate Holi with games and pranks, Sikhs have contests of horsemanship, wrestling etc. for both men and women, developing the idea of Sikh readiness to fight for just causes.

At all the above festivals the Guru Granth Sahib is read in its entirety by a relay of readers, taking 48 hours, followed by a service. Sikhs come and go during the proceedings. The langar is open continuously, and everyone helps to run it, and contributes food or money. Children may help in the langar, and may be taught hymns for the service. Afterwards everyone gathers in the langar for a meal.

New clothes are often bought for festivals, and money and sweets are given. Sikh children receive gifts of toys on their birthdays, not at festival time.

SIKH HOLY PLACES AND PILGRIMAGE

Sikh places of pilgrimage tend to be associated with bathing places; Guru Amar Das instituted a bathing well at Goiwindal and Guru Ram Das a bathing tank at Amritsar. The Sikh scriptures are nevertheless quite clear that bathing in such places does not purify or lead to salvation 'True pilgrimage is contemplation on God' (Adi Granth 687). Bathing and pilgrimage are seen as a discipline which enables the mind to concentrate on God.

Guru Ram Das also began building the holy city of Amritsar, in the Punjab. Here the Golden Temple houses the first copy of the Guru Granth Sahib. The city is the spiritual centre of Sikhism.

VISITING PLACES OF WORSHIP

A visit to a place of worship can provide the highlight of the children's work in many areas, and can help enormously to 'flesh out', for both pupils and teachers, what they have learnt about people's beliefs and worship. Most faith communities are delighted to welcome others to their building and have a chance to tell people about it. But a visit needs careful preparation if it is not to prove a disappointment. Here are some points to help you.

Choosing a place to visit

Give careful thought to deciding which building you want to visit. Many are converted houses or other buildings, and particularly if the faith community has not been long established in the area, may not have much for the children to look at, unless you are specifically studying the way buildings are converted for religious use. Do not forget that for many children a church is almost as unfamiliar inside as a mosque or gurdwara, and may provide many points of interest.

The most important thing is to establish good contact with a representative of the place you hope to visit. Do this well in advance, since it may be difficult for someone to be available to show you round during school hours. There are several ways to make contact: parents of children in your class may be able to put you in touch; there may be a noticeboard outside the building giving a name to contact; the local library may have information; hospital chaplaincies often have lists of contacts for non-Christian as well as Christian religious leaders; or you could write to one of the national organisations listed in this book to see if they can put you in touch with anyone locally.

Preparing for the visit

As early as possible, visit the building yourself, and meet the person who is going to act as your guide to the building. The success of your visit depends very largely on the guide, so take time establishing that you and he both understand each other over what is planned for the visit. Decide who will do most of the talking: the enthusiasm of someone who knows and loves the building and the faith it represents is invaluable, but if there are language difficulties or other reasons why he may be difficult for the children to listen to, you may prefer to do most of the talking yourself, using information discussed with your guide. Discuss how long you want the visit to last, how long you want the guide to speak, what topics to focus on.

Learn something of the history of the building, and its significance to those who use it. One difficulty about visiting a place of worship is that it usually has to be when the building is not in use. Find out if it is possible to visit during worship, and if so, check what will be going on, how long it lasts, whether you will be able to arrive or leave in the middle (in many faiths it is quite normal for people to come and go during the proceedings). If this is not possible, discuss ways to bring things more alive: it may be possible to play recordings of what goes on in a service, or show photos of the building when it is being used.

There are various practical points to check with your hosts:

★ What dress requirements are there? e.g. should the girls wear trousers (usually required for mosque and gurdwara); should everyone bring something to cover their head with; will they be asked to remove their shoes? (It can be embarrassing if you arrive at a mosque with holes in your socks!)

★ Will boys and girls be able to do and see the same things? Most mosques have separate areas for male and female, and in both synagogue and gurdwara men and women sit in different areas during services. The degree to which this is observed may depend on whether you are visiting when worship is going on or not.

★ Check that the activities you plan for the class in connection with the visit are acceptable to the faith community.

Inside the place of worship

Plan activities for the children to do while they are visiting. If there is a service going on, identify points for them to look out for. If not, as well as preparing questions for the children to answer, plan some 'sitting still' activities such as drawing something, copying Arabic or Hebrew writing which may be on the walls.

Make sure the children know what is expected of them during the visit. Emphasize that they are being invited into the 'home' of the faith community, and should act as guests in someone's house. Try to anticipate anything the children might find amusing or unpleasant (smells such as incense often arouse the strongest reactions), and discuss it with the class before your visit. If you are visiting during a service, make it clear that they are there as observers, and will not be expected to join in the prayers and actions of the worshippers, unless specifically invited to do so.

Finally, after your visit, maintain the contact with letters of thanks, preferably from the children as well as yourself, perhaps a contribution to the funds of the building, and by showing your hosts some of the work the children have produced in relation to the visit.

USEFUL ADDRESSES

JEWISH

Board of Deputies of British Jews, Woburn House, Upper Woburn Place, London WC1

Jewish Information Service, 34 Upper Berkeley Street, London W1H 7PG

Manchester Jewish Museum, 190 Cheetham Hill Road, Manchester M8 8LW

Jewish Education Bureau, 8 Westcombe Avenue, Leeds LS8 2BS

MUSLIM

Muslim Foundation, 223 London Road, Leicester LE2 1ZE

Islamic Cultural Centre, 146 Park Road, London NW8

Muslim Information Service, 233 Seven Sisters Road, London

BUDDHIST

Buddhist Society, 58 Eccleston Square, London SW1V 1PH

Manjushri Institute, Conishead Priory, Ulverston, Cumbria LA2 9QQ

The Buddhist Centre, Oaken Holt, Farmoor, Near Oxford OX2 9NL

CHRISTIAN

Church Information Office, Church House, Dean's Yard, London SW1P 3NZ

Council of Churches in Britain and Ireland, Interchurch House, 35-41 Lower Marsh, London SE1

SPCK (Society for Promoting Christian Knowledge) – publishers and booksellers with many bookshops throughout the UK. Headquarters at Holy Trinity Church, Marylebone Road, London NW1 4DU

HINDU

Swami Narayan Temple, 220 Willesden Lane, London NW2

India House, Aldwych, London WC2

Ramakrishna Vedanta Centre, Blind Lane, Bourne End, Buckinghamshire SL8 5LG

Institute of Indian Culture, 4A Castletown Road, London W14 9HQ

National Council of Hindu Temples, 3 Banksfield Avenue, Fulwood, Preston, Lancs. PR2 3RU

SIKH

Sikh Missionary Society (UK), 10 Featherstone Road, Southall, Middlesex UB2 5AA

CHINESE

Chinese Community, Education and Cultural Centre, 72 George Street, Manchester M1

General

Pictorial Charts Educational Trust, 27 Kirchen Road, West Ealing, London W13 0UD

SHAP Working Party on World Religions in Education, c/o The National Society's R.E. Development Centre, 23 Kensington Square, London W8 5HN

SHAP mailing, 81 St. Mary's Road, Huyton, Merseyside L36 5SR

Christian Education Movement, Royal Buildings, Victoria Street, Derby DE1 1GW

Books from India, 45 Museum Street, London WC1A 1LR

BIBLIOGRAPHY

Bastide, D. *Religious Education 5-12* (Falmer Press, 1989)

Cole, W.O. and Judith Evans *Religious Education in the Primary School* (Chanistor, 1992)

The F.A.R.E. Project *Forms of Assessment in Religious Education: The Main Report of the F.A.R.E. Project*

Grimmitt, M. (et al) *A Gift to the Child, Religious Education in the Early Years* (Simon and Schuster, 1991)

Grimmitt, M. *Religious Education and Human Development* (Mayhew Mcgrimmon, 1980)

Hull, J. *The Act Unpacked* (CEM, Derby, 1989)

Hull, J. *God-talk with Young Children* (CEM, Derby, 1991)

Jackson, R. *The Junior R.E. Handbook* (Stanley Thornes, 1990)

Lawton, C. *The Seder Handbook* (Board of Deputies of British Jews, 1984) also available from the Manchester Jewish Museum (see Useful Addresses p.00)

Rankin, J. (et al) *Religious Education Topics in the Primary School* (Longman, 1989)

Read, G. (et al) *How Do I Teach R.E.* (Mary Glasgow, 1988)

Read, G. (et al) *The Westhill Project Books and Photopaks* (Mary Glasgow, 1988)

Read, G. (et al) *Religious Education in the Early Years* (Stanley Thornes, 1992)

Further reading on world religions

An excellent starting point are books written for junior aged children such as *The Buddhist World, The Christian World* series (Macdonalds). Simpler series such as the *I am a Sikh*, etc. (Franklin Watts) are useful as a picture resource in school, though the texts are fairly limited. Pictorial Education Wall Charts on religion and accompanying notes are another useful resource.

Another very useful series is the *World Religions Series* (Stanley Thornes and Hulton) series editor W. Owen Cole e.g. *Sikhism* by Piara Singh Sambhi. These are written as G.C.S.E. texts and are accessible introductions to the faiths as well as useful sources for information.

Faiths and Festivals by Martin Palmer (Ward Lock Educational, 1983) is an invaluable introduction to festivals as it gives the stories behind them and briefly outlines their significance. It also gives a quite thorough introduction to the rites of passage in each major religion.

Worlds of Choice by Joanne O'Brien (Collins Educational, 1990) and *Worlds of Difference* by Esther Bisset and Martin Palmer (Blackie, 1985) both look at the relationship between religion and the environment through the stories and practice of the faith. Again, they are written for use in school and so are not heavy reading. *A Wealth of Faiths: Economics and Religion*, J. O'Brien (et al) (Worldwide Fund for Nature, 1992) is another useful title.

A new series *World Religions and Ecology* (Cassells, 1992) e.g. *Hinduism and Ecology* by Ranchor Prime provides an insight in the issue of religion and the environment and also a broader understanding of the faiths – these books are written for the non-specialist.

Approaching World Religions, series general editor Robert Jackson (John Murray) are introductions for teachers and have some suggestions for teaching about the faith in the primary school e.g. *Approaches to Islam* by Richard Thames, *Approaches to Hinduism* by Robert Jackson and Dirmit Killingley.

The Essential Teachings of ...... series (Rider) give extracts from sacred texts with a commentary and act as quite useful introductions (e.g. Kerry Brown ed. *The Essential Teachings of Hinduism* (Rider, 1988).

Other more specialized books:

Peter Harvey *An Introduction to Buddhism* (Cambridge University Press, 1990)

John Snelling *The Buddhist Handbook* (Rider, 1987)

R.C. Zaehner *Hinduism* (N.Y., 1966)

Goldberg and Raynor *The Jewish People* (Penguin, 1989)

Nicholas de Lange *Judaism* (Oxford, 1986)

Horrie and Chippendale *What is Islam?* (Virgin, 1991)

Sayid Abdul Ala Mawdudi *Towards Understanding Islam* (The U.K. Islamic Mission, 1980)

Singh and Cole *The Sikhs* (Routledge and Kegan Paul)

Ninian Smart *The World's Religions* (Cambridge University Press, 1989)

Edited by R.C. Zaehner, *The Concise Encyclopedia of Living Faiths* (Hutchinson, 1959).

CHILDREN'S BIBLIOGRAPHY

These books are recommended because they deal with concepts and questions central to R.E. They range from picture books suitable for younger juniors to novels for the older age group. The themes listed are just some of those in the books.

Dahl, R. *The BFG* (Puffin, 1982) Sophie is snatched from her bed by the Big Friendly Giant, and together they put a stop to the trogglehumping, bogthumping giants gobbling up little children. The issue of cultural customs is dealt with explicitly. Themes: cultural perspectives, friendship, coming to terms with dreams and nightmares.

Dejong, M. *The Wheel on the School* (Puffin, 1961) Six school children set about bringing the storks to their isolated Dutch fishing village and the whole community becomes involved in the project. In the common quest, young and old get to know each other for the first time. Themes: community, feelings, friendship, learning from each other.

Flournoy, V. *The Patchwork Quilt* (Picture Puffin, 1987) Grandma is too ill to work on the new patchwork quilt so all the family help. Themes: continuity, family life, co-operation, grandparents.

Herriot, J. *The Christmas Day Kitten* (Picture Piper, 1986) A mother stray cat nearing death brings her newly born kitten to a home where she has found food and warmth. Themes: death, hope.

Katsner, E. *Lottie and Lisa* (Puffin) Lottie and Lisa are identical twins with totally different personalities. Separated as babies when their parents divorce, they resolve to reunite them. This humorous book deals frankly with marriage breakdown, and also looks at parent/child relationships and the idea of balance in a personality. Themes: families, divorce, personality, fears, nightmares.

Kemp, G. *The Turbulent Term of Tyke Tyler* (Puffin, 1977) Medium bright Tyke and medium dim Danny add up to double trouble at school. A book written in the first person and which turns gender stereotypes on their head. Themes: friendship, responsibility.

King-Smith, D. *Martin's Mice* (Puffin) Martin is no ordinary cat because he keeps mice as pets instead of killing them. Unusually, for a children's book for this age, it shows a family where the child (Martin) does not get on with his parents and the parents do not get on with each other. *Saddlebottom*, another Dick King-Smith book, also skilfully deals with a child (a pig) being rejected by its mother. Themes: self-worth, families, freedom.

King-Smith, D. *The Sheep Pig* (Puffin, 1983) A pig learns to herd sheep. Falsely accused of the slaughter of the ewe who is his friend, he is narrowly saved from becoming bacon, and goes on to be champion at the sheep-dog trials. Themes: friendship, co-operation, prejudice, bereavement.

Lewis, C.S. *The Lion, The Witch and The Wardrobe* (Fontana Lions, 1950) and others in the Narnia series. Evacuee children go through the back of a wardrobe and find themselves in another world; one where it is always Winter and never Spring. The story tells how Spring returns. This classic story, made even more popular by a television series, picks up on many Christian motifs. Themes: redemptive love, sibling rivalry, trust, loyalty, seasonal symbols.

Pearce, P. *Tom's Midnight Garden* (Puffin, 1976) Tom, bored silly, staying in quarantine with his aunt and uncle, travels to a world in the past when the clock strikes thirteen. Themes: friendship, the relativity of time, loneliness.

Spyri, J. *Heidi* various editions. The well-known tale of the orphan girl left to live with her reclusive grandfather in the Swiss Alps. To the surprise of the villagers she is desperate to return to him when taken to be a companion to a rich invalid child in Frankfurt. It has some overtly Christian content, as reference is made to the parables of the Good Shepherd and the Prodigal son. Themes: homesickness, bereavement, forgiveness, wonder.

Varley, S. *Badger's Parting Gifts* (Picture Lions, 1985) Badger dies and his friends mourn for him and then remember together the things he has taught them. Borders on the sentimental but does just avoid it. Themes: death, loss, friendship, continuity.

White, E.B. *Charlotte's Web* (Puffin, 1952) Wilbur, the runt pig is saved from the slaughter house by the wit of his spider friend, Charlotte, but then Charlotte herself dies. Her death is written about in a sensitive but positive manner. Themes: outcast, friendship, death and bereavement.